Introduction to Logic
And Its Philosophy

Introduction to Logic
And Its Philosophy

Peter K. Schotch

ISBN 0-9780552-0-9

Library and Archives Canada Cataloguing in Publication

Schotch Peter K
  Introduction to Logic and Its Philosophy [electronic resource]
  Peter K. Schotch

  Includes bibliographical references and index.
  ISBN 0-9780552-0-9

  1. Formal Logic 2. Philosophy of Logic II. Schotch, Peter K.
  BC71.S42 2006   160   C2006-901677-1

Contents

Acknowledgements

This book is the result of many years of teaching several different introductory logic courses and trying to use many different textbooks. Some of them I liked and the students didn't. Some, not nearly so large a number, the students liked and I didn't. In each class I ended up learning something valuable—in fact I often think that I've learned at least as much as my students. So the debt that I acknowledge first, is to all those I have been privileged to teach—my students. Many of them pointed out mistakes and other infelicities in earlier versions of the text and thus saved me from embarrassment. In this regard I wish to single out Gillman Payette, and Julia Watt in particular.

The book was author-typeset using the LaTeX system, and I am pleased to record my gratitude to Leslie Lamport, the originator of LaTeX as well as to Donald Knuth for his TeX system upon which LaTeX is based. I have also used many "packages" written by other people. One in particular deserves special mention.

One might think that whatever one wanted to typeset, there must be (by now) at least one package which enables it. This turns out to be almost, but not quite, the case. The missing package is one that enables the typesetting of proofs in the so-called Fitch-style. Fortunately, for me, Guido Governatori (School of Information Systems, Faculty of Information Technology, Queensland University of Technology) was able to provide exactly the right package, which he has called natded. Later other packages came into being and I have used them here and there in this book, but without that very first one, I would have been stuck fast.

Several people read the manuscript at earlier stages and made suggestions. I wish to particularly acknowledge the contribution of Dorian Nicholson in this regard.

Finally, I acknowledge the *sine qua non* contribution of my wife, Cara, who provided a place from which I could take up the many projects, including this book, which had languished for years. Without her I couldn't have written this, nor would I even have wished to. It is fitting then, that I dedicate the book to her.

Chapter 1

Introduction

1.1 What this book is about, and why

There seem to be rather a lot of logic books about, these days. In view of this, a person should be clear in their own mind that there is sufficient reason for causing yet another of them to come into existence. In this sentence we see the concept of reason deployed in the sense of *motivation*. It's not a sense with which we shall be much concerned.

The sense that interests us, as well as most other philosophers who write books about it, is the sense in which reason is a *process* of a certain kind—a process which leads to *knowledge*.

There is some data. Our reason goes to work on this data. New knowledge appears in the output. Sir Isaac Newton glances out his window and chances to see an apple fall (in some versions of the story, the apple falls on his head). This event connects with other things that are present somehow in Sir Isaac (in his mind perhaps) and, after a decent interval, the theory of universal gravitation pops out. Such is the fable in any event, and we shall pretend that it is true.

This example raises quite a few questions. How is it that certain inputs get selected from a sea of such, as the 'data?' The apple fell and so did the odd leaf, bees buzzed, birds chirped etc., but the apple was what did it. How does that happen exactly?

What is the nature of this process which begins with the fall of the apple and ends with gravitation? Is it available to all, or does one need to be Sir Isaac Newton?

These are good questions to which we have no answers. Perhaps it would be better to say that *we* (meaning we philosophers) don't have the answers. These days we don't much trouble ourselves with questions like this. That's because these are questions about neuro-psychology or some related discipline, at least for the most part and so are outside of what we dare to claim as our speciality.

Evidently reason has something to do with rationality. Perhaps the connection is best explained in this fashion: A particular bit of reasoning is correct when it would be *irrational* not to accept the conclusion when the data has already been accepted. Setting aside certain problems already mentioned about determining just what constitutes the data, this pseudo-definition seems to work quite well. Of course, it requires that we be able to unpack the notion of irrationality in some non-controversial way. Sometimes we can, and sometimes we cannot.

The clearest example of this idea occurs when accepting the data is the same thing as accepting the conclusion. If we struggle with the notion for a moment or two, we can see that this will happen when the conclusion is also one of the data items—perhaps, but not necessarily, the only data item. Thus, for instance, if one of our data is represented by the sentence "Grass is green" which is also the sentence which represents the conclusion, then the connection between non-acceptance of the conclusion and irrationality is clear. In this case it would be irrational to accept the data but not the conclusion since it would be irrational to both accept and not accept *any* sentence, *at the same time*.[1] The last qualification is obviously required since we don't wish to rule out changing one's mind.

The relation between the data, (which we shall call the *premises*), and the conclusion when the reasoning is correct—what folk often call 'follows from,' forms the central part of our study in this work. We don't rule out the possibility that there might be other cases when it would be irrational to reject the conclusion having accepted the premises, (other

---

[1]This might be a bit brisk. Some readers have urged that it is *impossible* to both accept and not accept any sentence at the same time. Thus the irrationality lies not in the act (which is impossible) but rather in the *attempt* to do what is manifestly impossible.

than the case in which the conclusion is a premise that is), but that will be our central case. This brings us at length to the naming of names.

When a conclusion *follows from* its premises in the same way that it does when the conclusion *is* a premise, we call that kind of reasoning *deductive*, otherwise non-deductive.[2] Of course we now owe an explanation of the phrase 'in the same way.' It will turn out that there are two distinct ways to give that explanation.

That is the nutshell version of this book. We shall provide an introduction to the study of deduction and a discussion of some of the philosophical questions that arise in that study. This leaves out quite a few things that one commonly finds in beginning logic books.

There is no discussion of so-called informal logic, and in particular no catalogue of 'the fallacies.' Neither is there any account in this work of syllogistic reasoning and its extensions. It isn't that these other topics are disreputable or otherwise unworthy of study, but rather that they don't fit very well with the approach we shall use. In other words, this is intended to be a work squarely in the modern *symbolic* or *formal* tradition.

1.2 What Makes Logic Difficult

Logic classes in general, and symbolic logic classes in particular, usually have the reputation of being more difficult than other kinds of philosophy class, and it seems clear that many students have more difficulty with logic than they have with ethics or existentialism, *at the beginning of the class*. This can lead to loss numbers as high as 30% or more.

My own view is that students take their first symbolic logic class expecting to do well. Some of these have just come from a successful high-school career and are used to finding easy what many others find difficult. Then they get to their first assignments and they encounter difficulties. The problems are harder than they seemed in class. They

---

[2]Perhaps deduction might be characterized as the sense or use of 'follows from' when it would be irrational to both accept the premises and reject the conclusion while 'follows from' in general is characterized by saying that a conclusion follows from some premises when it would be *rational to accept* the conclusion, having already accepted the premises.

don't even know how to begin. This is an entirely unexpected and de-moralizing event.

Why are there these initial problems and how can the course be presented so that they don't occur? Sadly, there seems to be no mode of presenting a first logic class that can entirely dodge this early morale problem. Happily, we *do* know why even academic overachievers have the problems we have been discussing.

Roughly speaking, it's a memory problem. When we come to solve a problem there are two distinct categories of stuff to keep in our minds. The first is the data of the problem itself—in the case of logic, some sort of reasoning problem. The other is the technique or techniques which we shall use in solving the problem. It has now been shown[3] that if both of these kinds of thing, at least for reasoning problems, have to reside in *short-term memory*, performance in problem solving will be catastrophically degraded.

This result correctly predicts the hump that many students, even bright students, have to get over in the initial part of the class. It will be slow going, even *very* slow going before the students have internalized (which is to say *memorized*) the techniques. This in turn means that everything necessary to encourage such memorization should be done. Drills are indicated. So-called open-book examinations and quizzes are not.

And perhaps most important of all, the explanation should be given to students. Otherwise, they incorrectly identify the reason for their initial difficulties as an inadequacy in themselves. Even worse, far too often beginning students are told (by instructors, however well-meaning they might be) 'Some students just can't do logic, and there is no disgrace in being one of those.' Such 'explanations' do a huge disservice to the students as well as to the truth. In more than thirty years of logic teaching, I have found fewer than five students who, with sufficient effort and patience and goodwill on both sides, couldn't be taught introductory logic.

---

[3]In the work of F.M. Rabinowitz and his collaborators. See Howe and Rabinowitz (1996); Howe et al. (1998)

Part One:
The Classical Logic of Sentences

Chapter 2

Introducing Sentence Logic

2.1 overview

Logic is the science of reasoning, pure and simple. And things are never so pure as when the reasoning in question is carried entirely by sentences. We should hurry to qualify this assertion, by saying that the kind of sentences that do this important work are the kind known as *declarative* or sometimes *statements*. In other words, the sentences in question are those which are ordinarily used to *say* something. Such sentences make a claim, as opposed to asking a question, issuing an order, or exhorting our best efforts, to name just a few of the other things we use sentences to do.

The thing about sentences is that they are *concrete* objects—patterns of sound-waves in the air or patterns of ink on a page. Sentences are the kinds of things, like tables and chairs, that we can trip over out in the world. In other words, a sentence is a *physical object*. There are people who prefer it this way, and would like to prevent the consideration of any *abstract* entities in what we are doing. We shall be considering later, if such prevention is advisable or even possible.

For now, let's consider a specimen of the sort of reasoning that we shall be studying. We shall refer to this as an *inference*:

There is a tradition that refers to such hunks of reasoning as *arguments*. We avoid this usage more often than not, since we think of the term 'inference' as having a wider (and less agonistic) application.

Table 2.1: Example of an Inference

(P1) John is happy.
(P2) If John is happy, then Mary is sad.
(C) Therefore, Mary is sad.

Arguing nearly always requires some sort of *opponent* while inferring can be done in an entirely confrontation-free manner requiring no opponent or even audience. One's passions are often aroused in an argument while one's inferences mostly take place in an atmosphere of cool deliberation.

Nobody can understand these three sentences and sincerely tell us that C, the *conclusion*, doesn't follow from P1 and P2, the *premises*. In a certain sense, the whole science of deduction is founded on this fact about humans. We might imagine beings who did not immediately just *see* that the reasoning in the above snippet is correct but they would be different from us—perhaps even too different for us to understand.[1]

Sometimes, for some pieces of reasoning, human beings find the move from premises to conclusion compelling. Why is that? What explains this compulsion? Such a question is sometimes called *philosophical*. This is the sense of that term in which it contrasts with 'ordinary' or even 'normal'. When we ask somebody on the street whether or not the John and Mary inference is correct, she is liable to think that it was a trick question of some kind, since the reasoning is so obviously correct. But if we then go on to ask *why* the reasoning is correct, the most likely response is a blank stare. It is as if we have asked a question that was ill-formed in some way. If we press the matter, we might get the angry response 'Because it just *is*.'

We earlier made an attempt to answer this question in terms of an

---

[1]Ludwig Wittgenstein (Ludwig Wittgenstein, *Philosophical Investigations*, 2nd ed., tr. G.E.M. Anscombe (Oxford: Blackwell, 1958), p. 223.) famously remarks 'If a lion could talk, we could not understand him.' This draws attention to the fact that there is more to uptake than shared vocabulary. One of the other ingredients is surely something like shared logical intuitions.

account of rationality. We would say, on that view, that it would be irrational to accept the John and Mary premises, and not accept the conclusion. In fact, we would claim that it would be *as* irrational to do that as it would be to accept that John is happy and also *not* to accept it (at the same time). We should notice however, that we do not yet have an account of the 'as irrational as' relation.

Contemporary logic actually has such an account. In fact, it has *two* of them. These two correspond to the two theories of *logical consequence* or, more informally, of the *follows from* relation. There is also another *kind* of explanation which might be offered here—one that has little or nothing to do with reasoning, at least directly. We are thinking here of a biological, or evolutionary explanation.

It could have been the case, hundreds or thousands of generations ago, that there existed a tribe of proto-humans who did not in fact feel compelled to accept the conclusion of the John and Mary type of inference even after they had accepted the premises. But these hapless folk were all eaten by cave bears or other predators before their civilization could develop.

This is often a tempting kind of explanation, especially when it's not clear how else to explain something, but it is usually better to resist the temptation. Such evolutionary arguments tend to support the status quo.[2]

So then, back to our philosophical question. Why do people feel the compulsion we spoke of earlier, and that you yourself feel when you look at the sample deduction? We shall give the answer in two distinct ways, both of which seem to provide for the certainty with which deduction proceeds.

The first way, some think the most intuitive, is to propose that there are *basic forms* of reasoning, the correctness of which is not an issue. The reasoning from 'Grass is green' to 'Grass is green' is the most transparent, but not the only example. This is like answering 'Because it just *is!*' to the question 'Why is the John and Mary inference correct?' In

---

[2] Dorian Nicholson has suggested that the evolutionary argument implies that all those who do not accept the John and Mary inference should study logic, and in that sense does not *only* support the status quo.

order for some inference to be correct, on this view, there must be a way of getting from the premises to the conclusion using only the basic forms.

This strikes some people as pretty unsatisfying, since it amounts to saying that some basic kinds of inference are acceptable, without saying *why* (unless of course we are comfortable with the kind of evolutionary explanation mentioned above). We have the single (trivial) case in which the conclusion is a premise for which no explanation is needed as to why we are *compelled* to accept the conclusion on the basis of the premises, but what of the other cases? What of John and Mary? The conclusion in that case is definitely not among the premises except as a part. Saying that the two cases of rejecting conclusions are *equally* irrational is tempting but not entirely helpful since, as we mentioned already, we don't yet have any way of saying *exactly* what is meant by 'as irrational as.'

But there may be a way to repair that defect. We shall eventually frame a way of looking at deduction which will allow us to say when it would be as irrational to reject a conclusion having accepted certain premises as it would be to both accept and reject a single sentence.

Just what is it that characterizes the latter situation? Some have said that if we accept a certain sentence *as true*, which is another way of saying that we accept it as a premise, then if we take the conclusion to be the same sentence, we cannot ever be in the situation of accepting a false sentence as true. In other words, the truth of the premises provides an *absolute guarantee* of the truth of the conclusion when the conclusion is a premise. And it isn't hard to tell a story in which the truth of the John and Mary premises likewise provides an ironclad guarantee of the truth of its conclusion.

Going from premises to conclusion in those inferences *preserves truth*. Hence, this picture of deduction is sometimes called the *preservationist* picture.

We shall name these two ways of looking at consequence, the *syntactic perspective* (also called the *proof theoretic perspective*), and the *semantic perspective* (also called the *model theoretic* perspective). On the first approach the follows-from relation is reconstructed as the relation of *provability*. The second approach represents the follows-from relation as the relation of *semantic entailment*.

But before we examine these in detail, we need to say more about the way in which the two kinds of theory will be framed. If we think about our John and Mary example for a bit, we can see that its acceptability as an inference has nothing at all to do with most of what it is ostensibly *about*. Were we to change the names of those involved that would have no *logical* effect. And that goes for nearly any other change that we might ring, from 'is happy' to 'swims' for example—but not quite all. If, for instance, we were to change 'if ... then ...' to 'either ... or ...' the result would be an inference which is *not* correct.

2.2 A Formal Language

We usually explain the fact that our sample inference about John and Mary would still work if we changed it to a similar one involving Jack and Diane, by appeal to the idea of a *form*.

What is a form, exactly? The forms that we have to deal with (far too often) in our daily lives, have *blanks*, which is to say spaces that we have to fill in. Between the blanks are words and phrases that we normally can't (or at least shouldn't) change. So there are things we can change, and things we cannot. This is just like our example inference.

What we seem to have discovered so far about the example, is that everything is up for grabs—everything *except* 'if ... then ....' So the form will have blanks for everything except the conditional. If we agree to use *letters* to stand for blanks, then the form for our example will be something like that shown in table 2.2:

Now the question is bound to come up: 'Why are we using letters here to stand for the blanks? Why not just have actual blanks?' The reason is that we have to mark the blanks in order that the form produce the right pattern, once it is filled in. Such a thing is within our experience—as when a certain blank on a form is marked 'Name.'

It's crucial to the correctness of the John and Mary inference, that 'John is happy' be one of the premises *as well as* the beginning of the conditional sentence (i.e., the 'if, then' sentence). Using the same letter

Table 2.2: John and Mary Find a Form

(P1) A
(P2) If A then B
(C) Therefore B

for both of those blanks, the letter A in the example form, keeps us from putting in two different sentences.

The above form, with letters used for blanks, is a form of the earlier inference involving John and Mary, and any filled in version will be called an *instance* of that form. Why not call it *the* form of the inference? The answer is that forms are not unique. What counts as a form is *any* way of replacing sentences by blanks such that we could recover the starting point by replacing the blanks with sentences. So the one shown in table 2.3 is *also* a form of the John and Mary inference:

Table 2.3: Another Form for John and Mary

(P1) A
(P2) B
(C) Therefore C

If we replace A with 'John is happy' B with 'If John is happy then Mary is sad', and C by 'Mary is sad', we shall recover the original inference. Of course there are plenty of instances of this form which are *not* correct, though all of the instances of the earlier form are. That turns out to be quite rare—most forms have both correct and incorrect instances.

To distinguish a form, all of the instances of which are correct, from an ordinary form we shall refer to the former as a *valid* form. It is extremely important to notice that we are introducing a *technical use* of this term, as opposed to whatever uses it might have in ordinary speech. It is sometimes tempting to mix both technical and 'street' senses of a term, but this almost always leads to some kind of mistake.

We have allowed that a form might consist entirely of (named) blanks, but in other cases, what is allowed for non-blanks? To ask this question is to ask which words are crucial to the determination of validity. Such words, words which cannot be substituted for without destroying the validity of the form, have been called *logical words*.

Exactly which words are the logical ones turns out to be one of the more difficult philosophical questions. So difficult indeed, that many logicians prefer to side-step the issue and simply present a list.

We shall present a list too, but we never think of this list as anything more than preliminary. Since we are concerned with the sentences, we shall consider only those logical words which are used in connection with sentences (as opposed to *names*, for instance). These words are often called *connectives* or (sometimes) *junctives*. In table 2.4 we present the words that we have chosen as our logical vocabulary along with the name usually given to that kind of connective, the abbreviations we shall use for the connective.

Table 2.4: Logical Words for Sentence Forms

word(s)	name	abbreviation
both ... and ...	conjunction	$\wedge$
either ... or ...	disjunction	$\vee$
if ... then ...	conditional	$\supset$
... if and only if ...	biconditional	$\equiv$
not ...	negation	$\neg$

We, and most others use the name *conjuncts* to indicate the sentences which are conjoined while *disjuncts* serves the same function for those disjoined. The initial and final sentences in a conditional are called the *antecedent* and *consequent* respectively, and the sentence which gets negated is called the *negatum*.

Apart from the question of which words are logical, there is the question of how the logical words come to have that status. To put the question in this way is to assume that words *become* logical words, having started their careers in a less dramatic way. There is evidence to support this startling idea.[3] 'Or', for instance, seems to be a contraction of 'other' while most of the words we use for conjunction appear to have come from spatio-temporal words. As an example: The word 'but' once meant something like 'outside' or to use an older form: 'without.' This ancient usage persists in present day expressions like 'It never rains but it pours.' which means that it never rains *without* pouring.

We are almost ready to define a kind of language of sentence forms—the sort of thing called, for obvious reasons, a *formal language*. We have the alphabet, so to speak, which consists of the connectives together with the letters which serve as (the names of) blanks. All that is missing is punctuation. As matters now stand, most combinations of letters and connectives are ambiguous. Consider, as an example, $A \wedge B \vee C$.

We have no idea whether that expression is supposed to be the form of a conjunction or of a disjunction. We can resolve this ambiguity by using parentheses. So if the expression is supposed to stand for the form of a conjunction, we would write: $A \wedge (B \vee C)$. This is a standard way of disambiguating, but it isn't the only way.

An alternative, invented by the Polish logician Jan Łukasiewicz and usually referred to as 'Polish notation', is to put the connectives *before* the expressions they connect. For instance we might write our previous example as $\wedge A \vee BC$. The idea here is that we first read the $\wedge$ so we know that the entire expression is the form of a conjunction and then we read the next 'well-formed' bit—in the example A, as the first conjunct, while the rest of the expression is the second conjunct. We could get precisely the same disambiguation without using parentheses, by placing the connectives after the expressions they connect rather than before them. This approach has come to be known as *reverse* Polish notation.

So now we are ready to introduce our language of sentence forms, which we call SL in the following two stages.

---

[3]The leading authority on this interesting study is R.E. Jennings who argues in a series of papers that there is a process very like Darwinian evolution at work in how words change their status. The examples we consider were first discussed by Jennings.

Definition 2.2.1. The alphabet of *the language* SL consists of:

The infinite list $A, B, C, A_1, B_1, \ldots$ of *sentence letters*

the list $\wedge, \vee, \supset, \equiv, \neg$ of connective symbols

the punctuation symbols (,)

The concept of a *formula of* SL is defined:

Definition 2.2.2.

Every sentence letter is a formula

If P and Q are formulas, then so are

$(P \wedge Q)$

$(P \vee Q)$

$(P \supset Q)$

$(P \equiv Q)$

$(\neg P)$

Nothing else is a formula of SL except as defined by a finite number of applications of the above clauses.

Sometimes rigor is the enemy of clarity and we shall allow ourselves to omit parentheses when no ambiguity results. In particular we usually drop the outermost pair of parentheses which enclose the whole formula according to the definition.

The definition of formula, which we have just seen, is an example of what is called an *inductive* or *recursive* definition. We often use such a definition to define a class of items, even an infinite class, which can be arranged in a sequence (even an infinite sequence) of items, like the sequence of our formulas. We require some way of ordering the formulas and to do that, we define:

> **Definition 2.2.3.** The length of the formula P, of SL ($\ell(P)$) is the number of connectives in P.

First, in the *basis* of the definition, we define the concept for the first item (or items) in the sequence. In the example the first items are the sentence letters, which are the shortest possible formulas and having no connectives, are of length 0.

Next, in the inductive or recursive part we define those items at an arbitrary stage of the sequence *given* that previous items have already been defined. For formulas, the recursion begins by saying 'If P and Q are formulas'. So those letters represent formulas which have been defined so-far but there is no assumption that *all* formulas have been defined by the time P and Q make their appearance.

The recipe in definition 2.2 tells us that we define the next layer of formulas by taking all conjunctions, disjunctions, etc. of the formulas which have been constructed so far. And we keep on doing that over and over, until the whole infinite set of formulas has been defined. The point is that there is absolutely no essential difference between going from the first layer (the layer of sentence letters) to the second layer, and going from 1000th layer to the 1001th layer. It's that sameness which makes recursive definitions *work*.

This is another of those concepts which sound more complicated and difficult than they are. Here is another example, one which is a little more straightforward than our formula example.

We first define the function "'", *successor*

> x' is the next number after x, for every natural number x

Now we recursively define '+':

The Recursive Definition of '+'

[Basis] $k + 0 = k$

[Recursion] $k + n' = (k + n)'$

What makes this recursive as opposed to just a case of defining one function in terms of another, is that in the clause of the definition marked 'Recursion', the symbol '+' appears on both sides of the equation. We define addition in terms of addition, as well as successor but the sums in question have been defined at an earlier level, in just the way that P and Q range over formulas that have been constructed so far, and not over all formulas.

In the definition of formula, we use the letters P and Q as *variables* which range over formulas of SL. We shall continue to use capital Roman letters from the middle of the alphabet (with and without subscripts) for this purpose throughout the book. But this usage raises an important question.

With the aid of the definition we now have a complete account of the language of SL. But to what language do expressions like '$P \land Q$' belong? Only after the variables are assigned formulas of SL is this a formula, but what is it *before* such an assignment? It's in a language in which we *mention*, so to speak, SL, and this language has come to be called *the metalanguage of* SL. It is sometimes said that the metalanguage, for a given language L, is the language in which we talk about L.

This metalanguage idea turns out to be an extremely useful 20th Century coinage,[4] though it was not universally accepted.[5] Apart from the variables which we have just introduced, what else might the metalanguage of SL contain?

---

[4]Carnap is generally accorded the honor of having invented the concept of a metalanguage

[5]The 20th Century logician and philosopher Bertrand Russell , for instance seems to inveigh against the idea of using a metalanguage even before the concept was well and truly invented. See for instance *Principles of Mathematics* in which Russell announces that the concept of 'rule of inference' cannot be formalized

We choose not to answer this question in any complete way. In other words, we feel free to add features to our metalanguage whenever it strikes us as essential, or even useful, to do so. In particular we shall never give a rigorous definition of 'formula of the metalanguage of SL', and in this we follow the great majority of contemporary logicians.[6]

For now it is enough to say that we shall require a conjunction connective in the metalanguage and will use & to that end. We also need a conditional and biconditional and they will be represented in the metalanguage by $\Longrightarrow$ and $\Longleftrightarrow$. We shall also introduce variables over *sets* of formulas which will be represented by capital Greek letters like Γ, Δ, and Σ with and without subscripts. When we wish to say that a formula P *belongs to* the set Γ, we shall use the standard vocabulary of set-theory: $P \in \Gamma$. We shall also use the symbol $\varnothing$ to refer to the empty set, i.e., the unique set which has no members.

There are evidently different kinds of formula of SL depending upon which is the main connective. But there is also another difference in kind, between the formulas which contain connectives, the *compound* formulas, and those which don't, the *atomic* or sometimes *basic* formulas. Obviously every compound formula contains, as proper[7] parts, at least one other formula. The contained formulas are usually referred to as *subformulas*.

In the next couple of chapters we shall begin talking about the two accounts of the relation of logical consequence, which we mentioned earlier. In both cases we shall construct a theory of this relation in terms of the language SL. The reason for this is that many things are easier to state and easier to calculate for SL than they would be for a real live natural language. We might think of ourselves as dealing with a greatly simplified framework in order to discover the important basic principles in just the way that we begin our study of physics by ignoring many complications.

---

[6]We choose not to *formalize* the metalanguage because we have no project on hand which would require us to rigorously define metalinguistic forms. But we do not think that it would be a great evil, or even ill-advised in general. *This* position is probably a minority one.

[7]A part p of a whole w is said to be a *proper part* of w if and only if it is not equal to w.

2.3 SL and Natural Language

But if SL is not a natural language of the kind we (most of us) speak, then what is the point of studying it, if we wish to account for reasoning? Even if, as has been claimed, it is easier to frame or construct a theory of reasoning in an artificial language like SL, why should that interest the person who wants to understand reasoning in natural language?

The answer to this difficult question is that there is *no difference* between reasoning in natural language and reasoning in a formal language. If a bit of reasoning is correct, there isn't some special natural language *way* in which it is correct which we won't find in a formal language. What makes for right reason is the same across all languages formal and natural, object and meta. Given this fact about reasoning, it makes sense to evaluate reasoning in its natural habitat by *translating* into a formal language where the criteria of correctness are easier to deploy.

This is far from saying that worrying about the differences between formal language and ordinary language is misplaced or silly. We shall be carefully monitoring these differences as we develop our formal resources.

2.4 The Classical Perspective

Many hints have been dropped to the effect that there might be several different ways of laying out a theory of inference. The time has come to be a little more explicit about this matter. There are indeed many different ways to construct an account of the 'follows from' relation, and there have been from its earliest beginnings. In spite of that, there has emerged in the 20th Century one approach which has come to be called *classical*. The name is a bit ironic since it includes many features which would almost certainly have been firmly rejected by most ancient logicians, and several medieval ones as well.

What characterizes the classical approach perhaps above all, is its *simplicity*. Nearly every departure from the classical way of doing things is more difficult and more complicated. In spite of its obvious attractiveness however, simplicity is not always an automatic win. It might come to pass that the phenomena we seek to characterize are just not simple.[8] We might coin the term *classicality* at this point. It shares with simplicity the attribute of being difficult to characterize precisely and of being a matter of degree.

Perhaps the clearest and best way to talk about the classical account of reasoning is to say that there are certain hallmarks, and that once enough of these are accumulated, one is viewing things from the *classical perspective*.

Several of these hallmarks are themselves not exactly cut and dried. Most prominently, in this chapter, there is the list of logical words as presented in table 2.4. Some logicians and philosophers of logic[9] have asserted that the classical viewpoint requires that the logic of sentences recognize no other words as logical except the ones in the table, and those which might be defined in terms of them.

Certainly if an account of sentence logic failed to recognize any of the words in the table, no one would think the account in question classical. However there are many logicians and philosophers who think that the table might be augmented without thereby torpedoing classicality.[10]

Essay or Discussion Questions and Topics

1. Suppose that the term 'logical word' is defined as a word, the meaning of which is crucial to the determination of the correctness or otherwise, of at least one inference. Are there any other conditions that should be placed on the notion?

2. Without placing further conditions on the term, it is clear that the usual list of sentence connectives are indeed logical words. What new words would also qualify?

3. Is it the case that virtually *any* word could be a logical word, on the 'no further conditions' view?

---

[8] A story sometimes told about Einstein has him saying that he wanted his theory of relativity to be as simple as possible, but no simpler than that.

[9] Perhaps the most emphatic of these was the 20th Century philosopher, W.V.O. Quine.

[10] A popular example is furnished by the connectives that correspond to the words 'necessary' and 'possible', but there are many other examples.

Chapter 3

Proof Theory of Sentence Logic

3.1 Overview

We have noted earlier that in constructing a theory of the deductive version of the relation 'follows from', also known as the *consequence* relation, there are two distinct paradigms under which we may choose to fall. We shall consider the so-called preservationist paradigm in the next chapter. Now it is time for the other, the *rule compliance* paradigm. According to this view of the matter, what makes for correct (deductive) reasoning is strict adherence to a set of *rules* usually called rules of inference or rules of *proof*. It is normally part and parcel of this approach that such rules should be presented in a rigorous way. In particular, it should always be clear what the rules are, and when some 'step' in a piece of reasoning complies. These are formal requirements.

There are also informal requirements. Naturally there won't be a rigorous account of these, but we should mention at least ease of use and what we might call 'goodness of fit' with generally accepted principles of problem solving. We shall also be interested in promoting a system of rules which minimizes the kind of memory problem we identified in the introductory chapter.

In what follows we shall construct a system of rules which characterizes the consequence relation of the logic CSL from the *syntactical* point of view. To be perfectly rigorous we should use different names for the semantic and syntactical presentations of classical sentence logic, but our level of rigor will fall somewhat short of perfection.

3.2 Introducing the rules of CSL

For now, we shall begin to describe a system of rules in the manner
of so-called Fitch-style natural deduction (after the American logician
 Frederick B. Fitch, see Fitch (1952)). The experience of many logic
teachers seems to support the view that Fitch's system is the easiest to
use, for beginners. The heart of the system is the concept of a *subderivation*. In other words, for this system, inference is, built up in
layers. Which is to say that the task of getting from the premises to the
conclusion is a matter of solving a number of sub-tasks, each of which
may be easier (and certainly less intimidating) than the main job.

A subderivation is a piece of reasoning which begins with an assumption (or assumptions)—this (or these) assumption(s) is (or are) in
effect or *hold* for the duration of the subderivation. This period during
which the assumption(s) of the subderivation is(are) in effect is called
the *scope* of the assumption(s). The central feature of the Fitch system
is a graphical representation of this notion of the scope of an assumption. Each subderivation extends from 'North' to 'South' on the page
with the assumption(s) at the top. The extent of the scope of the assumptions is indicated by a *scope line* which is a vertical line like:

$$\begin{array}{|l} P \\ \hline \vdots \\ Q \end{array}$$

In each subderivation, the convention is to underline the assump-
tion(s).

An important feature of this system, is that subderivations can be
nested, which is to say that we can have assemblies of subderivations
like:

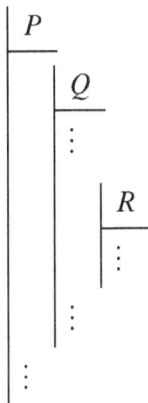

So that whenever, as sometimes happens, we are required to assume something in the middle of a piece of reasoning—'for the sake of argument' as people say, we simply introduce a new subderivation, beginning with the new assumption.

The line at the far left is called the *main* scope line of the derivation. Take note though, that there is no 'main derivation.' The main scope line is simply the scope line of a subderivation (if necessary, we might think of it as the *main subderivation*). The derivation proper, is the whole assembly of subderivations.

Whenever a rule of inference ends, or *terminates* a subderivation, the scope line of that subderivation will end. In such a case, the assumption of the subderivation which was terminated is said to be *discharged*. It is important to realize that not every rule of inference terminates a subderivation—some do all their work inside one single subderivation without reference to any other. All this sounds more arcane than it really is, as a few examples will make clear.

The general idea is that when we engage in complex reasoning what we are doing can be represented as having been put together out of certain simpler atoms of reasoning. This means, among other things, that we don't have to have *all* of the reasoning before our minds at any one time, in order to be successful reasoners. Given what we know about memory and the way it limits our ability to perform reasoning tasks, this is a superior way to solve reasoning problems. And it may well be, as Descartes asserts,[1] a superior way of problem solving in general

In what follows we shall use the capital Greek letters Γ (gamma), and Δ (delta), with and without subscripts, as variables which range over sets of formulas in the manner introduced in the previous chapter. For the most part, the sets in question will be premise sets.

So let Γ be a set of premises. We write '$\Gamma \vdash P$' to represent that our proof-theoretic version of the follows-from relation holds between the premises Γ and the conclusion P. The symbol $\vdash$, usually read 'proves', is part of the metalanguage.

A *natural deduction* system, as opposed to some other sort of system based on inference rules,[2] has a pair of rules for each connective. One rule to *introduce* a formula which has that connective as its main operator, and another to *eliminate* a formula of that sort.[3] Here are the rules which govern conjunctions.

Conjunction Introduction ([$\wedge$I])

$$
\begin{array}{l|l}
& \vdots \\
& P* \\
& \vdots \\
& Q* \\
& \vdots \\
& P \wedge Q
\end{array}
$$

This rule is sometimes called *adjunction*. In the schematic presentation of the rules, note that the lines which are marked with an asterisk are the premises of the rule, the things that must have been derived before the rule is invoked, while the conclusion appears without adornment. Even though only one scope line appears in the presentation, it is

---

[1] See his *Discourse on Method*

[2] The *sequent logic* pioneered by Gentzen, for instance, has only introduction rules and structural rules. See Gentzen (1969)

[3] For this reason, such a system of rules is sometimes called an *intelim* system.

intended that the rule functions in the same manner in an embedded sub-derivation. Finally, and most importantly, the order in which premises occur before the rule is invoked is unimportant. This means that the following is also a way to represent the rule of Conjunction Introduction:

$$\begin{array}{|l} \vdots \\ Q* \\ \vdots \\ P* \\ \vdots \\ Q \wedge P \end{array}$$

Conjunction Elimination ([∧E])

This rule is captured by either of the following schemes:

$$\begin{array}{|l} \vdots \\ P \wedge Q* \\ \vdots \\ P \end{array}$$

$$\begin{array}{|l} \vdots \\ P \wedge Q* \\ \vdots \\ Q \end{array}$$

The idea here is that there is no magic to the order in which the conjuncts appear in the conjunction.[4] The rule Conjunction Elimination is often called *simplification* .

---

[4]This is another part of the classical perspective. In a different setting, say one involving the determination of the truth of a conjunction by a computer program, the order in which the conjuncts appear might make a great deal of difference to the length of time taken to evaluate the expression.

It is also useful to be able to write out the rules linearly, for certain purposes—most notably in studying metalogic. We can easily do that if we allow ourselves a bit of metalinguistic formality. In particular, we shall use the symbol $\Longrightarrow$, as we remarked earlier, to stand for the metalinguistic conditional (which we now stipulate has the same behavior as the $\supset$ in the object language). We shall also use the symbol & to represent conjunction in the metalanguage. Dressed up in their metalinguistic finery, the rules for conjunction look like:

$[\wedge I] (\Gamma \vdash P \ \& \ \Gamma \vdash Q) \ \Longrightarrow \ \Gamma \vdash P \wedge Q$

$[\wedge E] \ \Gamma \vdash P \wedge Q \ \Longrightarrow \ (\Gamma \vdash P \ \& \ \Gamma \vdash Q)$

In these horizontal forms of the rules, the Γ represents all the assumptions upon which depend the derivation of the premises of the rule, i.e., P and Q in $[\wedge I]$. Let us give ourselves a metalanguage biconditional: $\Longleftrightarrow$ which will consist of two metalanguage conditionals in just the way that happens in the object language. Then it should be obvious that we can collapse these two rules into a single one:

$[\wedge] (\Gamma \vdash P \ \& \ \Gamma \vdash Q) \ \Longleftrightarrow \ \Gamma \vdash P \wedge Q$

This is particularly nice, having one 'proof-condition' we might call it.[5]

Next let us take up the rules for introducing and eliminating disjunctions. The first one, captured by either scheme, is easy—nearly trivial in fact.

Disjunction Introduction ($[\vee I]$)

$$
\begin{array}{|l}
\vdots \\
Q* \\
\vdots \\
Q \vee P
\end{array}
$$

---

[5]This condition exactly matches the truth-condition for conjunction which will be introduced in the next chapter. Alas, none of the other connectives enjoy such a close connection to their semantic presentation.

$$\begin{array}{|l} \vdots \\ P* \\ \vdots \\ P \vee Q \end{array}$$

This rule is also known as *addition*. [6] The horizontal form would be written:

[∨I] $\Gamma \vdash P$ or $\Gamma \vdash Q \implies \Gamma \vdash P \vee Q$

Several words of caution are in order concerning this rule. When one passes from the premise to the conclusion, the step is entirely warranted, but a great deal of information is lost. Disjunction is often used in ordinary speech to offer choices or to indicate that there are choices. In our formal logic, the classical perspective goes far beyond that. Indeed it would be possible to argue that there are hardly any instances in natural discourse in which 'or' has the meaning which we give it.[7]

To take an example of what this information loss comes down to, let us assume that your grade in this class is the arithmetic mean of your scores on the mid-term exam and the final exam. Further, assume that you have scored 95% on both, so that your average is 95%. In fact you can now deduce that your final grade in the class will be A+. You can also make a further deduction using the Disjunction Introduction rule: you can deduce that either you will receive an A+, or you will fail the class. In this way we take a palatable conclusion, and turn it into a not-so palatable one. The point is that it is silly to assert a disjunction when we already know which of the disjuncts is true. This is an example of retreating from something (logically) stronger, to something (logically) weaker. It's important to realize this because there will be times when one must derive a disjunction as a step in some derivation, and one's first impulse will be to do that by first deriving one of the disjuncts. If we are trying to do this on the main scope line, then we are almost certainly

---

[6]In the late 19th and early 20th Centuries, disjunction was most often called 'logical sum.' Hence 'addition' is an obvious name for the rule which brings into being such a sum.

[7]The interested reader should consult R.E. Jennings' excellent book *The Genesis of Disjunction* for more on the deeply mysterious nature of this connective.

making a mistake. For if we could derive the disjunct, why would we go on to derive the weaker disjunction? Let us make this into a rule of thumb:[8]

Rule of Thumb for Disjunction Introduction

Never use Disjunction Introduction on the main scope line.

So far, things have been within sight of our intuitions, broadly speaking. In the next rule things get a little more remote, since this will be our first encounter with subderivations:

Disjunction Elimination ($[\vee E]$)

$$
\begin{array}{|l}
P \vee Q* \\
\quad \begin{array}{|l} P \\ \hline \vdots \\ R \end{array} \\
\quad \begin{array}{|l} Q \\ \hline \vdots \\ R \end{array} \\
R
\end{array}
$$

This rule is also called *Constructive Dilemma*, or more generally *dilemma-type* reasoning. If you stare at it long enough the rule will

---

[8] Many people, when asked to explain the phrase 'rule of thumb,' will mutter something about not being allowed to beat one's spouse with a stick thicker than one's thumb. This is wrong as well as offensive. The origin of the phrase, which seems to have come originally from Danish, involves approximation accomplished by the carpenter using her thumb as a 'rule'—in the sense of 'ruler.' Thus a rule of thumb is only an approximate rule in exactly the way that a thumb is only an approximate ruler.

eventually make sense. The idea is that you dispose of a given disjunction, say $A \vee B$, by saying that it doesn't matter which of the two disjuncts actually obtains, the same thing will inevitably follow. Thus we may discharge the disjunction in favor of that 'in either event' consequence. Notice that this rule requires the introduction of two subderivations, each headed by a distinct disjunct (the order is not important) one directly above the other. When the rule is invoked it acts to terminate *both* of these subderivations at the same time.

Another thing to keep in mind concerning this rule, is that more often than not we use the rule to reason from one disjunction to a different one. So it only eliminates one specific disjunction and we mustn't start thinking that there will be no disjunction in the conclusion.

For the horizontal form we have:

$[\vee E]\ (\Gamma \vdash P \vee Q\ \&\ \Gamma, P \vdash R\ \&\ \Gamma, Q \vdash R) \implies \Gamma \vdash R$

In this formulation we are using expressions like 'Γ, P' to represent the addition of P to the assumptions that already exist in Γ.[9]

Next we encounter the elimination and introduction rules for the conditional.

Conditional Elimination ($[\supset E]$)

$$
\begin{array}{l}
\vdots \\
P \supset Q* \\
\vdots \\
P* \\
\vdots \\
Q
\end{array}
$$

This rule is often referred to as *modus ponens*[10] (MP). In horizontal form, the rule is:

$[\supset E]\ (\Gamma \vdash P \supset Q\ \&\ \Gamma \vdash P) \implies \Gamma \vdash Q$

---

[9]The proper way to represent adding a formula, say P to set of formulas say Γ is: $\Gamma \cup \{P\}$. We shall take expressions like Γ, P to be abbreviations of the proper set-theoretic expressions.

[10]Such usage is not correct however. Historically, the rule *modus ponendo ponens* applied only to the case in which the premises of the rule do not depend upon any assumptions.

The companion rule is another of those which introduce a subderivation.

Conditional Introduction ($[\supset I]$)

$$
\begin{array}{l}
\vdots \\
\left|\begin{array}{l}
\underline{\quad P \quad} \\
\vdots \\
Q
\end{array}\right. \\
P \supset Q
\end{array}
$$

This rule also goes by the name of *Conditional Proof* (CP) or, in a somewhat older setting, the *deduction theorem*. The result of applying the rule is to immediately terminate the subderivation headed by the assumption represented by P. The horizontalized version is:

$[\supset I]$ $(\Gamma, P \vdash Q)$ $\Longrightarrow$ $\Gamma \vdash P \supset Q$

The rules for the biconditional work as expected given that the biconditional is simply two conditionals (in opposite directions) pasted together.

Biconditional Elimination ($[\equiv E]$)

Either of the following:

$$
\begin{array}{l}
\vdots \\
P \equiv Q* \\
\vdots \\
P* \\
\vdots \\
Q
\end{array}
$$

$$
\begin{array}{l|l}
& \vdots \\
& P \equiv Q* \\
& \vdots \\
& Q* \\
& \vdots \\
& P
\end{array}
$$

The horizontal form is: [≡E] [(Γ ⊢ $P \equiv Q$ & Γ ⊢ Q) $\implies$ Γ ⊢ P]
or
[(Γ ⊢ $P \equiv Q$ & Γ ⊢ P) $\implies$ Γ ⊢ Q] [≡I] (Biconditional Introduction)

$$
\begin{array}{l|l}
& \vdots \\
& \quad P \\
& \quad \vdots \\
& \quad Q \\
& \quad Q \\
& \quad \vdots \\
& \quad P \\
& P \equiv Q
\end{array}
$$

Invoking the rule immediately terminates the two subderivations, just as in the case of [∨E].

The negation rules are quite easy to formulate, and even seem to be intuitively what we expect of such rules, but the form in which we give them has generated a great deal of controversy since the ancient beginnings of the science of logic.

Before we get to negation proper, we introduce a new bit of language which might seem counterintuitive at first. An *absurd* formula, or absurdity is defined:[11]

Definition 3.2.1. The formula A is absurd if and only if $A \vdash B$ for every formula B of SL.

Why do we need such a thing? The short answer is that we don't need it strictly speaking but that it proves technically convenient to have this notion. The convenience in the first place is furnished by our having a very general way to talk about the (classical) consistency of sets of formulas, and of talking about inconsistency in a similarly general way.

When we first begin to think about inconsistency we think of it in terms of some pair of sentences both of which should not be provable.[12] If a set Γ *does* prove both members of the pair, then it is inconsistent. The paradigm is a pair of formulas consisting of some formula P and its negation $\neg P$. This is the touchstone of inconsistency because, whatever else negation is supposed to do, it must *exclude* or perhaps *deny* the formula it negates. We cannot, at the same time, both affirm and deny the same formula without inconsistency.[13]

But which pair of formulas should we pick to stand for inconsistency? The answer of course, is that it doesn't matter in the least. The pair P and $\neg P$ is just as bad as the pair Q and $\neg Q$ etc.

For this reason we introduce a formula[14] $\bot$, read *falsum* or sometimes *the false*, which will stand for an arbitrary absurdity. It has the property that all of the infinitely many pairs of formulas and their negations have in common. And what property is that? This question is answered by providing the following rules.

---

[11] Strictly speaking, the notion of absurdity is understood only relative to some notion of provability. Since we are only dealing with one such notion, it makes no pedagogical sense to be this precise.

[12] Or in semantic mode, both of which cannot be *true* at the same time

[13] This is a quick and dirty gloss but a detailed treatment of these issues would take us beyond the material of a first course in formal logic.

[14] Strictly speaking this introduction requires an amendment to the earlier definition of 'formula of SL' conferring formulahood on $\bot$, which we will assume has been made

Falsum Introduction ($[\perp\text{I}]$)

$$
\begin{array}{l}
\vdots \\
P* \\
\vdots \\
\neg P* \\
\vdots \\
\perp
\end{array}
$$

Here P is a variable, in case a reminder is needed, so all that is required to introduce falsum, is *any* formula and its negation, in either order.

The horizontal form is:

$[\perp\text{I}]\ (\Gamma \vdash P\ \&\ \Gamma \vdash \neg P)\ \Longrightarrow\ \Gamma \vdash \perp$

Falsum elimination ($[\perp\text{E}]$)

$$
\begin{array}{l}
\vdots \\
\perp\ * \\
\vdots \\
P
\end{array}
$$

which says that any sentence whatever may be derived from falsum. This is what we might expect of a sentence which does duty as a kind of arbitrary contradiction. Certainly, to hark back to our earliest musings in this book, it would be no more irrational to accept P, no matter what sentence be substituted, than it would be to accept $\perp$.

In horizontal form the rule is:

$[\perp\text{E}]\ \Gamma \vdash \perp \Longrightarrow\ \Gamma \vdash P$

Now for the negation rules:

Negation Introduction ([¬I])

$$
\begin{array}{c|l}
 & \vdots \\
 & \quad \begin{array}{|l} P \\ \hline \vdots \\ \bot \end{array} \\
 & \neg P
\end{array}
$$

Anything from which we can derive the falsum, must itself be false. This is a principle which has been known from antiquity by the name *reductio ad absurdum.* In this context we are using a very strong sense of absurdity, in which it means not simply something which is not accepted, but indeed something which cannot even *possibly* be accepted—which nicely characterizes $\bot$, in an informal way.

In horizontal form: $[\neg I]$ $\Gamma, P \vdash \bot \implies \Gamma \vdash \neg P$

And the elimination rule is practically the same thing:

Negation Elimination ([¬E])

$$
\begin{array}{c|l}
 & \vdots \\
 & \quad \begin{array}{|l} \neg P \\ \hline \vdots \\ \bot \end{array} \\
 & P
\end{array}
$$

At least it is another form of *reductio.* In horizontal form:

$[\neg E]$ $\Gamma, \neg P \vdash \bot \implies \Gamma \vdash P$

Both rules terminate their respective subderivations.

In practice, we shall allow as a shortcut the derivation of some formula P and its negation $\neg P$ without having to take the further step of introducing ⊥, even though strictly speaking that is what the rules require.

The rule of Negation Elimination should be regarded as a last resort, something to be avoided unless its use is absolutely necessary. Whenever you derive something by showing that the assumption of its falsehood leads to contradiction, you are said to be using an *indirect* proof. And make no mistake, there is a definite whiff of the pejorative when a proof is so-described. Many logicians will work for hours, or even years, to try to discover a direct proof when all they have is an indirect one.

The reasons for the prejudice against indirect proof seem to be a mixture of aesthetics, psychology and a certain viewpoint in the philosophy of logic and of mathematics called the *constructive* viewpoint.

From a widely-shared[15] aesthetic perspective, direct proofs are more beautiful, or at least prettier than indirect proofs.

From a psychological perspective, direct proofs tend to be more convincing, especially to the untutored lay person.

According to the constructive viewpoint, no mathematical object, (e.g. number, function, etc.) may be said to exist without giving a method whereby the object in question can be constructed (at least in principle—for soft-constructivists). For example, if we show that the assumption that such and such a number doesn't exist leads to contradiction, then we have shown by indirect proof that the number exists without having shown it constructively. Like 'indirect,' the expression 'non-constructive' has come to be a kind of mathematical/logical synonym for 'second rate.'

If you must use indirect proof, use it sparingly. And be aware that some people will look down on your efforts—even to the point of refusing to accept them. The official position of classical logic, is that negation elimination is acceptable, but that doesn't stop many classical logicians from trying to avoid it as much as possible. Maybe it would be better to state the official position as 'It is not always possible to avoid the use of indirect proof.'

---

[15] Widely-shared here means shared across a number of distinct schools in the philosophy of logic

Even though we call negation elimination the rule of last resort, it ought to be realized that there *is* a resort now, even if it is the last. When one is stuck in the middle of some derivation, take comfort in the fact that 'There's always negation elimination.'

Even though we have uttered a pair of rules for each of our connectives, we aren't quite done. There remain the rules which don't mention any connective; which are not, that is, either introduction or elimination rules. Such rules are usually called *structural*.

There is, for example, the rule which allows us to derive the very first inference that struck us as correct under the 'irrational to accept the premises and not the conclusion' model of reasoning. We are referring of course to the case in which the conclusion is one of the premises. In particular then, we require a rule which would justify this:

$$\begin{array}{|l} P \\ \hline P \end{array}$$

No rule in our current collection justifies this, perhaps the most obvious move in all of deduction. We shall soon repair that deficiency, but we notice that there is a nearly as obvious move that we ought to be able to make, namely:

$$\left\| \begin{array}{|l} \vdots \\ P \\ \vdots \\ P \end{array} \right.$$

In both cases we bring a formula (within the scope of which we are working—as indicated by the scope lines) down. In the first case we bring it straight down i.e., within the same subderivation. In the latter case we bring the formula down which we had derived in another subderivation. The important point here is that the subderivation in question is still *active*. Its scope line is still with us in the place that we want to relocate the formula—P in this example.

We should take the trouble to define this notion with as much precision as we can muster, since it will be crucial to some of our later studies, as well as to our understanding of the rules.

Let i be a line of some derivation D.

Definition 3.2.2. A subderivation $D*$ of D is *active* at line i in D if and only if the scope line of $D*$ extends to i.

Now it may not be obvious, but these two cases are actually different rules. It is in fact possible to have a system of rules which allows the first kind of bringing down without the second, and vice versa. But it is traditional in constructing the kind of system that we use, to say that both moves are justified by a rule called [R], the *rule of reiteration* .

We shall allow ourselves to use this rule, especially in its second form, *implicitly*, which is to say without explicit citation. In other words we shall allow the use of rules, Conditional Elimination for instance, in which the premises are derived in active subderivations rather than the subderivation in which the rule is invoked. Strictly speaking, in such a case, we should first use [R] one or more times in order that the premises of the rule are listed in the same subderivation in which the rule is used—that is the way the rule is stated. But this can get in the way of *momentum*, which is usually a bad idea, practically speaking.

3.3 Annotating Derivations

When writing out derivations, all that is strictly necessary are the lines. Once the line is written down, it is a mechanical matter to check if there is a rule of inference which would justify that line. However the mechanics might be extremely time consuming, so we shall adopt some conventions which will be of great assistance to the person who is checking to make sure that a sequence of lines actually is a derivation.

First, each time an assumption is introduced, it is underlined. This is all that is necessary to flag that the line is an assumption although some proof systems require that the word 'assumption' be written beside the formula in question. We shall make no such demands.

We shall require of each line justified by appeal to a rule, that the line be annotated with the name of the rule. Generally, the rule which introduces a connective δ will be named with '$[\delta I]$' while the rule which eliminates that connective will be named with '$[\delta E]$' although most of the rules also have alternative (two-letter) names, and using those instead is entirely acceptable. Except for the rule [R] of reiteration, the rule [$\wedge$E] of conjunction elimination and the rule [$\vee$I] of disjunction introduction, every rule of CSL requires two or more *premise* lines which must be present earlier in the derivation in which the rule is invoked. We require that the line annotation cite these earlier lines as well as the name of the rule.

Some rules, like [$\supset$E], require two premise lines. Suppose for example that the rule is being invoked on line l of the derivation and that the premise lines are derived on j and k. In such a case the annotation for line l would be something of the form '$[\supset E]\,j,k$'. Other rules, like [$\supset$I] for instance, require one or more previous subderivations. The rules terminate those subderivations. When annotating the lines in which rules of this kind are invoked, we shall require citing the subderivation (or subderivations) as well as the name of the rule. So if, in a certain derivation, $A \supset B$ is derived on line n by [$\supset$I] from a subderivation which extends from line $n - j$ to line $n - 1$, then the annotation beside line n would be something of the form '$[\supset I]\,(n - j)—(n - 1)$'.[16]

Each use of the rule [R], is to be annotated with its name, together with the number of the line from which the formula is being brought down. See the 'quick rules of reference' below for CSL for the annotation method for each rule.

3.4   Some Formal Definitions

The time has come to make precise certain ideas that we have been using in an intuitive way, as well as to frame the definitions of the key logical terminology, in its syntactical guise. As we expect, the centerpiece is

---

[16]For a concrete example, see the derivation on page 44.

the definition of the inference relation. On the way to that, we require some preliminaries. This makes precise the notion of a *derivation* in CSL and the *assumptions* which are active at a given line of a derivation.

Definition 3.4.1. A finite sequence of steps is a *derivation* in CSL *of* its last line, *from* assumptions (if any) listed on its initial lines if and only if each line in the sequence is either an assumption or is justified by a rule of CSL.

Definition 3.4.2. The formula P *belongs to the set of assumptions* of line number i in derivation D (in CSL) ($P \in \mathcal{Q}(D, i)$) if and only if P is an assumption of any subderivation D' of D which is active at line i.

Definition 3.4.3. $\Gamma \vdash P$ (Gamma *proves* P) if and only if there is a derivation of P from a set of assumptions which are included in Γ.

And now we can finally say just what is the logic CSL from the syntactical perspective:

Definition 3.4.4. The logic CSL is, from the syntactical perspective, defined to be the set of pairs Γ, P such that $\Gamma \vdash P$.

Definition 3.4.5. $\vdash P$ (P is a *theorem* of CSL) if and only if there is a derivation in CSL of P from no assumptions.

An alternative version of definition 3.4.5 would be:
$\vdash P$ if and only if $\varnothing \vdash P$

Definition 3.4.6. Two formulas P and Q are (syntactically) *equivalent* (in CSL), written $P \dashv\vdash Q$ if and only if each formula can be derived from the assumption of the other (in CSL).

Evidently the definition just given is itself equivalent to saying the biconditional between the two formulas is a theorem (of CSL).

Definition 3.4.7. A set Γ of formulas, is (syntactically) *consistent* if and only if there is a formula P such that $\Gamma \nvdash P$.

This definition of syntactical consistency is due to the American logician E.L. Post and while it is the most technically convenient one, it may look a little odd at first glance. The thing to keep in mind is that if we could derive a contradiction from Γ, some formula P together with its negation $\neg P$ for instance, then we could derive every formula (by indirect proof). Similarly, if we could derive any formula, then we could derive $\bot$. It follows that if we cannot derive every formula, then our set must be consistent in the usual sense.

It may not be evident, but a little thought shows that the definition just given is equivalent to:
$\Gamma \nvdash \bot$ which is itself equivalent to:
There is no formula P such that $\Gamma \vdash P$ & $\Gamma \vdash \neg P$.

3.5 Using the Rules

The Importance of Learning the Rules

It will take a certain amount of practice before these rules have been internalized and doing derivations seems natural. The beginning student should start doing exercises as soon as possible in order to facilitate that process. In particular, a certain amount of hands-on experience is strongly recommended *before* reading this section and the next. Otherwise, the scarce resources of short-term memory must be devoted to these helpful hints in addition to the rules and, finally, the data of the actual problems. As remarked in the preface, studies have shown beyond doubt that such (short-term) memory-intensive approaches degrade performance catastrophically.

Winning Strategies

The most valuable piece of advice is:

Principal Rule of Thumb for Derivations

Work *backward* from the conclusion to the assumptions as far as you can.

This is often quite far. The idea is to let the rules do as much of the work as they can, so you don't have to. Many derivations look very daunting because of their evident complexity. Our feeling of unease, if not outright panic, when we look at one of these all at once can now be explained as our intuitive worry that we shall exhaust our short-term memory before we get to the end of the task. It is just this kind of thing that the Fitch-style system avoids by breaking up the derivation into subderivations. For the most part that analysis of the problem is done mechanically.

Nowhere is this more evident than in the task of deriving conditionals. This is indeed a useful property since human beings easily get lost when they try to understand a complex conditional. Using the Fitch method, you never have to deal with a nested conditional. As an example of this, let us show that '$(A \supset (B \supset C)) \supset ((A \supset B) \supset (A \supset C))$' (sometimes called *the self-distribution law for the conditional*) is a theorem of CSL.

In the first place, since a theorem is a derivation from no assumptions, we *must* work backward having nothing at all from which to work forward. The particular work-backward strategy which the Fitch system promotes, comes from having only one way to introduce a connective. So what we do is look at what we want to derive from above and ask ourselves 'How did we get that?' So long as what we want is a compound formula, we shall be able to answer the question with 'By using the rule for such-and-such introduction.'

We keep on doing this, until we are asking about formulas consisting of sentence letters, and it is only at that point, that we can begin working from what we have (if anything). If we follow this advice faithfully, we shall find that what seem very complex and daunting problems, fall apart into easy to solve sub tasks. Let's try this on the problem at hand:

Here the technique works particularly easily since the only connective we encounter is the conditional. Starting from the last line, we ask 'How did we derive this?', and the answer is 'By the rule of conditional introduction!' In other words, at the outermost level we must have a derivation that looks like this:

$$
\begin{array}{l}
A \supset (B \supset C) \\
\vdots \\
(A \supset B) \supset (A \supset C) \\
((A \supset (B \supset C)) \supset ((A \supset B) \supset (A \supset C)) \qquad [\supset I]
\end{array}
$$

Things seem more manageable already and we've hardly done more than answer a single question. So let's ask ourselves how we got the penultimate line. The answer is the same as it was before: Conditional Introduction—which means that we must have had *another* subderivation along the lines of:

$$A \supset (B \supset C)$$

$$A \supset B$$

$$\vdots$$

$$A \supset C$$

$$(A \supset B) \supset (A \supset C) \qquad [\supset\text{I}]$$

$$((A \supset (B \supset C)) \supset ((A \supset B) \supset (A \supset C)) \qquad [\supset\text{I}]$$

Now we ask of the third line from the bottom, whence that came, and we receive the expected answer, since it too is a conditional. And that means another subderivation:

$$A \supset (B \supset C)$$

$$A \supset B$$

$$A$$

$$\vdots$$

$$C$$

$$A \supset C \qquad [\supset\text{I}]$$

$$(A \supset B) \supset (A \supset C) \qquad [\supset\text{I}]$$

$$((A \supset (B \supset C)) \supset ((A \supset B) \supset (A \supset C)) \qquad [\supset\text{I}]$$

But now we are down to letters and it's time to work forward. Before we do that however, we should stop to notice that more than half the derivation has been written out in a completely mechanical fashion. What looked complicated and frightening, now looks like it might even be *easy*.

How can we derive the letter C? If we look at what we have to work with at that point, we can see that the assumptions A, $A \supset B$, and $A \supset (B \supset C)$ are all active. Some people are confused, at first, by the fact that the last line has no assumptions. They think that must mean that there are no assumptions allowed *anywhere* in the derivation, but that is not true. All that the 'no assumption' provision means, is that no assumption can be active at the last line, which is a far cry from not allowing any assumptions at any line. And in this case, even though we are proving a theorem, by the innermost subderivation, we have accumulated the three assumptions just mentioned.

But if we have A and $A \supset B$ then we must have B by a single application of [$\supset$E] and if we also have $A \supset (B \supset C)$ then we must have $B \supset C$ by one application of that same rule, and since we previously derived B, we have C by one last application of the elimination rule. If we put it together we shall obtain this derivation:

1	$A \supset (B \supset C)$	
2	$\quad A \supset B$	
3	$\quad\quad A$	
4	$\quad\quad B$	[$\supset$E], 2, 3
5	$\quad\quad B \supset C$	[$\supset$E], 1, 3
6	$\quad\quad C$	[$\supset$E], 4, 5
7	$\quad A \supset C$	[$\supset$I], 3–6
8	$(A \supset B) \supset (A \supset C)$	[$\supset$I], 2–7
9	$((A \supset (B \supset C)) \supset ((A \supset B) \supset (A \supset C))$	[$\supset$I], 1–8

Of course this is an illustration which has been carefully chosen, and no one method will crank out a derivation for you in a mechanical fashion every time. Sometimes, the method of working backwards will fail, as when we must derive a disjunction on the main scope line, and at other times we will find ourselves grinding to a halt after working backwards as far as possible.

The key thing in deriving is *momentum*. By this is meant the sense of being busy; of writing things down; of having something to *do*. This is a source of energy, one which is often needed to carry you through the difficult parts. To put the matter another way, one of the *least* useful things one can do on the way to producing a derivation, is staring at a blank piece of paper.[17] Fortunately, the Fitch-style system we are using nearly always keeps us busy. Even if we are worried about being able to solve a difficult problem, there will be things we can be writing down, almost automatically, and by the time we get to the hard bits we may find that they aren't nearly as hard as we thought.

In aid of momentum conservation, it is often a good idea to skimp on writing out line justifications, at least in full detail. Rigor is sometimes the enemy of momentum as well as of clarity. One can always come back and annotate the steps later. And if, when we come back, it turns out that one or more of the steps is not quite justifiable, not in accord with the rules of inference after all, at least there is a rough idea of how to proceed. Perhaps some different combination of rules will accomplish what was attempted in the suspect portion of the derivation. The point is, if we stop to make sure that everything we are writing down is correct, we are almost certain to lose momentum and end up staring at a blank piece of paper. Experience will teach us that it is usually better to be writing down something rather than nothing, even if the something in question is less than entirely correct.

It isn't long after the novice begins working on derivations that she notices something disturbing: The derivation *she* produced is different from the one her friend produced. Perhaps when asked about it, the instructor produced a derivation which was distinct from both! How is such a thing possible? Surely if one can derive a certain conclusion C from a certain set of assumptions Γ, then there must be only one way to do that. In many cases this is not true—even in most cases. Nor is it the case in general that one particular derivation will be *the best* or even that one will be better than another.

---

[17]What Hemingway called 'The Great White Bull.'

Obviously, there are some pairs of derivations for which we can judge one is better—perhaps one is indirect and the other not. One might be longer than the other, though if the longer one is direct and the shorter not, then the former might still be judged superior. Many of the judgements are really aesthetic, and so there will be considerable variation from one person to the next.

And this is not a bad thing, though it is certainly something of which the beginner should be aware. Often, and without meaning to, an instructor will steer the students in a certain direction by showing them how to do this or that derivation. The students are quick to pick up, however much it is unintended, that the 'right' way to do this or that, is the way the instructor usually does it. But this is bad; it puts yet another layer of stuff between the student and the skill that she is attempting to master. Actually, it may be worse than that.

Left to their own devices, people tend to develop an *individual style* of doing derivations. Doing things in this particular way feels more natural to them than doing things some other (equally correct) way. It is probably a mistake to attempt to interfere very much with this beyond correcting actual errors.[18] It is of a piece with somebody's individual prose style.

When somebody begins writing prose she might emulate her favorite writers, but she comes by and by into a kind of writing which is peculiar to her—she finds her own *voice*. People can and do write prose outside of their own distinctive style—and indeed we encourage fledgling writers to try out as many distinct styles as possible. But in the course of conducting a writing workshop, we don't insist that the students go away writing like Conrad or Dickens or Hemingway. In fact if they did, we might count our efforts a failure.[19]

---

[18]Of course the author attempts to do a certain amount of interfering when he insists, from time to time, that indirect proofs are inferior to direct proofs. In this he is actually attempting to short-circuit his influence in lectures where he nearly always thinks of the indirect proof first—perhaps because of the way he was trained!

[19]All of which is to say that too much 'showing how to do it' sessions in the classroom, may actually be harmful, in just the way that one wouldn't normally think of showing somebody how to write by reading them the collected works of D. H. Lawrence, or even one's own works. Of course there will always be a place for doing examples, but that shouldn't be the majority of lecture content.

The Special Problems of Negation Elimination

The place where momentum is most likely to drop and where the 'work backwards' strategy is most likely to fail is in the last resort— negation elimination. Working backwards is not a useful piece of advice in this case because what we must derive in the [¬E] subderivation is some formula P, and its negation $\neg P$. The whole art of using this inference rule, is selecting *which* formula to try to derive. Only after we have made this selection, does it make sense to start working backwards because which formulas we have on hand, in that part of the derivation, should influence our choice. In other words, we should work *forwards* from the materials on hand before we try working backwards. In particular, keep in mind the following rule of thumb:

Rule of Thumb for using Negation Elimination

Try to derive formulas for which the negations are easily derived.

Obviously one should begin with those negations which are easiest to get, for instance a negation standing alone or as a conjunct. After that, a negation as a consequent of a conditional or one side of a biconditional. Negations which are disjuncts or the antecedents of conditionals should be regarded as hard to derive.

Once the decision has been taken to use the rule of last resort, that is often not the end of the matter. Suppose that it *still* doesn't work? In this case, it is possible that one is attempting to derive the underivable, but it is also possible that one can make a change to the overall structure of the derivation so far attempted.

It may be that one stalls out deep in some interior sub-derivation and in that case one would be best advised not to invoke [¬E] *there*, but rather *earlier* in the derivation. Thinking of Negation Elimination as a last resort; as a kind of *dirty hands* rule, once we have decided to get our hands dirty, there is no point in putting it off, our hands will not thereby be less dirty somehow. And doing [¬E] earlier in the derivation will give us one more assumption to use that wasn't available to us before we decided to use *reductio*.

So the advice takes this form:

Avoid Negation Elimination as far as possible, but once you have decided that you cannot avoid it, use it earlier in the derivation rather than later.

Common Mistakes, Pitfalls, and Other Problems

Some of the most common mistakes made by beginners are demonstrated in the following derivation fragments:

Conditional Elimination is a very intuitive rule—so much so, that beginners are often in too much of a hurry to use it. Consider:

$$
\begin{array}{ll}
1. & A \vee (B \supset C) \\
2. & B \\
3. & A \vee C \quad ; 1,2\,[\supset E] \quad (MISTAKE!) \\
  & \vdots
\end{array}
$$

In the above fragment the mistake is that line 1 is *not a conditional* although it has a conditional as one of its disjuncts. The rule, [⊃E], requires that (at least) one of its premises must be a conditional. It often seems to beginners that the rules of CSL are too lax in that one may assume anything. Of course, it's quite true that one is always allowed to make an assumption, but it is *emphatically not true* that one is allowed to *discharge* any assumption once it has served its purpose.

Consider:

```
1              │A
2              │ │B
(MISTAKE!)   │ A ∧ B        [∧I], 1, 2
```

In the above fragment an attempt is made to derive a conjunction by assuming both conjuncts. What keeps this from being correct is that the rule [∧I], of conjunction introduction does not terminate a subderivation, and thus it cannot, as attempted, terminate either of the two subderivations which introduce the assumptions. A correct use of the rule in these circumstances would be:

```
1    │ │A
2    │ │ │B
3    │ │ │A ∧ B        [∧I], 1, 2
```

although this usage leaves us two subderivations away from the main scope line. In another kind of mistake it's not that there are too many scope lines, but rather too few:

$$n \qquad \begin{array}{|l} \begin{array}{|l} A \\ \hline \vdots \\ B \end{array} \\ A \supset B \qquad [\supset I] \\ \vdots \end{array}$$

$(MISTAKE!) \quad \begin{array}{|l} A \end{array} \qquad [R], n$

In this we attempt to bring down the sentence A, but our attempt to do so is rendered forlorn by the fact that the subderivation from which we wish to do the bringing down is not active at the line in which we try to invoke [R], and hence A is no longer available for reiteration by that point of the derivation.

All of the previous may be thought of as making moves which are not in accord with the rules. Another type of mistake, perhaps a more subtle type, results when the beginner fails to use a move which *is* allowed by the rules. Of course such behavior is mistaken only when there in no other way to accomplish a given derivation.

The difference between the two kinds of mistake is that only the latter kind might actually be *excused*, on philosophical grounds. Consider, for instance, the following fragment:

$$\begin{array}{|l} \vdots \\ P \\ \begin{array}{|l} \vdots \\ \neg P \\ \begin{array}{|l} \vdots \\ A(?) \end{array} \end{array} \end{array}$$

In this the line $A(?)$ represents that we wish to derive A on that line, but don't see how this might be accomplished. This might not actually be a mistake, as was noted above, provided that there are a number of alternative ways. If there is only one way to proceed, then that way requires that A be derived by [¬E]. In other words, the actual derivation should be done as shown schematically:

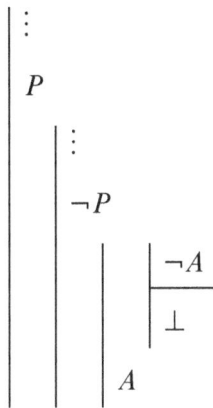

$$
\begin{array}{l}
\vdots \\
P \\
\quad\begin{array}{l}
\vdots \\
\neg P \\
\quad\begin{array}{l}
\quad\begin{array}{l}
\neg A \\
\hline
\bot
\end{array} \\
A
\end{array}
\end{array}
\end{array}
$$

Here A may be derived because *any* formula could be derived at that point, a point at which we are within the scope of a *contradiction*. In other words: for some formula P, both that formula and its negation have been derived in active subderivations. Hence both are available by [R].

This much is obvious, but what is often not obvious to beginners is that we are *allowed* to use the rule of negation introduction. No few have been bewitched by its common name: *reductio ad absurdum*. It seems to these people that A shouldn't be derived by [¬E] because it does not *lead* to an absurdity. In particular, the assumption of $\neg A$ does not lead to a contradiction since that contradiction existed in the derivation *before* we assumed $\neg A$, hence the latter has not been shown to lead to any absurdity—at least none that wasn't lying around already.

There are enough people in the world who feel this way, that there has been constructed an alternative to CSL, which doesn't allow this kind of appeal to *reductio*.[20]

Another pitfall or error which beginners sometimes commit in their attempts to use [¬E], involves thinking that the contradiction to which an assumption leads must take the form of a sentence letter and its negation. Now it *is* true that all contradictions are interderivable, so that if an assumption leads to any contradiction at all, it must lead, if only eventually, to some single letter and its negation, but this is not the way to actually apply the rule in practice. It is certainly not the way to apply the rule in accord with its Rule of Thumb. Consider for example, the derivation which shows that $A \lor \neg A$ is a theorem.

We begin with:

$$\vdots$$
$$A \lor \neg A$$

with no assumptions at the top of the main scope line and no idea how to begin. This is because we recall that we shouldn't use Disjunction Introduction on the main scope line. If ever we needed a last resort, this is the place. Having made the decision to use Negation Elimination, we must have:

$$\neg(A \lor \neg A)$$
$$\vdots$$
$$?$$
$$A \lor \neg A \qquad\qquad [\neg E]$$

The ? marks the place where we must produce some formula and its negation—but which? The rule of thumb enjoins us to derive some formula for which we already *have* the negation. A typical beginner's error in the current derivation is to think that A is such a formula. We do *not* in fact have $\neg A$. The latter formula is *buried* inside a disjunction, which is in turn inside a negation. Mark that hard to get. The rule of thumb tells us to start with negations which are easier to get, those

---

[20]The alternative approach is usually called *Intuitionism* although there is a great deal more to Intuitionism than its criticism of the classical negation rules.

which stand alone or are conjuncts perhaps. There is only one formula which is a negation standing alone, and that is $\neg(A \vee \neg A)$.

If we obey the rule of thumb then, we must try to derive $A \vee \neg A$, the negatum of the one and only negation which is easy to get. This is liable to strike the beginner as at least bizarre, and perhaps even absurd. After all, the negatum in question is exactly what we are trying to derive on the main scope line! If we can derive it in the subderivation, couldn't we derive it on the main scope line?

We could not, because in the subderivation we have more assumptions than we do in the main derivation. In the main derivation we don't have any assumptions at all. So far, this is where we are:

$$
\begin{array}{|ll}
\quad\begin{array}{|ll}
\neg(A \vee \neg A) & \\
\vdots & \\
A \vee \neg A?? & \\
\end{array} \\
A \vee \neg A & [\neg E]
\end{array}
$$

where the ?? indicate that we haven't decided how to derive this line. In point of fact, since we are not on the main scope line, we can now go back to our usual strategy and say that we must have obtained this line by Disjunction Introduction. Further, let's suppose that we obtained the disjunct A first and then used the rule [$\vee$I] to get what we want. In other words, let's assume that we can turn the following fragment into a derivation:

$$
\begin{array}{|ll}
\quad\begin{array}{|ll}
\neg(A \vee \neg A) & \\
\vdots & \\
A?? & \\
A \vee \neg A & [\vee I] \\
\end{array} \\
A \vee \neg A & [\neg E]
\end{array}
$$

At this point, since we are down to letters again, we can see that we must resort once more to [¬E]. This means that we must assume '¬A and derive some contradiction or other—finding which one, is the art of using *reductio* reasoning. The rule of thumb tells us to be guided by which negations we already have, or can easily get. In this case, there are two such negations: $A \lor \neg A$ and $\neg A$. It might seem that the latter is simpler, and hence easier to use, but that would not be true. The question which will decide the issue of which negation to use is: 'Which *un-negated* formula will be easier to derive?' Remember that to use *reductio* we must derive both a formula *and* its negation. This comes down to: "Which of 'A' and '$A \lor \neg A$' is easier to derive (at this point of the derivation)?"

We can derive the disjunction in one step by [∨I], while it would take three steps to derive A. So wrapping the whole derivation up and properly annotating it, we get:

1		$\neg(A \lor \neg A)$	
2		$\neg A$	
3		$A \lor \neg A$	[∨I], 2
4		$\bot$	[⊥I], 1, 3
5		A	[¬E], 2–4
6		$A \lor \neg A$	[∨I], 5
7		$\bot$	[⊥I], 1, 6
8	$A \lor \neg A$		[¬E], 1–7

This particular derivation is nearly always the cause of tears, or at least of bad language when it is first assigned to beginning students. There isn't any doubt that it is difficult, although more or less blindly following rules of thumb can carry one nearly all the way through to the end. It may be that this is a difficult (early) exercise, not only because we must resort to *reductio* immediately, even before we can try some other way, but also that we must use one *reductio* subderivation inside the scope of another.

If we think about it for a bit, it will be hard not to see this as a kind of watershed for the Classical approach to logic. Perhaps nowhere else in the very beginnings of logic, do we sail quite so close to the wind or travel quite so far away from our immediate intuitions. If, for instance, we think that *reductio* reasoning is only allowable when the assumption may be seen to contribute to the production of a contradiction, then nesting of [¬E] subderivations one inside another will not be legitimate in most cases. If the exterior subderivation really does lead to a contradiction, then that contradiction must be there before we start the interior subderivation.

In other words, if we were to try to fix the classical negation rules by placing a condition on its application to only consistent (without the assumption which is being reduced) sets of formulas—perhaps along the lines of:

$$\Gamma \nvdash \bot \ \& \ \Gamma, A \vdash \bot \Longrightarrow \Gamma \vdash \neg A$$

we can never perform a reductio within the scope of another. It would follow from this that any derivation which required the use of a reductio subderivation inside the scope of another could be done in the new system. It is beyond the scope of this book to answer the question of whether there are any such derivations in CSLand exactly which logic would result from the restriction on the classical negation rules.[21]

3.6 Exercises

Show that each of the following derivability claims hold, by constructing a derivation of the conclusion from the premises.

1. $(A \supset B) \supset A / \therefore (B \supset A) \supset A$

2. $(A \supset B) \supset C / \therefore (C \supset A) \supset A$

---

[21] In an earlier version of this book I was rather more careless in my discussion of these matters. This was pointed out to me by Calvin Ostrum, who thereby earned my gratitude

3. $\{(A \supset C) \supset C, B \supset C\} / \therefore (A \supset B) \supset C$

4. $\{((A \supset B) \supset C) \supset D, B \supset D\} / \therefore A \supset D$

5. $\{((A \supset B) \supset C) \supset D, B \supset C\} / \therefore A \supset D$

6. $\{A \supset B, A \wedge \neg B\} / \therefore C$

7. $\{A \supset (B \supset C), A \supset (B \supset D), A, C \supset \neg D\} / \therefore \neg B$

8. $\{(((A \supset B) \supset (\neg C \supset \neg D)) \supset C) \supset E, E \supset A, D\} / \therefore A$

9. $A \wedge B / \therefore \neg(A \supset \neg B)$

10. $\neg A \supset B / \therefore A \vee B$

11. $A \vee B / \therefore \neg A \supset B$

12. $\{A \supset \neg B, \neg A \supset B\} / \therefore A \equiv \neg B$

13. $A \wedge B / \therefore \neg(\neg A \vee \neg B)$

14. $\neg(\neg A \vee \neg B) / \therefore A \wedge B$

15. $A \vee B / \therefore (A \supset B) \supset B$

16. $(A \supset B) \supset B / \therefore A \vee B$

17. $(A \supset B) \supset C / \therefore (A \wedge (B \supset C)) \vee C$

18. $\{(A \equiv B) \equiv (A \equiv C), B\} / \therefore C$

19. $\{A \equiv B, C\} / \therefore (A \wedge C) \equiv (C \supset B)$

20. $\{(A \equiv B) \vee C, C \vee A\} / \therefore C \vee B$

21. $\{A \equiv B, B \equiv C\} / \therefore ((A \wedge B) \wedge C) \vee ((\neg A \wedge \neg B) \wedge \neg C)$

22. $\{(\neg V \supset W) \wedge (X \supset W), \neg(\neg X \wedge V)\} / \therefore W$

23. $\{(D \wedge E) \supset F, (D \supset F) \supset G\} / \therefore E \supset G$

24. $\{(E \supset F) \wedge (G \supset \neg H)\} / \therefore (\neg E \vee F) \wedge (G \supset \neg H)$

25. $\{(F \supset G) \wedge (H \supset I), (J \supset K), (F \vee J) \wedge (H \vee L)\} / \therefore G \vee K$

26. $\{(G \supset \neg H) \supset I, \neg(G \wedge H)\} / \therefore I \vee \neg H$

27. $\{(J \vee K) \supset \neg L, L\} / \therefore \neg J$

28. $\{(K \vee L) \supset (M \vee N), (M \vee N) \supset (O \wedge P), K\} / \therefore O$

29. $\{(M \supset N) \wedge (O \supset P), \neg N \vee \neg P, \neg(M \wedge O) \supset Q\} / \therefore Q$

30. $\{(Q \vee R) \supset S\} / \therefore Q \supset S$

31. $\{(X \vee Y) \supset (X \wedge Y), \neg(X \vee Y)\} / \therefore \neg(X \wedge Y)$

32. $\{(Z \supset Z) \supset (A \supset A), (A \supset A) \supset (Z \supset Z)\} / \therefore A \supset A$

33. $\{[(A \vee B) \supset C], [(C \vee B) \supset [A \supset (D \equiv E)]], A \wedge D\} / \therefore D \equiv E$

34. $\{A \supset B), A \vee (C \wedge D), \neg B \wedge \neg E\} / \therefore C$

35. $\{A \vee (B \vee C), B \supset (A \supset \neg C), (A \equiv C)\} / \therefore A \equiv \neg B$

36. $\{[(M \wedge N) \wedge O] \supset P, Q \supset [(O \wedge M) \wedge N]\} / \therefore \neg Q \vee P$

37. $\{\neg A \supset B, C \supset (D \vee E), D \supset \neg C, A \supset \neg E\} / \therefore C \supset B$

38. $\{\neg D \supset (\neg E \supset \neg F), \neg(F \wedge \neg D) \supset \neg G\} / \therefore G \supset E$

39. $\{\neg F \vee \neg[\neg(G \wedge H) \wedge (G \vee H)], (G \supset H) \supset [(H \supset G) \supset I]\} / \therefore F \supset (F \wedge I)$

40. $\{A \supset \neg B, \neg(C \wedge \neg A)\} / \therefore C \supset \neg B$

41. $\{A \supset B, C \supset D, A \vee C\} / \therefore (A \wedge B) \vee (C \wedge D)$

42. $\{A \vee (B \wedge C), \neg E, (A \vee B) \supset (D \vee E), \neg A\} / \therefore (C \wedge D)$

43. $\{C\}/ \therefore D \supset C$

44. $\{H \supset (I \wedge J)\}/ \therefore H \supset I$

45. $\{J \supset K, K \vee L, (L \wedge \neg J) \supset (M \wedge \neg J), \neg K\}/ \therefore M$

46. $\{J \vee (\neg J \wedge K), J \supset L\}/ \therefore (L \wedge J) \equiv J$

47. $\{M \supset N, M \supset (N \supset O)\}/ \therefore M \supset O$

48. $\{N \supset O\}/ \therefore (N \wedge P) \supset O$

49. $\{T \supset (U \wedge V), (U \vee V) \supset W\}/ \therefore T \supset W$

50. $\{T \supset U, T \supset V\}/ \therefore T \supset (U \wedge V)$

51. $\{W \supset X, Y \supset X\}/ \therefore (W \vee Y) \supset X$

52. $\{Z \supset A, A \vee Z\}/ \therefore A$

3.7   Derivable Rules in CSL

Historically, there have been many other rules apart from ones we have introduced so far. We now consider how many of these alternative rules might be added to the existing stock.

Definition 3.7.1. An introduction or elimination rule is said to be *derivable* in a logic L, if and only if any line of a derivation justified by the rule, could have also been derived by means of the original rule set alone.

Derivable rules don't allow any derivations that weren't allowed already—don't give us anything *new*. In that case, why use them? There are two reasons.

There are several rules which have been important historically and it is important to show that such rules are indeed derivable. Also, there are rules which can often be used in place of their less intuitive official rules. An example of these two motivations together is an alternative version of disjunction elimination which usually goes by the name of *disjunctive syllogism* ([DS]). It is represented by either of the following:

$$P \vee Q*$$
$$\neg P*$$
$$\vdots$$
$$Q$$

$$P \vee Q*$$
$$\neg Q*$$
$$\vdots$$
$$P$$

In horizontal form: $(\Gamma \vdash A \vee B \, \& \, \Gamma \vdash \neg A) \implies \Gamma \vdash B$

The word syllogism here and in the next rule is used to mean any rule with two premises.

It has often seemed to reasoners that the conditional can be *composed* in the manner of the following rule of *Hypothetical Syllogism* ([HS]).[22]

$$P \supset Q*$$
$$\vdots$$
$$Q \supset R*$$
$$\vdots$$
$$P \supset R$$

---

[22]The word 'hypothetical' is the word for the conditional form which is derived from Greek. The *parts* of the conditional in that tradition (as opposed to the Latin whence come antecedent and consequent) are hypothesis and apodisis.

There are many situations in which we wish we could reason backwards from the consequent to the antecedent of a conditional. It turns out that there is indeed a way to do that, but it involves negation. This is the burden of the rule *Modus Tollens*[23] ([MT]).

$$
\begin{array}{|l}
\vdots \\
P \supset Q* \\
\vdots \\
\neg Q* \\
\vdots \\
\neg P
\end{array}
$$

Rules of Replacement

All the rules of inference we have seen thus far work on *whole formulas*. In order to use a such-and-such elimination rule, we must begin with a formula for which the such-and-such connective is the *main connective*. In fact we warn against the attempt to use rules on parts of formulas. There are however rules which work on subformulas as well as formulas. These kinds of rules are known as *rules of replacement*.

Not only are we allowed to use these rules on subformulas, all the rules are *bidirectional*. Consider a rule like:

[Xrep] $X \longleftrightarrow Y$

The double-headed arrow indicates that we can replace the left side by the right side or *vice versa*, in any formula or subformula.

How can this be? Surely the addition of replacement rules takes us beyond what we can derive using only connective rules? In fact they do not. We can show, though not in this chapter, that if a rule licenses the replacement of equivalents by equivalents, we can derive the result of applying the rule, within our original rule set. More precisely: Let X and X' and Y and Y' be any four formulas such that Y' is like Y except that it contains X' as a subformula at zero or more places where

---

[23]This rule is as misnamed, historically speaking, as the rule [MP]. In the first place the ancient rule was named *Modus Tollendo Tollens* and in the second place, that rule applied *only* to the case in which the premises of the rule were both theorems.

Y contains X. It then follows that if we can derive in CSL that X and X' are equivalent, then we can likewise derive that so are Y and Y'. In view of this result, all we need do to demonstrate that a rule of replacement is derivable, is to show that the two sides are equivalent (in CSL).

Here is the list of replacement rules that we allow:

Contraposition [Contra] $P \supset Q \longleftrightarrow \neg Q \supset \neg P$

Implication [Impl] $P \supset Q \longleftrightarrow \neg P \vee Q$

Double Negation [DN] $P \longleftrightarrow \neg\neg P$

De Morgan [DeM]

$$\neg(P \wedge Q) \longleftrightarrow \neg P \vee \neg Q$$
$$\neg(P \vee Q) \longleftrightarrow \neg P \wedge \neg Q$$

Commutativity [Com]

$$P \vee Q \longleftrightarrow Q \vee P$$
$$P \wedge Q \longleftrightarrow Q \wedge P$$

Idempotence [Id]

$$P \vee P \longleftrightarrow P$$
$$P \wedge P \longleftrightarrow P$$

Exportation [Exp] $P \supset (Q \supset R) \longleftrightarrow (P \wedge Q) \supset R$

Associativity [Assoc]

$$P \wedge (Q \wedge R) \longleftrightarrow (P \wedge Q) \wedge R$$
$$P \vee (Q \vee R) \longleftrightarrow (P \vee Q) \vee R$$

Distribution [Dist]

$$P \wedge (Q \vee R) \longleftrightarrow (P \wedge Q) \vee (P \wedge R)$$
$$P \vee (Q \wedge R) \longleftrightarrow (P \vee Q) \wedge (P \vee R)$$

Equivalence [Equiv]

$$P \equiv Q \longleftrightarrow (P \supset Q) \wedge (Q \supset P)$$
$$P \equiv Q \longleftrightarrow (P \wedge Q) \vee (\neg P \wedge \neg Q)$$

3.8   Exercises

Construct a derivation of the conclusion from the premises in each of the following: (You are permitted to use derivable rules).

1. $A \supset (B \supset C)/ \therefore B \supset (A \supset C)$

2. $A \supset (A \supset B)/ \therefore A \supset B$

3. $\{(A \supset B) \supset (A \supset C), B\}/ \therefore A \supset C$

4. $(A \supset B) \supset (B \supset C)/ \therefore B \supset C$

5. $\{A \supset (B \supset \neg A), A \supset B\}/ \therefore \neg A$

6. $A \supset (B \supset \neg A)/ \therefore B \supset \neg A$

7. $\neg A \supset \neg B/ \therefore B \supset A$

8. $\{\neg\neg A, B \supset \neg A\}/ \therefore \neg(A \supset B)$

9. $\neg(A \wedge \neg B)/ \therefore A \supset B$

10. $A \wedge \neg B/ \therefore \neg(A \supset B)$

11. $\{A \supset (C \wedge D), B \supset (\neg C \wedge \neg D)\}/ \therefore \neg(A \wedge B)$

12. $\{(A \supset \neg B) \wedge (B \supset \neg C), D \supset B\}/ \therefore D \supset (\neg A \wedge \neg C)$

13. $\{A \vee B, A \supset C, B \supset D\}/ \therefore C \vee D$

14. $\{A \vee B, B \supset C\}/ \therefore \neg A \supset C$

15. $\{A \supset B, \neg(B \vee C)\}/ \therefore \neg(A \vee C)$

16. $\{A \vee B, (A \supset C) \wedge (\neg C \supset \neg B)\}/ \therefore C$

3.9 Solutions to Selected Exercises

selected solutions to exercises 3.6

1. The derivation starts, as they all do with a vertical line. At the top we write the assumptions, and at the bottom the conclusion we hope to derive. That would look like:

$$
\begin{array}{c|l}
1 & (A \supset B) \supset A \\
\vdots & \vdots \\
n & (B \supset A) \supset A
\end{array}
$$

(In this the three dots stand for a *lot* of room.)

Noticing that we must derive a conditional as the conclusion, we begin that in the most direct way, a subderivation ending just above the conclusion which we hope to derive by means of conditional introduction. So our derivation evolves into something like:

$$
\begin{array}{c|l}
1 & (A \supset B) \supset A \\
2 & \quad B \supset A \\
\vdots & \quad \vdots \\
n-1 & \quad A \\
n & (B \supset A) \supset A \qquad [\supset I], 2\text{-}n-1
\end{array}
$$

At this point we observe that what we need, namely A, is available as the consequent of two different conditionals—the conditional of line 1 and the conditional of line 2. So now we consider which of those we might be able to use to give us our A by conditional elimination.

The shortest one, on line 2, would yield us A if only we can derive B, while the conditional on line 1 requires an additional $A \supset B$ in order to produce the A that we are looking for on line n-1. So we should ask ourselves "How hard is it going to be to derive B?" The answer would seem to be "very hard", since B is available only in the antecedents of the two conditionals we already have. Getting formulas out of antecedents is a mug's game at best. When we look closely, we see that both ways of getting A by conditional elimination involve deriving B. It's just that the 'long' way requires that we derive B having assumed A and the shorter way gives no other resources than we already have. If we put this all together it looks like our best shot is represented by:

1	$(A \supset B) \supset A$	
2	$\quad B \supset A$	
3	$\quad\quad A$	
$\vdots$	$\quad\quad \vdots$	
$n-3$	$\quad\quad B$	
$n-2$	$\quad A \supset B$	$[\supset\text{I}], 3\text{–}n-3$
$n-1$	$\quad A$	$[\supset\text{E}], 1, n-2$
n	$(B \supset A) \supset A$	$[\supset\text{I}], 2\text{–}n-1$

But no amount of staring at the paper or head-scratching will deliver to us a method of deriving B, even though we are allowed to use the extra information A. At this point we grind to a halt and admit that we are stuck. The time has come for the rule of last resort. Our untutored impulse is to apply the strategy at our current stopping point which is to say that we have in mind something like:

$$
\begin{array}{lll}
1 & (A \supset B) \supset A & \\
2 & \quad B \supset A & \\
3 & \quad\quad A & \\
4 & \quad\quad\quad \neg B & \\
\vdots & \quad\quad\quad \vdots & \\
n-4 & \quad\quad\quad \bot & \\
n-3 & \quad\quad B & [\neg\text{E}], 4\text{--}n-4 \\
n-2 & \quad A \supset B & [\supset\text{I}], 3\text{--}n-3 \\
n-1 & \quad A & [\supset\text{E}], 1, n-2 \\
n & (B \supset A) \supset A & [\supset\text{I}], 2\text{--}n-1
\end{array}
$$

To make this approach work we need to derive some formula and its negation in order to introduce the false at line n-4. The standing advice we have is to look first for whatever negations we have "on hand" and then try to derive the negatum. Alas the only negation we have on hand is $\neg B$ and so we're back to trying to derive B, at which task we have already failed (more than once). So it seems that our rule of last resort has let us down.

Actually it hasn't. Beginners and others who flinch from the use of negation elimination are often inclined to wait as long as possible before using the dreaded rule. It's as if using deep inside a derivation is less reprehensible somehow than using it at the start. But the truth is that once we have decided to dirty our hands, we should plunge right in and get them dirty right away.

So what we need to do is use negation elimination earlier. How early? Well, if we use it on the main scope line, we shall have the negation of a nested conditional to work with. The prospect is unpleasant enough that we drop that idea and decide that we shall derive A on line n-1, not by conditional elimination which now seems to us to be a snare and a delusion, but rather by using negation elimination instead.

In other words our derivation will look like this:

$$
\begin{array}{lll}
1 & (A \supset B) \supset A & \\
2 & \quad B \supset A & \\
3 & \quad\quad \neg A & \\
\vdots & \quad\quad \vdots & \\
n-2 & \quad\quad \bot & \\
n-1 & \quad A & [\neg E],\ 3\text{--}n-2 \\
n & (B \supset A) \supset A & [\supset I],\ 2\text{--}n-1
\end{array}
$$

To derive the false at line n-2, we need to first derive some formula and its negation, and the rule of thumb is to see what negations we already have. There is only one of those, $\neg A$. So in order to get the false, we must derive A. But before we fall into the slough of despond at the idea of once again trying to derive A, something we failed utterly to do a few moments ago, we are suddenly heartened by the idea that we have more information than we did last time, we now have the negation of A.

If we look back now at our previous attempt, we came to grief in trying to derive B under the assumption that A—we couldn't see how to get some formula and it's negation that time, but this time it is immediately obvious. Once we assume A *now* then since we already *have* the negation of A as a previous assumption, we can use negation elimination to derive anything we want. What we want is B. So really, what we are doing is taking the old and failed derivation, and inserting most of its steps into our new derivation. Let's put these ideas together in stages. First:

1	$(A \supset B) \supset A$	
2	$B \supset A$	
3	$\neg A$	
⋮	⋮	
$n-3$	A	
$n-2$	$\bot$	$[\bot I], 3, n-3$
$n-1$	A	$[\neg E], 3\text{–}n-2$
n	$(B \supset A) \supset A$	$[\supset I], 2\text{–}n-1$

Next to derive A on line n-3 we shall use the previous strategy, which is to say we will use conditional elimination by deriving $A \supset B$. In other words:

1	$(A \supset B) \supset A$	
2	$B \supset A$	
3	$\neg A$	
⋮	⋮	
$n-4$	$A \supset B$	
$n-3$	A	$[\supset E], 1, n-4$
$n-2$	$\bot$	$[\bot I], 3, n-3$
$n-1$	A	$[\neg E], 3\text{–}n-2$
n	$(B \supset A) \supset A$	$[\supset I], 2\text{–}n-1$

The difference between this time and last we can see how to fill in the blank. To derive $A \supset B$ we must assume A and derive B under that assumption. But if we assume A we can introduce $\bot$ anywhere after that, since we have earlier assumed $\neg A$. But let's not get ahead of ourselves. First we do this:

1	$(A \supset B) \supset A$	
2	$\quad B \supset A$	
3	$\quad\quad \neg A$	
4	$\quad\quad\quad A$	
$\vdots$	$\quad\quad\quad \vdots$	
$n-5$	$\quad\quad\quad B$	
$n-4$	$\quad\quad A \supset B$	$[\supset I], 4\text{–}n-5$
$n-3$	$\quad\quad A$	$[\supset E], 1, n-4$
$n-2$	$\quad\quad \perp$	$[\perp I], 3, n-5$
$n-1$	$\quad A$	$[\neg E], 3\text{–}n-4$
n	$(B \supset A) \supset A$	$[\supset I], 2\text{–}n-1$

And as for deriving B, nothing could (now) be easier.

1	$(A \supset B) \supset A$	
2	$B \supset A$	
3	$\neg A$	
4	A	
5	$\neg B$	
6	$\bot$	[$\bot$I], 3, 4
7	B	[$\neg$E], 5–6
8	$A \supset B$	[$\supset$I], 4–7
9	A	[$\supset$E], 1, 8
10	$\bot$	[$\bot$I], 3, 9
11	A	[$\neg$E], 3–10
12	$(B \supset A) \supset A$	[$\supset$I], 2–11

2. This one will turn out to be quite similar to the first. But let's just blast away and see what happens. First the main outline:

1	$(A \supset B) \supset C$	
$\vdots$	$\vdots$	
n	$(C \supset A) \supset A$	

The conclusion is a conditional, so we assume we got it by conditional introduction, which is to say:

$$
\begin{array}{ll}
1 & (A \supset B) \supset C \\
2 & \quad C \supset A \\
\vdots & \quad \vdots \\
n-1 & \quad A \\
n & (C \supset A) \supset A \qquad [\supset\!\text{I}], 2\text{–}n-1
\end{array}
$$

But how to get A? Well, A is the consequent (always good) of the conditional at line 2. If we could derive the antecedent of that conditional, we'd have what we want by conditional elimination.

So we're thinking along these lines:

$$
\begin{array}{ll}
1 & (A \supset B) \supset C \\
2 & \quad C \supset A \\
\vdots & \quad \vdots \\
n-2 & \quad C \\
n-1 & \quad A \qquad\qquad\quad [\supset\!\text{E}], 2, n-2 \\
n & (C \supset A) \supset A \qquad [\supset\!\text{I}], 2\text{–}n-1
\end{array}
$$

And this C that we need is itself a consequent of the conditional at line 1. So we might hope to derive the antecedent of *that* conditional too which would give us

1	$(A \supset B) \supset C$	
2	$C \supset A$	
3	A	
⋮	⋮	
$n - 4$	B	
$n - 3$	$A \supset B$	[$\supset$I], 3–$n - 4$
$n - 2$	C	[$\supset$E], 1, $n - 3$
$n - 1$	A	[$\supset$E], 2, $n - 2$
n	$(C \supset A) \supset A$	[$\supset$I], 2–$n - 1$

Alas our headlong rush to proof has now gone off the rails. We need to find some way of getting B and there just isn't any. Since we're stuck we shall invoke the rule of last resort but having our previous experience in mind, we know that we backtrack and start using it earlier in the derivation. In particular, we notice a parallel with the previous derivation, namely that if we only had the negation of A to work with, as soon as we assume A, we'd then be able to derive anything at all since we would be within range of a formula and its negation.

In other words, instead of deriving A by conditional elimination, as we tried to do, we shall instead get it by negation elimination. Like this:

$$
\begin{array}{ll}
1 & (A \supset B) \supset C \\
2 & \qquad C \supset A \\
3 & \qquad\qquad \neg A \\
\vdots & \qquad\qquad \vdots \\
n-2 & \qquad\qquad \bot \\
n-1 & \qquad A \qquad\qquad\qquad [\neg E],\ 3,\ n-2 \\
n & (C \supset A) \supset A \qquad [\supset I],\ 2\text{--}n-1
\end{array}
$$

Knowing how the previous one went, this one is pretty much on rails. We're going to get the false by getting A to go with the negation of A on line 3. And the way we get A is by first getting C which together with the conditional on line 2 will give us what we want by conditional elimination (as in our previous try). And to get C we must first get $A \supset B$ so we can use the conditional on line 1. Last time that was hard but this time it's easy. As soon as we assume A we can get anything. So filling in all this, we get:

1	$(A \supset B) \supset C$	
2	$C \supset A$	
3	$\neg A$	
4	A	
5	$\neg B$	
6	$\bot$	$[\bot I]$, 3, 4
7	B	$[\neg E]$, 5–6
8	$A \supset B$	$[\supset I]$, 4–7
9	C	$[\supset E]$, 1, 8
10	A	$[\supset E]$, 2, 9
11	$\bot$	$[\bot I]$, 10, 3
12	A	$[\neg E]$, 3, 11
13	$(C \supset A) \supset A$	$[\supset I]$, 2–12

6. This one looks quite puzzling.

1	$A \supset B$
2	$A \wedge \neg B$
$\vdots$	$\vdots$
.	C

There is no C in the premises so how on earth can we derive it from them? This must be a mistake of some sort, mustn't it? Well, in a word, no. This is not a mistake and we can indeed derive C but only because from those premises, we can derive anything at all. In other words, this is a setup for negation elimination. To be more accurate, given that C does not occur in the premises, there is no other way to derive it except for negation elimination. That would make the derivation look like:

$$
\begin{array}{c|l}
1 & A \supset B \\
2 & A \wedge \neg B \\
\hline
3 & \quad\begin{array}{|l} \neg C \\ \vdots \\ \bot \end{array} \\
\cdot & C
\end{array}
$$

At this point we know that we must derive some formula and its negation in the subderivation starting with $\neg C$ in order to apply the rule [$\bot$I]. Further, the way we select which formula plus negation to try to derive, is to see which negations we already have, or can easily get. We notice that in the second premise we have the negation of B as a conjunct. Conjuncts are easy to get so we settle on trying to derive the pair B and $\neg B$. That would look like:

$$
\begin{array}{c|l}
1 & A \supset B \\
2 & A \wedge \neg B \\
3 & \quad\quad \neg C \\
4 & \quad\quad \neg B \\
\vdots & \quad\quad \vdots \\
\cdot & \quad\quad B \\
\cdot & \quad\quad \bot \\
\cdot & \quad C
\end{array}
$$

But we see we have B as the consequent of the conditional premise 1 and that we have the antecedent of that conditional as a conjunct of premise 2. This now looks easy. First we get the A by simplifying 2.

$$
\begin{array}{c|l}
1 & A \supset B \\
2 & A \wedge \neg B \\
3 & \quad\quad \neg C \\
4 & \quad\quad \neg B \\
5 & \quad\quad A \\
\vdots & \quad\quad \vdots \\
\cdot & \quad\quad B \\
\cdot & \quad\quad \bot \\
\cdot & \quad C
\end{array}
$$

We don't need the "dots" at this point since we see that B follows at once from the first premise by [$\supset$E] since we have derived the antecedent of the conditional at step 5. In other words here is the first draft of the completed derivation:

$$
\begin{array}{c|l}
1 & A \supset B \\
2 & A \wedge \neg B \\
3 & \quad \neg C \\
4 & \quad \neg B \\
5 & \quad A \\
6 & \quad B \\
7 & \quad \bot \\
8 & C
\end{array}
$$

All we need to finish the derivation are the line justifications. We know what they are, but we must make them explicit.

$$
\begin{array}{c|l l}
1 & A \supset B & \\
2 & A \wedge \neg B & \\
3 & \quad \neg C & \\
4 & \quad \neg B & [\wedge E], 2 \\
5 & \quad A & [\wedge E], 2 \\
6 & \quad B & [\supset E], 1, 5 \\
7 & \quad \bot & [\bot I], 4, 6 \\
8 & C & [\neg E], 3\text{--}7
\end{array}
$$

7. In this exercise we have a lot of premises to work with, but what we want, $\neg B$ isn't in any of them. Still we aren't to the point of even

thinking about that. We see we are supposed to derive a negation and so we shall begin using the rule of negation introduction. Like this:

$$
\begin{array}{ll}
1 & A \supset (B \supset C) \\
2 & A \supset (B \supset D) \\
3 & A \\
4 & C \supset \neg D) \\
5 & \quad B \\
\vdots & \quad \vdots \\
. & \quad \bot \\
. & \neg B
\end{array}
$$

We know, by now, that the key to deriving $\bot$ is to locate some negation that we can easily derive. In this case there is such a thing—the $\neg D$ which forms the consequent of premise 4. This means that we think of the derivation as evolving in this manner:

$$
\begin{array}{ll}
1 & A \supset (B \supset C) \\
2 & A \supset (B \supset D) \\
3 & A \\
4 & C \supset \neg D) \\
5 & \quad B \\
\vdots & \quad \vdots \\
. & \quad \neg D \\
. & \quad \bot \\
. & \neg B
\end{array}
$$

But how did we dig out that $\neg D$? We must have used [$\supset$E], but in order to use that rule, we must first have derived the antecedent of 4, namely C. In other words, our derivation would be of the form:

$$
\begin{array}{l|l}
1 & A \supset (B \supset C) \\[4pt]
2 & A \supset (B \supset D) \\[4pt]
3 & A \\[4pt]
4 & C \supset \neg D) \\[4pt]
5 & \quad\quad B \\
\vdots & \quad\quad \vdots \\
\cdot & \quad\quad C \\
\cdot & \quad\quad \neg D \\
\cdot & \quad\quad \bot \\
\cdot & \neg B
\end{array}
$$

Now we must consider how to derive C. As a bonus, the answer to that question also tells us how to derive D, which we need in order to derive $\bot$. The answer in both cases is that we use premise 3, A, together with premises 1 and 2 in order to derive $B \supset C$ and $B \supset D$ respectively. Then, since we already have B which we assumed at step 5, we must have both C and D by two uses of [$\supset$E]. So the nearly finished derivation must be:

1	$A \supset (B \supset C)$
2	$A \supset (B \supset D)$
3	A
4	$C \supset \neg D)$
5	B
6	$B \supset C$
7	$B \supset D$
8	C
9	D
10	$\neg D$
11	$\bot$
12	$\neg B$

All that remains is to supply annotations for the lines still need them.

1	$A \supset (B \supset C)$	
2	$A \supset (B \supset D)$	
3	A	
4	$C \supset \neg D)$	
5	B	
6	$B \supset C$	[∧E], 1, 3
7	$B \supset D$	[∧E], 2, 3
8	C	[∧E], 5, 6
9	D	[∧E], 5, 7
10	$\neg D$	[∧E], 4, 8
11	$\perp$	[⊥I], 9, 10
12	$\neg B$	[¬I], 5–11

12. In this exercise we must derive a biconditional. We know that requires two subderivations—one in each direction. So the overall structure would look like this:

$$
\begin{array}{r|l}
1 & A \supset \neg B \\
2 & \neg A \supset B \\ \hline
3 & \quad \boxed{\begin{array}{l} A \\ \vdots \\ \neg B \end{array}} \\
\vdots & \\
\cdot & \\
\cdot & \quad \boxed{\begin{array}{l} \neg B \\ \vdots \\ A \end{array}} \\
\vdots & \\
\cdot & \\
\cdot & A \equiv \neg B
\end{array}
$$

The top subderivation is trivial. We already have $A \supset \neg B$ as the first premise, and we have just assumed A. So we get $\neg B$ by one application of the rule $[\supset E]$.

$$
\begin{array}{r|l}
1 & A \supset \neg B \\
2 & \neg A \supset B \\ \hline
3 & \quad \boxed{\begin{array}{l} A \\ \neg B \end{array}} \\
4 & \\
\cdot & \\
\vdots & \quad \boxed{\begin{array}{l} \neg B \\ \vdots \\ A \end{array}} \\
\cdot & \\
\cdot & A \equiv \neg B
\end{array}
$$

But deriving A in the second subderivation isn't so easy. The only A (apart from the assumption in line 3 which is now out of range) is in the antecedent of premise 1—not a good place! So we must fall back on the rule of last resort:

$$
\begin{array}{ll}
1 & A \supset \neg B \\
2 & \neg A \supset B \\
3 & \quad A \\
4 & \quad \neg B \\
5 & \quad \neg B \\
6 & \quad\quad \neg A \\
\vdots & \quad\quad \vdots \\
\cdot & \quad\quad \bot \\
\cdot & \quad A \\
\cdot & A \equiv \neg B
\end{array}
$$

In order to derive the false under the assumption that $\neg A$ we must derive some formula and its negation. The way we pick which pair to try to derive is to see which negation we can derive most easily. We seem to be faced with a tie on this occasion since both $\neg B$ and $\neg A$ are immediately available as assumptions which are still "live." In such a case we must decide between the two candidates by asking how difficult it would be to derive the *un-negated* formulas. In other words if we pick $\neg A$ as the basis of our derived contradiction, how hard is it going to be to derive the A part?

The answer is: very hard! Recall that we have just been forced to use [$\neg$E] because we couldn't see how otherwise to derive A. If we had some notion of how to derive A now, we would use it earlier and save ourselves some trouble. So it's going to have to be B which we derive. We see that we have B as the consequent of the second premise. This is very useful because we have earlier, at line 7, assumed the antecedent of that premise. Thus we get what we want, B, by one use of [$\supset$E].

Putting this together:

$$
\begin{array}{r|l}
1 & A \supset \neg B \\
2 & \neg A \supset B \\
\hline
3 & \quad A \\
4 & \quad \neg B \\
5 & \quad \neg B \\
6 & \qquad \neg A \\
7 & \qquad B \\
8 & \qquad \bot \\
9 & \quad A \\
10 & A \equiv \neg B
\end{array}
$$

And finally we put in the annotations.

1	$A \supset \neg B$	
2	$\neg A \supset B$	
3	A	
4	$\neg B$	[∧E], 1, 3
5	$\neg B$	
6	$\neg A$	
7	B	[∧E], 2, 6
8	$\bot$	[⊥I], 5, 7
9	A	[¬E], 6–8
10	$A \equiv \neg B$	[≡I], 3–4, 5–9

34. This is another of those in which "work backwards" doesn't seem so promising since we are working from a single letter.

1	$A \supset B$
2	$A \vee (C \wedge D)$
3	$\neg B \wedge \neg E$
$\vdots$	$\vdots$
n	C

We look for the C which we are trying to derive and we can see it only in the second disjunct of premise 2. This suggests that we should eliminate that disjunction in order to get what we want. In order to eliminate a disjunction we introduce two subderivations just above the thing that we want, and make that thing, in this case C the conclusion of both subderivations. After we do that, we are entitled to conclude C by

disjunction elimination. In other words, we next write down something
that looks like this:

$$
\begin{array}{lll}
1 & A \supset B & \\
2 & A \lor (C \land D) & \\
3 & \neg B \land \neg E & \\
4 & \quad A & \\
\vdots & \quad \vdots & \\
m & \quad C & \\
m+1 & \quad C \land D & \\
\vdots & \quad \vdots & \\
n-1 & \quad C & \\
n & C & [\lor E],\ 2,\ 4\text{--}m,\ m+1\text{--}n-1
\end{array}
$$

The bottom sub-derivation is trivial—we simply conclude C by eliminating the conjunction in $C \land D$. When something is this easy, it is often
a sign that you are on the right track. So what we have as the next stage
is:

1	$A \supset B$	
2	$A \vee (C \wedge D)$	
3	$\neg B \wedge \neg E$	
4	A	
$\vdots$	$\vdots$	
m	C	
$n - 2$	$C \wedge D$	
$n - 1$	C	$[\wedge E], n - 2$
n	C	$[\vee E], 2, 4{-}m, n - 2{-}n - 1$

So how shall we get C from A in the first sub-derivation? We can see that having A gives us B by eliminating the conditional in the first premise. And if we have B then, by eliminating the conjunction in the third premise, we can derive $\neg B$. The second conjunct isn't any use to us but the first conjunct is the negation of B which we have already derived. Since we have both B and its negation we can justify introducing $\bot$ and from that, anything follows (by False-elimination) including the C that we want.

Here's the whole thing written out with line numbers and proper annotations:

1	$A \supset B$	
2	$A \vee (C \wedge D)$	
3	$\neg B \wedge \neg E$	
4	$\quad A$	
5	$\quad B$	$[\supset E]$, 1, 4
6	$\quad \neg B$	$[\wedge E]$, 3
7	$\quad \bot$	$[\bot I]$, 5, 6
8	$\quad C$	$[\bot E]$, 7
9	$\quad C \wedge D$	
10	$\quad C$	$[\wedge E]$, 9
11	C	$[\vee E]$, 2, 4–8, 9–10

Selected Solutions to Exercises 3.8

In these exercises we are permitted to use derived rules and rules of replacement. But you should notice that use of these rules doesn't automatically make everything easier. It will generally be clear when there is an advantage, but the clarity can only be acquired by experience.

12. In this problem the conclusion looks to be a good candidate for replacement. We begin as usual.

1	$(A \supset \neg B) \wedge (B \supset \neg C)$
2	$D \supset B$
$\vdots$	$\vdots$
n	$D \supset (\neg A \wedge \neg C)$

Since the conclusion is a conditional, we should assume that we derived it by conditional introduction. In other words:

1	$(A \supset \neg B) \wedge (B \supset \neg C)$	
2	$D \supset B$	
3	D	
$\vdots$	$\vdots$	
$n-1$	$\neg A \wedge \neg C$	
n	$D \supset (\neg A \wedge \neg C)$	$[\supset I], 3{-}n-1$

At this point let's try a replacement rule. We can see that the conclusion of the subderivation, the conjunction of two negations, is the same thing, by a replacement rule, as the negation of a disjunction. Let's decide to get the latter form. This means we're going to do:

1	$(A \supset \neg B) \wedge (B \supset \neg C)$	
2	$D \supset B$	
3	D	
$\vdots$	$\vdots$	
$n-2$	$\neg(A \vee C)$	
$n-1$	$\neg A \wedge \neg C$	$[rep], n-2$
n	$D \supset (\neg A \wedge \neg C)$	$[\supset I], 3{-}n-2$

It should occur to us to try to get the negation of anything, by the rule of negation introduction. If the derivation went that way, it would look like this:

1	$(A \supset \neg B) \wedge (B \supset \neg C)$	
2	$D \supset B$	
3	D	
4	$A \vee C$	
⋮	⋮	
$n-3$	$\perp$	
$n-2$	$\neg(A \vee C)$	$[\neg I], 4\text{--}n-3$
$n-1$	$\neg A \wedge \neg C$	$[\text{rep}], n-2$
n	$D \supset (\neg A \wedge \neg C)$	$[\supset I], 3\text{--}n-2$

Evidently we're going to need to use disjunction elimination to make the derivation work. It will have to look like this:

1	$(A \supset \neg B) \wedge (B \supset \neg C)$	
2	$D \supset B$	
3	D	
4	$A \vee C$	
5	A	
$\vdots$	$\vdots$	
m	$\bot$	
$m+1$	C	
$\vdots$	$\vdots$	
$n-4$	$\bot$	
$n-3$	$\bot$	$[\vee\mathrm{E}], 4, 5\text{--}m, m+1\text{--}n-4$
$n-2$	$\neg(A \vee C)$	$[\neg\mathrm{I}], 4\text{--}\vdots$
$n-1$	$\neg A \wedge \neg C$	$[\mathrm{rep}], n-2$
n	$D \supset (\neg A \wedge \neg C)$	$[\supset\mathrm{I}], 3\text{--}n-1$

For the subderivation that begins with A we evidently need to bring down the first conjunct of premise 1, since it is a conditional with antecedent A. The correct rule to do that is conjunction elimination. And once we have the conditional, we can immediately derive $\neg B$ by conditional elimination.

1	$(A \supset \neg B) \wedge (B \supset \neg C)$		
2	$D \supset B$		
3		D	
4			$A \vee C$
5			A
6			$A \supset \neg B$ [∧E], 1
7			$\neg B$ [⊃E], 5, 6
⋮			⋮
m			$\bot$
$m+1$			C
⋮			⋮
$n-4$			$\bot$
$n-3$		$\bot$ [∨E], 4, 5–7, ∴–$m+1$
$n-2$		$\neg(A \vee C)$ [¬I], 4–6
$n-1$		$\neg A \wedge \neg C$ [rep], $n-4$
n	$D \supset (\neg A \wedge \neg C)$ [⊃I], 3–$n-3$

Now, since we're trying to derive $\bot$ and we already have $\neg B$, we must derive B. But this is trivial by conditional elimination since we have the ingredients on hand in lines 2 and 3. So the completed sub-derivation looks like this:

1	$(A \supset \neg B) \land (B \supset \neg C)$			
2	$D \supset B$			
3		D		
4			$A \lor C$	
5				A
6				$A \supset \neg B$	$[\land E], 1$
7				$\neg B$	$[\supset E], 5, 6$
8				B	$[\supset E], 2, 3$
9				$\bot$	$[\bot I], 7, 8$
m				C
$\vdots$				$\vdots$
$n - 4$				$\bot$
$n - 3$			$\bot$		$[\lor E], 4, 5\text{–}9, m\text{–}n - 4$
$n - 2$		$\neg(A \lor C)$			$[\neg I], 4\text{–}n - 3$
$n - 1$		$\neg A \land \neg C$			$[\text{rep}], n - 2$
n	$D \supset (\neg A \land \neg C)$				$[\supset I], 3\text{–}n - 1$

For the subderivation beginning with C, we shall pursue the same strategy except we use the second conjunct of premise 1. So the first stage is to bring down that conjunct:

1	$(A \supset \neg B) \wedge (B \supset \neg C)$	
2	$D \supset B$	
3	D	
4	$A \vee C$	
5	A	
6	$A \supset \neg B$	$[\wedge E], 1$
7	$\neg B$	$[\supset E], 5, 6$
8	B	$[\supset E], 2, 3$
9	$\perp$	$[\perp I], 7, 8$
10	C	
11	$B \supset \neg C$	$[\wedge E], 1$
$\vdots$	$\vdots$	
$n - 4$	$\perp$	
$n - 3$	$\perp$	$[\vee E], 4, 5\text{–}9, 10\text{–}n - 4$
$n - 2$	$\neg(A \vee C)$	$[\neg I], 4\text{–}n - 3$
$n - 1$	$\neg A \wedge \neg C$	$[rep], n - 2$
n	$D \supset (\neg A \wedge \neg C)$	$[\supset I], 3\text{–}n - 1$

But we already know how to derive B from our earlier experience in the previous subderivation. We need only use conditional elimination on lines 2 and 3 (both of which are within range of the prospective line 12. But then we'd have both C and $\neg C$—the latter by yet another conditional elimination. So once we put all this together we get the completed derivation.

1	$(A \supset \neg B) \wedge (B \supset \neg C)$	
2	$D \supset B$	
3	D	
4	$A \vee C$	
5	A	
6	$A \supset \neg B$	[∧E], 1
7	$\neg B$	[⊃E], 5, 6
8	B	[⊃E], 2, 3
9	$\bot$	[⊥I], 7, 8
10	C	
11	$B \supset \neg C$	[∧E], 1
12	B	[⊃E], 2, 3
13	$\neg C$	[⊃E], 11, 12
14	$\bot$	[⊥I], 10, 13
15	$\bot$	[∨E], 4, 5–9, 10–14
16	$\neg(A \vee C)$	[¬I], 4–15
17	$\neg A \wedge \neg C$	[rep], 16
18	$D \supset (\neg A \wedge \neg C)$	[⊃I], 3–17

14. This one looks a bit simpler than the previous one.

1	$A \vee B$
2	$B \supset C$
⋮	⋮
n	$\neg A \supset C$

The conclusion of this looks very tempting to anybody who wants to try out some rules of replacement. In particular we can see that it is equivalent to a disjunction with the antecedent negated. In other words:

$$
\begin{array}{r|l}
1 & A \vee B \\
2 & B \supset C \\
\vdots & \vdots \\
\hline
n-1 & \neg\neg A \vee C \\
n & \neg A \supset C \qquad \text{[rep]}, n-1
\end{array}
$$

But of course, the "double negations" cancel out so we can back up one step further to:

$$
\begin{array}{r|l}
1 & A \vee B \\
2 & B \supset C \\
\vdots & \vdots \\
\hline
n-2 & A \vee C \\
n-1 & \neg\neg A \vee C \qquad \text{[rep]}, n-2 \\
n & \neg A \supset C \qquad \text{[rep]}, n-1
\end{array}
$$

So it turns out that we are trying to derive a plain old disjunction, and we see that we already have a disjunction as premise 1. Our experience guides us in the direction of thinking that disjunction elimination would be our best bet since most reasoning from disjunctions leads to other disjunctions. Saying that would be saying that we expect the pattern to be:

1	$A \vee B$	
2	$B \supset C$	
3	$\quad A$	
⋮	$\quad$ ⋮	
m	$\quad A \vee C$	
$m + 1$	$\quad B$	
⋮	$\quad$ ⋮	
$n - 3$	$\quad A \vee C$	
$n - 2$	$A \vee C$	[∨E], 1, 3–m, $m + 1$–$n - 3$
$n - 1$	$\neg\neg A \vee C$	[rep], $n - 2$
n	$\neg A \supset C$	[rep], $n - 1$

The top subderivation is trivial. We don't need the dots since we can go directly from A to $A \vee C$ by means of disjunction introduction (since we aren't working on the main scope line).

1	$A \vee B$	
2	$B \supset C$	
3	A	
4	$A \vee C$	[$\vee$I], 3
5	B	
$\vdots$	$\vdots$	
$n - 3$	$A \vee C$	
$n - 2$	$A \vee C$	[$\vee$E], 1, 3–4, 5–$n - 3$
$n - 1$	$\neg\neg A \vee C$	[rep], $n - 2$
n	$\neg A \supset C$	[rep], $n - 1$

The second subderivation—the one starting with B is nearly as trivial. We can see at once that using premise 2 along with the assumption, gives us C by conditional elimination. But from C we can infer $A \vee C$ immediately by (the other form of) disjunction introduction. So the whole derivation is:

1	$A \lor B$	
2	$B \supset C$	
3	$\quad A$	
4	$\quad A \lor C$	[$\lor$I], 3
5	$\quad B$	
6	$\quad C$	[$\supset$E], 2, 5
7	$\quad A \lor C$	[$\lor$I], 6
8	$A \lor C$	[$\lor$E], 1, 3–4, 5–7
9	$\neg\neg A \lor C$	[rep], 8
10	$\neg A \supset C$	[rep], 9

3.10 Rules of CSL Quick Reference

Conjunction Introduction ($[\wedge I]$)

$$
\begin{array}{c|l}
\vdots & \vdots \\
n & P \\
\vdots & \vdots \\
m & Q \\
\vdots & \vdots \\
k & P \wedge Q \qquad [\wedge I], n, m
\end{array}
$$

or

$$
\begin{array}{c|l}
\vdots & \vdots \\
n & Q \\
\vdots & \vdots \\
m & P \\
\vdots & \vdots \\
k & Q \wedge P \qquad [\wedge I], n, m
\end{array}
$$

Conjunction Elimination ($[\wedge E]$)

$$
\begin{array}{c|l}
\vdots & \vdots \\
n & P \wedge Q \\
\vdots & \vdots \\
k & P \qquad [\wedge I], n
\end{array}
$$

or

$$
\begin{array}{c|c}
\vdots & \vdots \\
n & P \wedge Q \\
\vdots & \vdots \\
k & Q \qquad [\wedge\text{I}], n
\end{array}
$$

Disjunction Introduction ([∨I])

$$
\begin{array}{c|c}
\vdots & \vdots \\
n & P \\
\vdots & \vdots \\
k & P \vee Q \qquad [\vee\text{I}], n
\end{array}
$$

or

$$
\begin{array}{c|c}
\vdots & \vdots \\
n & Q \\
\vdots & \vdots \\
k & Q \vee P \qquad [\vee\text{I}], n
\end{array}
$$

Disjunction Elimination ([∨E])

$$
\begin{array}{c|l}
\vdots & \vdots \\
n & P \vee Q \\
n+1 & \quad\boxed{\;P} \\
\vdots & \quad\vdots \\
m & \quad R \\
m+1 & \quad\boxed{\;Q} \\
\vdots & \quad\vdots \\
k & \quad R \\
l & R \qquad [\vee\text{E}], n, n+1\text{--}m, m+1\text{--}k
\end{array}
$$

Conditional Elimination ([⊃E])

$$
\begin{array}{c|l}
\vdots & \vdots \\
n & P \supset Q \\
\vdots & \vdots \\
m & P \\
\vdots & \vdots \\
k & Q \qquad [\supset\text{E}], n, m
\end{array}
$$

Conditional Introduction ([⊃I])

$$
\begin{array}{c|c}
\vdots & \vdots \\
n & \quad\boxed{\begin{array}{l} P \\ \hline \vdots \\ Q \end{array}} \\
m \\
m+1 & P \supset Q \qquad [\supset\!\text{I}],\, n\text{--}m
\end{array}
$$

Biconditional Elimination ([≡E])

$$
\begin{array}{c|l}
\vdots & \vdots \\
n & P \equiv Q \\
\vdots & \vdots \\
m & P \\
\vdots & \vdots \\
k & Q \qquad\quad [\equiv\!\text{E}],\, n,\, m
\end{array}
$$

or

$$
\begin{array}{c|l}
\vdots & \vdots \\
n & P \equiv Q \\
\vdots & \vdots \\
m & Q \\
\vdots & \vdots \\
k & P \qquad\quad [\equiv\!\text{E}],\, n,\, m
\end{array}
$$

[≡I] (Biconditional Introduction)

$$
\begin{array}{c|l}
\vdots & \vdots \\
n & \quad\boxed{\;P\;} \\
\vdots & \quad\;\vdots \\
m & \quad\;Q \\
m+1 & \quad\boxed{\;Q\;} \\
\vdots & \quad\;\vdots \\
k & \quad\;P \\
k+1 & P \equiv Q \qquad [\equiv\mathrm{I}],\, n\text{–}m,\, m+1\text{–}k
\end{array}
$$

Falsum Introduction ([⊥I])

$$
\begin{array}{c|l}
\vdots & \vdots \\
n & P \\
\vdots & \vdots \\
m & \neg P \\
\vdots & \vdots \\
k & \bot \qquad [\bot\mathrm{I}],\, n,\, m
\end{array}
$$

Falsum elimination ([⊥E])

$$
\begin{array}{c|l}
\vdots & \vdots \\
n & \bot \\
\vdots & \vdots \\
m & P \qquad [\bot\text{E}], n
\end{array}
$$

Negation Introduction ([¬I])

$$
\begin{array}{c|l}
\vdots & \vdots \\
n & \\
& \quad \underline{P} \\
\vdots & \quad \vdots \\
m & \quad \bot \\
m+1 & \neg P \qquad [\neg\text{I}], n\text{--}m
\end{array}
$$

Negation Elimination ([¬E])

$$
\begin{array}{c|l}
\vdots & \vdots \\
n & \\
& \quad \underline{\neg P} \\
\vdots & \quad \vdots \\
m & \quad \bot \\
m+1 & P \qquad [\neg\text{E}], n\text{--}m
\end{array}
$$

The Structural Rule [R] of reiteration

$$
\begin{array}{c|l}
n & P \\
  & \overline{} \\
\vdots & \vdots \\
m & P \qquad \text{[R]}, n
\end{array}
$$

or

$$
\begin{array}{c|l}
\vdots & \vdots \\
n & P \\
\vdots & \\
  & \quad \vdots \\
m & \quad P \qquad \text{[R]}, n \\
\vdots & \quad \vdots \\
\vdots & \vdots
\end{array}
$$

3.11 Definitions Quick Reference

A finite sequence of steps is a derivation in CSL *of* its last line, *from* assumptions (if any) listed on its initial lines if and only if each line in the sequence is either an assumption or is justified by a rule of CSL.

The formula P belongs to the set of assumptions of line number i in derivation D (in CSL) ($P \in \mathcal{Q}(D, i)$) if and only if P is an assumption of any subderivation D' of D which is active at line i.

$\Gamma \vdash P$ (Gamma proves P) if and only if there is a derivation of P from a set of assumptions which are included in Γ.

The logic CSL is, from the syntactical perspective, defined to be the set of pairs Γ, P such that $\Gamma \vdash P$.

$\vdash P$ (P is a *theorem* of CSL) if and only if there is a derivation in CSL of P from no assumptions.

Two formulas P and Q are (syntactically) *equivalent* (in CSL), written $P \dashv\vdash Q$ if and only if assuming one formula the other can be derived (in CSL).

A set Γ of formulas, is (syntactically) *consistent* if and only if there is a formula P such that $\Gamma \nvdash P$.

3.12   Derivable Rules Quick Reference

The Rule [DS], of Disjunctive Syllogism

$$
\begin{array}{ll}
& \vdots \qquad\quad \vdots \\
n & \qquad P \lor Q \\
& \vdots \qquad\quad \vdots \\
m & \qquad \neg P \\
m+1 & \qquad Q \qquad\qquad [\text{DS}], n, m
\end{array}
$$

or

$$
\begin{array}{ll}
& \vdots \qquad\quad \vdots \\
n & \qquad P \lor Q \\
& \vdots \qquad\quad \vdots \\
m & \qquad \neg Q \\
m+1 & \qquad P \qquad\qquad [\text{DS}], n, m
\end{array}
$$

The rule [HS] of Hypothetical Syllogism

$$
\begin{array}{ll}
& \vdots \qquad\quad \vdots \\
n & \qquad P \supset Q \\
& \vdots \qquad\quad \vdots \\
m & \qquad Q \supset R \\
m+1 & \qquad P \supset R \qquad\quad [\text{HS}], n, m
\end{array}
$$

The rule [MT] of Modus Tollens

$$
\begin{array}{c|ll}
 & \vdots & \\
n & P \supset Q & \\
 & \vdots & \\
m & \neg Q & \\
m+1 & \neg P & \text{[MT]}, n, m
\end{array}
$$

3.13   Replacement Rules Quick Reference

Contraposition [Contra] $P \supset Q \longleftrightarrow \neg Q \supset \neg P$

Implication [Impl] $P \supset Q \longleftrightarrow \neg P \vee Q$

Double Negation [DN] $P \longleftrightarrow \neg \neg P$

De Morgan [DeM]

$$\neg (P \wedge Q) \longleftrightarrow \neg P \vee \neg Q$$
$$\neg (P \vee Q) \longleftrightarrow \neg P \wedge \neg Q$$

Commutativity [Com]

$$P \vee Q \longleftrightarrow Q \vee P$$
$$P \wedge Q \longleftrightarrow Q \wedge P$$

Idempotence [Id]

$$P \vee P \longleftrightarrow P$$
$$P \wedge P \longleftrightarrow P$$

Exportation [Exp] $P \supset (Q \supset R) \longleftrightarrow (P \wedge Q) \supset R$

Associativity [Assoc]

$$P \wedge (Q \wedge R) \longleftrightarrow (P \wedge Q) \wedge R$$
$$P \vee (Q \vee R) \longleftrightarrow (P \vee Q) \vee R$$

Distribution [Dist]

$$P \wedge (Q \vee R) \longleftrightarrow (P \wedge Q) \vee (P \wedge R)$$
$$P \vee (Q \wedge R) \longleftrightarrow (P \vee Q) \wedge (P \vee R)$$

Equivalence [Equiv]

$$P \equiv Q \longleftrightarrow (P \supset Q) \wedge (Q \supset P)$$
$$P \equiv Q \longleftrightarrow (P \wedge Q) \vee (\neg P \wedge \neg Q)$$

Chapter 4

Semantics of Sentence Logic

4.1 Overview

In this chapter we shall begin to study the concept of logical consequence from the semantic perspective. To say semantic in this context is to say that the theory we present here defines consequence in terms of *truth*.

The notion of truth is subtle and difficult, but we can avoid these difficulties, for the most part. This is because we don't require a complete account of truth, but only that part of the theory which bears on inferential relations among sentences. In other words, we require the following:

> There are two *truth values* called *true* and *false*.
>
> *Every* sentence is either true or false.
>
> *No* sentence is both true and false.

The mathematical concept of a *function* can be used to say this more succinctly. If the relationship between sentences and truth-values is functional, then every sentence must receive a value (usually called the requirement of *totality*) which is *unique*—i.e., each sentence is related to exactly one truth-value (usually called the requirement of *single-*

111

valuedness). But these requirements for functionality are exactly the conditions mentioned above.

In fact, these two conditions/requirements have been around in some form since antiquity. Their more familiar names are: *the law of excluded middle* and *the law of non-contradiction*. Together, they form part of what we have called the classical perspective on logic.

It has seemed to many, that the requirements are too strict. Some, notably the 19th Century philosopher John Stuart Mill, have announced that not only are these principles not laws, they aren't even true.

For excluded middle Mill was just one of a large number of those, before and after him, who have seen fit to complain. Mill thought there were clearly *other* semantic categories, besides truth and falsehood, his own example was 'meaningless.' Something might be an obvious sentence and yet not be meaningful, Mill thought. There are examples of so-called sortal mistakes for instance—sentences like 'The smell of bacon is unbreakable.'

In this example we can see the first line of defense, which would be to require that all meaningless sentences simply be assigned the value false, is not available. Assigning our example sentence false, makes it *true* that the smell of bacon is breakable.

Defenders of the classical way of looking at things have also proposed something a bit more sweeping in response to the problems raised by alternative semantic categories. Two of the best known of the 20th Century defenders, Bertrand Russell[1] and W.V.O. Quine[2], suggest we make 'being true or false' part of the *definition* of the items under study— declarative sentence, statement, proposition, are the usual ones. It certainly wouldn't be the first time that what we call a law, is more properly thought of as a definition.[3] To suggest that what counts as a (declarative) sentence might not be entirely a matter of syntax is sometimes regarded by linguists as a radical position.

People often think that the first of the boxed requirements, the requirement that there be only two truth-values, is also part and parcel of

---

[1] see Russell (1903)

[2] see Quine (1970)

[3] This is one of the themes of H. Poincaré's *Science and Hypothesis* Poincaré (1960)

the classical perspective, but that claim is on very shaky ground.[4]

4.2 The Connectives in Terms of Truth-Values

Words like 'and', 'or,' and 'if ... then ... ' often present a problem when their *meaning* must be explained. They aren't like nouns and verbs or other homely parts of speech. For that reason, they were called *syncategorematic* (belonging to their own category) by the grammarians and logicians of the Middle Ages.

In terms of their function, they are like *operations* in algebra, in that they combine or attach to items to form new ones. This analogy with algebra was used to such good effect by George Boole in the 19th Century, that to this very day connective words like 'and' are often referred to as *sentence operators*. It certainly gives us a way to distinguish them from one another, namely in terms of their truth-value output given certain truth-value inputs.

We shall use the letters T and F to stand for the two truth-values truth and falsehood, respectively. We should note however that there is absolutely no magic to this choice. We *could have* used *any* two distinct symbols for this purpose (including using F to stand for 'true'). Another, equally common choice, is 1 and 0.

Conjunction

The easiest way to describe the connectives in terms of their truth-value outputs for various inputs, is to use a *table*. Here, for instance, is the classical table for the conjunction connective.

Definition 4.2.1.

$P \wedge Q$	T	F
T	T	F
F	F	F

The cell of the table in the top left shows which connective is being described. The truth-values taken on by the Q conjunct are listed along

---

[4]This issue is discussed in more detail in Chapter 6

the top (above the double line), directly after the Q in $P \wedge Q$. The values taken on by the P conjunct are listed down the left side (to the left of the double line) directly under the P in $P \wedge Q$. To find out the value taken on by the whole compound sentence when its P component takes on value V_1 and its Q component takes on value V_2 we simply find the row of the first column in which V_1 occurs and the column of the first row in which V_2 occurs and the cell in which the two intersect in the table, contains the required value.

For conjunctions then, we can see that the only true ones have both conjuncts true and that if either conjunct is false, so is the whole conjunction. We can also see at a glance that the table is symmetric about the diagonal, which is to say if we rotate it on the diagonal and thus exchange columns for rows (or vice versa depending upon which diagonal is our axis), we get the same table. And this, with a bit of thought, confirms what we already knew, that the order of the conjuncts in a conjunction makes no difference—not in terms of the truth-value account at least.[5]

This account is the classical truth-value semantics for conjunction. It is also the same account most non-classical logics use as well. Many people hold that conjunction has the most intuitive, and least controversial semantics of any of the connectives. We have only to think of somebody who refused to accept a conjunction after accepting both conjuncts or who was satisfied that a conjunction was true after having determined that the first conjunct was false. Wouldn't we call a person like that irrational or at least call into question such a person's understanding of 'and?'

That, or something like it, is the way the truth table for 'and' is usually justified, but perhaps it is a bit too brisk. It is certainly true

---

[5]Which is not to say that the order never makes a difference with the classical conjunction. Suppose that we are evaluating a conjunction by discovering the truth-values of the conjuncts working from left to right. Further, let's suppose that the first conjunct is true while the second is false. After we test the first, we still don't know the value of the conjunction so we must go on to test the second one as well. But if we had started with the second, which corresponds to the case of the conjunction $Q \wedge P$, we could have stopped after the first test, since we would know that the whole compound must be false. Thus in terms of length of time it takes to determine the truth-value of a conjunction from the truth-values of its components, the order of the conjuncts might make a great deal of difference.

that there is a *sense* or perhaps *use* of and which has the properties depicted in the table. Is it the most common use? Is it even a particularly common use? These questions are not to be settled by rhetoric, they require serious study by linguists of a particularly statistical bent. This much we can say even without the benefit of those studies:

[AND1] Do that again, and I'll be leaving without you.

[AND2] I'm going to go to the store and buy a can of beans.

[AND3] I wish you would try and remember what you are doing.

are the sort of thing we say to one another every day, and none of those uses obeys the table in definition 4.2.1. AND1 is obviously some sort of conditional,[6] while AND2 clearly embeds some reference to time, or to the temporal order at least. AND3 is rather mysterious and linguists have been going back and forth in allowing as grammatical, conjunction replacing the preposition 'to' as part of the complement of the verb 'try', since at least the nineteenth Century. Currently, the usage is reckoned to be grammatical. In all of these uses the order of the conjuncts is significant.

What do these examples show? They certainly do *not* show that the table definition of conjunction is wrong or even misguided. They do show, on the other hand, that many textbooks and other purveyors of logic instruction are oversimplified to the point of being misleading. What we actually do when we present our account of conjunction is single out *one* use of the word. In the case of the other connectives, we are occasionally forced to *invent* a use when it isn't clear that there is one lying around in natural language that will suit us.

Disjunction

In the case of disjunction, it is often suggested that the following table depicts the most natural use.

---

[6]Using 'and' as a form of 'if' might be familiar to us from even a brief acquaintance with Elizabethan English. While that use may have withered entirely, using 'and' as a form of *then*, and thus still as a conditional, seems, as the example shows, to have survived to the present day.

	$P \vee Q$	T	F
Definition 4.2.2.	T	T	T
	F	T	F

According to this definition, the only false disjunctions are those with both disjuncts false and a single true disjunct is enough to render any disjunction true. It is customary to say at this point, that there are actually two sorts of disjunction in common use: the *inclusive* as above, and the *exclusive*. Before we too make the distinction, it is important to realize that 'or' in natural language, is a *much* more mysterious connective than is generally acknowledged in textbooks. Consider for instance:

[OR3] John is taller than either Mary or Bill.

There is nothing disjunctive here at all—the sentence clearly means that John is taller than Mary *and* John is taller than Bill.[7] Were we to make a serious logico-linguistic study of the matter we would probably find a nest of other uses of 'or' as well—meaning other than the ones for which we have neat tables. The moral here is that what we are *not* doing is discovering interesting and useful facts about language. That doesn't prevent what we *are* doing from being interesting and useful, we should hasten to add.

If we aren't getting our data from natural language, as so many of our illustrious predecessors have claimed, then where are we getting it? Perhaps from what we have already done, from our definition of $\wedge$ that is. We can explain the truth-table for disjunction in terms of the one for conjunction, if we appeal to the concept of *duality*.

What is typically meant by saying that two connectives are duals (of each other) is that one can be converted into the other (and vice versa) by applying some specified transformation.[8] In the case of conjunction and disjunction, we are interested in the transformation that interchanges T

---

[7]In his *The Genesis of Disjunction*, R.E. Jennings argues that what we claim to represent in natural language by disjunction, is actually really best seen as a kind of conjunction.

[8]This transformation normally involves negation.

and F. If we stare at the table in definition 4.2.2 we see that it just *is* the table in definition 4.2.1 with T and F swapped. So disjunction does to F what conjunction does to T and to T what conjunction does to F.

It will prove to be extremely useful to have a connective which is dual in this sense to $\wedge$. So much so, that we can probably be forgiven a bit of overstatement when claiming a rich natural language heritage for this definition.

A variation, what we have called the exclusive sense of disjunction represented by the symbol $\underline{\vee}$, is also usually 'derived' from natural language.

	$P \underline{\vee} Q$	T	F
Definition 4.2.3.	T	F	T
	F	T	F

This table matches the one for the previous (inclusive) connective except for the case in which both disjuncts are true. In the previous table the whole disjunction was true in that case, and in this table the whole disjunction is false.

Certainly Boole seems to have thought that this was altogether more natural than the earlier version. One popular example[9] from natural language used to bolster the exclusive interpretation is what R.E. Jennings has called 'the argument from confection.' Examine this sentence:

You may have either pie or cake.

This is supposed to be the most transparent case in which we would agree that *normally* only one of the alternatives is being offered. Perhaps this is because if somebody were to ask for both pie and cake she would be making a complete pig of herself. But this is just crazy. As it stands, there just is no presumption of exclusivity. There is also a problem for interpreting the 'or' in the example as *any* sort of disjunction. It seems

---

[9]It is alleged that this example can be found in many textbooks

to follow from 'You may have either pie or cake.' that 'you may have pie.' That looks more like conjunction.

Waiving that worry, we may be able to specify a *context* which would incline toward the exclusive reading, but it would take some work. We could start by saying:

> You may have *either* pie or cake.

where the italicized word represents a similarly emphatic tone of voice. That by itself might not be enough to carry the day. We could imagine extending a plate containing a piece of cake in one hand at the same time as we uttered the word 'cake' while simultaneously holding the plate containing a piece of pie behind our backs. Then when we uttered 'pie' we could reverse hands. Even that might not be enough for an audience composed of somebody hungry enough or greedy enough not to take the hint. Such a person might say with perfect justice 'But you *never said* that I couldn't have both!,' might she not?

There is of course an easily specified context in which nothing but an exclusive interpretation is possible. We use such a context when we say:

> [Excl] You may have either pie or cake, but you may not have both!

However, if this is the *only* context[10] which secures exclusivity, then there really isn't any such thing as an exclusive sense of 'or' in natural language. There is instead the inclusive sense conjoined with a denial of the conjunction of the disjuncts. Of course there is nothing to stop us from introducing $\underline{\vee}$ as we have. It's another very convenient connective. We can think of it, if we must have a natural language connection, as a kind of abbreviation for expressions of the sort marked [Excl] above.

---

[10]It is tempting to speculate that the argument from confection fails in part because we can imagine somebody wanting both alternatives. Perhaps if we had unattractive alternatives, that possibility would be so much smaller that the exclusive sense would really appear. For instance 'You will either be hanged by the neck or burned at the stake.' may well contain the implication that we shall not string you up and then light you on fire. But this is a matter for empirical linguistic research.

Limits on Defining Connectives

We have defined a truth-table for two connectives and are clearly on the way to defining tables for the remaining ones. How far can this process extend? It often seems to beginners that the possibilities are limitless; that we can define *anything*. In fact there are quite severe limitations, given the nature of truth-tables.

In a table we are given the truth-values of the component formulas and we use these to determine the value of the whole compound by looking it up in the table. There is never any doubt about the value of the whole given the value of the parts; never a case when a value fails to be determined or when more than one value corresponds to just one set of values of the components. We have already had occasion to use the mathematical concept of a *function* and it can be used here too for the description of the kind of tabular relationship in which there is exactly one output for every distinct combination of inputs. Such a relationship is said to be *functional*.

This has found its way into standard logic terminology as follows:

Definition 4.2.4. The semantic definition of a connective in terms of truth-values is said to be *truth-functional* if and only if for any distribution of truth-values to the component formulas, the definition determines exactly one truth-value for the whole compound which has the connective in question as its main connective.

Some authors prefer to say of this or that connective that it is truth-functional (or a truth-function) as opposed to reserving this terminology for the semantic definition. We allow ourselves this liberty when convenient.

Evidently *any* definition given in the form of a table will be truth-functional provided there are no blank cells. This is sometimes called the requirement that there be no *truth-value gaps*. It is part of the classical viewpoint, that all the definitions we produce for sentence connectives be truth-functional.[11]

So, if we are restricted to uttering only truth-functional definitions, then the limits on what we can define are determined by the number of truth-functions which are available. In the case of a binary connective, we must select a table for that connective from among the only 16 possible tables.[12]

The Conditional

Even those who believe that the definitions for conjunction and disjunction merely codify linguistic intuitions, even those people admit that we must abandon some or all of those same intuitions if we are to give a truth-functional definition of the conditional.

The intuitions on which we are attempting to float, those concerning the behavior of the (English language) conditional in the indicative, are obviously not amenable to a truth-functional treatment. We can see that the table for the indicative conditional must have blank cells for those rows in which the antecedent is false. When (we know that) the antecedent of a conditional is false, the standard rules of grammar require that we use the subjunctive. We are not allowed to say: 'If Granny has wheels then she's a trolley' but only 'If Granny had wheels then she would be a trolley.'

If we consult our intuitions concerning the conditional we find one very clear case. If the antecedent of a conditional is true and the consequent is false, then the whole compound must be false. What a conditional *says* after all is that the truth of the antecedent (the condition) leads to the truth of the consequent (the conditioned). In case the antecedent is true (the condition is fulfilled or obtains) and the consequent

---

[11] W.V.O. Quine has argued that the requirement of truth-functionality is a consequence of the more general requirement of *extensionality* which is, very roughly speaking, the requirement that we can always substitute equals for equals without changing a truth into a falsehood or vice versa.

[12] How do we derive this number? It represents the fact that there are two truth-values and 2^2 distinct distributions of truth-values to the 2 components of a formula compounded with a binary connective. Each of those distributions must correspond functionally to one of the two truth-values—the value in the table of the compound. The formula for the number of functions from a set containing Y objects to a set containing X objects, is X^Y.

is not true, what the conditional asserts must be false. There is no clearer linguistic intuition to be had in the whole of logic.

Some hold that there is another intuition, nearly as compelling as the one just surveyed. In case the antecedent is true and the consequent is also true, then wouldn't the previous intuition concerning what the conditional says, apply to make the whole compound true? At first it might seem so, but nearly as long as there have been logicians, there have been logicians who held that it isn't enough for the consequent to be true when the antecedent is true. The truth of a conditional requires in addition that the consequent be true *because* the antecedent is true. In other words, the truth of a conditional requires not merely that the truth-values of the antecedent and consequent line up in a certain way but that there be some kind of intelligible relationship, a causal relationship for instance, between the components.

We can easily agree with the critics that the genuine indicative conditional is not just a matter of truth-values, but the connective we shall define *is* to be definable in terms of the truth-values of its components alone—to have a truth-functional definition. And the classical theory of the connectives requires that only truth-functional definitions be used. Once again, what happens in natural language can only guide us so far. Since the value of the conditional must be either T or F when all we know is that both antecedent and consequent are T, it would seem crazy to require that the compound be F especially since we *know* that in at least some of those cases, the conditional will be true,[13] so in our truth-functional approximation of the natural language indicative conditional, we shall assign the whole conditional T when both antecedent and consequent are T. But we have only filled in two out of the four cells of the table, and the requirement of truth-functionality requires that there be no empty cells. How shall we fill out the remaining two cells? Let's examine all of the possible ways of doing that:

---

[13] And it may well make the most sense that it not take any value, rather than be F when both the antecedent and consequent are T and the whole conditional is not true. Consider for instance 'If 2+2 = 4 then grass is green.' This seems more bizarre than out and out false. We feel annoyed by the sentence and want it not to be true, but we don't want it to be false either.

$P \supset_1 Q$	T	F
T	T	F
F	T	F

$P \supset_2 Q$	T	F
T	T	F
F	T	T

$P \supset_3 Q$	T	F
T	T	F
F	F	T

$P \supset_4 Q$	T	F
T	T	F
F	F	F

We should immediately rule out $\supset_1$ and $\supset_4$. The first defines the conditional to always take the same value as it's consequent, which seems an odd way to define a conditional. The last defines the conditional so that it takes the same value as the conjunction of the antecedent with the consequent, which seems even odder.

As for the middle two proposals, $\supset_2$ makes every conditional with a false antecedent, true. This does not seem very intuitive. Why should a conditional get to be true just because it's antecedent is false, independent of the truth-value of the consequent? $\supset_3$ has the virtue of varying the truth-value of the conditional so that it depends upon values of both the antecedent and consequent, rather than just one of them, like $\supset_2$. Unfortunately the third possibility makes true only the conditionals in which the antecedent and consequent have the *same* truth value. We can see that a connective which is defined that way would be very useful but it wouldn't be a conditional. It would not distinguish the order of the components, and we have already noticed that 'If A then B' is, in general, a different assertion from 'If B then A.'

This leaves us with $\supset_2$ as the least worst definition. It should be very clear that we have paid a heavy price, the price of savaging our intuitions about the conditional, in order to purchase the truth-functionality of the definition. Is it worth that price? Many logicians and philosophers have said 'No!' Some have made a career out of vilifying this definition of the conditional, which has been with us since the definition was first uttered by logicians of the Hellenistic period of philosophy.[14] But we now know that any departure from the definition can only be in the direction of non-truth-functionality. Let us make it the official definition:

Definition 4.2.5.

$P \supset Q$		T	F
T		T	F
F		T	T

Notice that the *only* false conditionals, on this definition are those with true antecedent and false consequent.

Negation

Negation is another of those seemingly straight-forward ideas that comes apart in our hands and leaves us with a mystery. We have a very strong intuition that negation should turn truth into falsehood *and* vice versa. After all, if it's true that grass is green, then it must be false that grass is not green, since it cannot both be and not be, *anything*. Similarly if it's false that I am green, then it must be true that I am not green. It all sounds very reasonable. It's also entirely truth-functional:

---

[14]One of the most famous logical debates of the Hellenistic period took place in Athens between Diodorus and his ex-student Philo and the subject under debate was whether or not the $\supset_2$ definition of the conditional was correct. Philo took the pro side and Diodorus the con. When Philo was judged the winner, it proved to be a blow to Diodorus' career from which he was never able to recover.

	P	$\neg P$
Definition 4.2.6.	T	F
	F	T

In addition to being intuitive this definition supports what we have always been told about negatives—that a double negative is a positive. In fact $\neg\neg P$ is not just a positive, it is *exactly* the same as P.

So where does the mystery come in? In matching the definition to natural language uses of negation the problem is that, no matter what we were told in high-school, we often use double negative constructions which we do *not* take to be positive. As for more theoretical issues, this turning of true into false and false into true is extremely powerful. If we consider the sentence:

[S] This sentence is true.

we might find it a bit puzzling, but hardly the sign of any deep problem. On the other hand the sentence $\neg$ S is an entirely different matter. It has the property of being true if it's false and false if it's true. This kind of unstable tail-biting behavior is often called *paradoxical*. The moral is that negation can be used to turn a non-paradoxical sentence into a paradoxical one.

A New Connective

Throughout this chapter we have been referring to the truth-values true and false, by means of the symbols T and F. These symbols belong to what we earlier called the metalanguage of SL. It will prove useful to also have a way of referring to the truth values in the object language. In order to do that we shall use the $\bot$ formula that we introduced previously. This formula is actually a limiting case of a connective. We have already seen both binary and unary connectives and now we introduce a zero-ary one.

We don't need a table to give a definition:

> **Definition 4.2.7.** The symbol $\perp$ always takes the truth-value F.

Evidently there is something the same about $P \wedge \neg P$, $Q \wedge \neg Q$, $R \wedge \neg R$, etc. All of them are contradictions, formulas which couldn't possibly be true. We can think of $\perp$ as the formula which expresses exactly that one thing all these different contradictions have in common. It is an *arbitrary contradiction*.

We could also define another constant, *the true* which always takes the value T, but rather than utter another definition, we shall simply use $\neg \perp$ when we require an expression which is never false.

Biconditional

We have already seen the definition for $\equiv$ in terms of truth values. We encountered it briefly when we examined the four possibilities for the definition of $\supset$. We rejected it for the conditional since it made the compound sentence true exactly when the two components have the same truth value. This won't do at all as a notion of conditionality, but it is precisely what we want for the biconditional. In fact the expression $\equiv$ is the nearest we can get to equality for sentences. This is a technical idea and about as remote from an ordinary language motivation as we could get. Of course, we often use the biconditional to translate the expression 'if and only if' but this is a similarly technical way of talking. This means that so long as the definition meets the technical requirements, we shall have no complaints regarding misuse of language or the cost of truth-functionality, or the like. With a sigh of relief, here is the definition:

Definition 4.2.8.

$P \equiv Q$	T	F
T	T	F
F	F	T

A bit of work with pencil and paper will show that the above table is exactly the same as one would compute for the formula

$(P \supset Q) \wedge (Q \supset P)$

which gives some reason for the name of this connective.

4.3   The Key Logical Terms: CSL

With the definition in terms of truth-values for all of our connectives, we are nearly ready to similarly define the concept of *follows from*. Giving a precise definition of this term is usually described as *defining a logic*. The logic defined in this semantic way will again be called CSL. We shall avoid confusion with the syntactical approach by keeping the notation for the various notions distinct from their syntactical counterparts. There is just one thing to do before we can produce our central definitions. Using the connective definitions we are now in the position of being able to calculate the truth-value of any compound formula, no matter how complex, so long as we know the truth-values of the atomic components of the formula. In other words, if we know the values of the sentence letters in a formula then we can eventually work out the value of the whole formula since formulas are required to be of finite length. And it follows from this that if we knew the values of all (infinitely many) sentence letters then we would know the value of every formula. This evidently raises the question: How do we know the values of the sentence letters?

In a certain sense, this is not a logical question. If, for instance, we happen to be using the letter *A* to represent the sentence 'John is happy,' then we wouldn't normally ask a logician if we wanted to know what the truth-value of that sentence is. We might ask John. If the matter were sufficiently important we might ask a whole battery of people, including psychologists, neuroscientists, and philosophers to determine the answer to the question 'Is John happy, or not?' But it is important to realize that whether or not some conclusion follows from some premises—which *is* a logical question, does not depend upon getting the correct truth-value for sentences like 'John is happy.'

What it *does* depend upon is determining whether or not it is possible for the premises to be true and the conclusion false. For that, we must be able to consider all possible distributions of truth values to the formulas which represent the premises, which in turn requires looking at *all possible distributions* to the sentence letters.

Sometimes beginners have the idea that there is only one such distribution. Perhaps they are thinking that there is one *correct* distribution, the one which assigns to each letter the truth-value that it really has. However attractive this idea may be, there are two things wrong with it. First, none of the letters have any *real* truth-value—the letters are used to stand for sentences in a particular application of SL, but before that, they don't have any association with natural language. Second, as we have already observed, the question of which is the correct truth-value for any actual atomic sentence, is not a logical question.

This much is clear: Questions about the truth-value of any given atomic sentence cannot be answered in a vacuum. If we are asked to determine whether or not 'Mary is sad' is true, we shall not have any idea of how to begin in general. If *all* we have is the sentence then there are too many unanswered questions before we can say with any confidence that Mary is sad, or conversely. We need the context, the background information, a complete set of facts—in other words we need to be able to settle all the questions about who Mary is, and what her mental state might be. It ought to be clear that there is more than just one possible way for that determination to be made.

So if there isn't just one distribution of truth-values to sentence letters, how many are there? There are infinitely many![15] Not to worry though, we shall never be in a position where we actually have to use all of them. We shall now be more precise concerning just what a distribution of truth-values to the sentence letters of SL is.

To begin with, we recognize then in most applications we aren't going to be using all infinitely many of the sentence letters. We shall refer to the set of letters that we actually do use at any one time as an *index*. So an index is simply a subset of the set of all atomic sentences. We shall use letters like *I* to stand for indices.

---

[15]In fact there are more such distributions than there are integers. There are as many distributions as there are points on the line.

Definition 4.3.1. A *truth-value assignment*, represented by one of
the letters $v, v_1, \ldots, v_i, \ldots$, is a function which assigns to each
sentence letter in I, exactly one of the values T or F.

We might think of each value assignment v as representing a complete set of facts, or a total context, or as a representation of whatever it
takes for us to be able to give every atomic sentence in I a truth-value.

Recall that calling v a function means (1) every sentence letter in I
gets either T or F and (2) no sentence letter in I gets both T and F.
These are, of course, exactly the conditions that we imposed on *all* sentences at the start of this chapter. We have ensured that every compound
formula (relative to I)[16] has a value which depends on the value of its
components in a *functional* way, through a table, so all formulas must
satisfy the conditions because the sentence letters do.

Every value assignment v determines the value of every formula,
through the application of the truth-value definitions of the connectives,
even though it explicitly gives truth-values to the sentence letters alone.
We now make this determination precise in the following recursive definition:

Definition 4.3.2. The notion of a formula of being *true relative to
the truth-value assignment* v, written $\models_v$, is defined by:

$$\models_v P \iff v(A) = T \text{ if } P \text{ is a sentence letter.}$$

$$[\wedge] \models_v P \wedge Q \iff (\models_v P \ \& \ \models_v Q)$$
$$[\vee] \models_v P \vee Q \iff (\models_v P \text{ or } \models_v Q)$$
$$[\supset] \models_v P \supset Q \iff (\models_v P \implies \models_v Q)$$
$$[\equiv] \models_v P \equiv Q \iff (\models_v P \iff \models_v Q)$$
$$[\neg] \models_v \neg P \iff \not\models_v P$$

---

[16]From this point on we shall tacitly assume that any set of formulas under consideration is
constructed using as its atomic components, only members of some index I, explicit mention of
which will be suppressed so long as no confusion results.

$$[\perp]\ \nvDash_v \perp$$

We also use the terminology 'the formula P is true *on v*' as well as 'the formula P is true *at v*' and even 'v makes P true.'

It may not be apparent at first glance, but the definition we have just given exactly matches the earlier definitions of the connectives in terms of truth-values. In particular, the various clauses for each connective in the recursive part of the definition, usually called *truth-conditions*, are each an alternative way of saying precisely what the corresponding table says.

Consider the truth-condition for $\wedge$ as an example. If both conjuncts are true, the conjunction is true, says the condition, and this is also what the table says. The condition goes on to say that a conjunction is true *only if* both conjuncts are true, which is to say that in every other case, the conjunction is not true. Put these two together and we have precisely described the table for conjunction. The same reasoning shows that the truth-condition for disjunction is likewise just another way of specifying precisely the same thing as the table for that connective.

But in what way does the clause [⊃] match the table for that operator? In this case we simply stipulate that the metalinguistic conditional $\implies$ behaves exactly the way its object language counterpart ⊃ does. In particular, it is true when its antecedent is false and false only when its antecedent is true and consequent false. It's easy to see that this simply amounts to a stipulation that the table which we gave earlier for ⊃ is correct.

And if such a move secures the coincidence of the truth-condition with the table, then clearly the same coincidence must obtain between the truth-condition for $\equiv$ and its table. We must simply say that what we mean by the metalinguistic biconditional is the conjunction of two metalinguistic conditionals (going in either direction).

Once we have defined truth for sentences (relative to an assignment), the other definitions are easy to construct. Of course the main definition is the one for the semantic version of 'follows from.' On the way to this we first define what we mean for a whole set of sentences to be true, on an assignment.

Definition 4.3.3. 'True relative to v' for sets Γ of formulas, written $\models_v \Gamma$, is defined:
If Γ is the set of formulas $\{P_1, P_2, \ldots\}$ then $\models_v \Gamma$ if and only if $\models_v P_1, \models_v P_2, \ldots$.

In other words, a set is true relative to a value assignment, if and only if each and every formula in the set is true on that assignment. Although it is seldom noticed, this is another of the hallmarks of classical logic. One might imagine a departure from classical ways of doing things according to which it was sets which were true and false in the first instance and formulas (sentences) were assigned truth values according to the truth-values of the sets to which they belonged.[17]

Here then is our central definition.

Definition 4.3.4. The set Γ of formulas is said to *semantically entail* the formula P (written $\Gamma \models P$) if and only if for every truth-value assignment $v, \models_v \Gamma \implies \models_v P$.

We also say more simply that the set Γ entails P, especially when it is clear that the semantic approach is being used.

An equivalent way of talking, but one which focuses on the inference is often useful:

Definition 4.3.5. The inference from premises Γ to conclusion P is *semantically valid* if and only if $\Gamma \models P$.

There is a special case of entailment which results when the set of formulas which is doing the entailing is empty. Sometimes beginners

---

[17]As a matter of fact this kind of approach seems never to have been tried in formal logic, but it appears to be quite close to what has been called the *coherence* approach to truth.

think that such a thing is impossible, that the empty set cannot possibly entail any formula, but a little thought shows that, however bizarre it might seem, it can indeed happen that a formula is entailed by $\varnothing$.

Consider what it would take to show that a formula P is *not* entailed by a set Γ, in general. From the definition we can see that what is required is the existence of an assignment v such that, $\models_v \Gamma$ and $\not\models_v P$. We shall call such a value assignment a *counterexample* to the statement that Γ semantically entails P, since it shows that it is possible for the premises Γ all to be true, while the conclusion P is false.

So that if it is impossible to find such a counterexample v then it must be the case that Γ semantically entails P. When we examine the definition of entailment carefully, we see that there is a case, which we might think of them as a loophole in the definition, in which things do not go according to our intuitions. Suppose that it is impossible that the conclusion P be false. In such a case it will likewise be impossible for the premises of Γ to be true while the conclusion P is false, *for any set* Γ including the empty set. So that gives us the formulas which are semantically entailed by the empty set, the formulas which are true on every value assignment. Such formulas are called *logical truths* or *tautologies*.

Definition 4.3.6. A formula P is a *logical truth* (written $\models P$) if and only if for every value assignment v, $\models_v P$.

The negation of a logical truth, is a *logical falsehood*, a formula which is false on every value assignment. Beginners often make the mistake of thinking that the phrase 'negation of a logical truth' means the same thing as 'not logically true.' But in order for a formula to be not logically true it is only required that there be at least one value assignment on which the formula is false. This is a long way from requiring that the formula be false on *every* value assignment! Logical truth and logical falsehood are extremes. Between them, exist the majority of formulas which are true on some value assignments and false on others and so are neither logically true nor logically false.

Apart from the case which gives rise to the logical truths, we can see that there is another loophole in the definition of entailment. It might turn out that there is no counterexample to the claim that Γ entails P because it is impossible for all the formulas in Γ to be true on any value assignment. If that is so, then it will be impossible to find an assignment on which Γ is true and P is false, *for any P*. Such a set entails *everything* and is sometimes said to *explode* inferentially.

We next define a concept which relates to this second loophole.

Definition 4.3.7. A set Γ of formulas is said to be *semantically consistent* if and only if there is at least one value assignment v on which $\models_v \Gamma$. If a set is not semantically consistent, it is said to be semantically *inconsistent*.

We often drop the qualification 'semantically' when no confusion is likely to result.

So every inconsistent set explodes, given the definition of entails. Clearly an inconsistent set is pathological, and we would prefer to deal with consistent sets whenever possible. In view of that, perhaps it makes sense to arrange for them all to explode. Such an explosion signals our contempt for inconsistency and our determination to avoid it.

There is a difficulty with this, otherwise admirable, hard line on inconsistency. The only way to convert an inconsistent set into a consistent one, is to throw away some of its members. The idea is to throw out the 'bad guys' and keep throwing them out until we get down to a consistent set.[18]

Sometimes the bad guys are obvious, logical falsehoods for instance, and then this plan makes perfect sense. At other times, there are no obvious villains. All we have is a set of sentences or formulas not all of which can be simultaneously true. In such a case we would be reduced to throwing out things at random until we achieve consistency and that strategy had very little appeal.

One might argue that for exploding sets, the distinction between what follows from the set and what doesn't, has become moot since

---

[18]This is the method recommended by W.V.O. Quine in his famous *Web of Belief*.

there isn't any longer a significant contrast. We would get the same effect by requiring that no formula or sentence follows from an inconsistent set. But this approach to inconsistency, the approach which makes all inconsistent sets trivial, is another hallmark of classical logic. Perhaps it would be best to say that a tacit assumption of the classical approach is that premise sets are consistent, and there is no provision for any other case.[19]

This notion of consistency, which seems quite close to our intuitive use of that notion, is very rich. In fact we could just as well have chosen to define it first, and then the other notions could easily have been defined in terms of it. Some logic books do exactly that, defining entailment as the inconsistency of the set consisting of the premises together with the negation of the conclusion, and logical truth as the inconsistency of the set consisting of the negation of the formula.

Next we define a kind of metalinguistic identity.

Definition 4.3.8. Two formulas P and Q are *semantically equivalent* written $P :: Q$, if and only if for every value assignment v, $\models_v P \iff \models_v Q$.

This amounts to saying that the two always take the same truth-value, on every value assignment, and that the equivalence of P and Q is the same thing as the logical truth of the biconditional $P \equiv Q$.

Finally, we can say what a logic *is* in general, and what our classical logic of sentences (from the semantic perspective) is in particular. For us, a logic is identified with the inferences that it licenses. So a logic is a set of pairs (Γ, P) such that Γ is a set of formulas and P is a formula. The logic CSL is, from the semantic perspective, the set of such pairs such that Γ semantically entails P.

This definition of a logic is not universally accepted, nor is it even the majority position. The majority view is to identify a logic with its set of logical truths. This is a bit of 19th Century logical lore which has

---

[19] A number of logicians became dissatisfied with this particular classical failing, and determined to provide an alternative account in which not every classically inconsistent set explodes. Such approaches have come to be called *paraconsistent*.

shown amazing persistence. Perhaps the explanation lies in the fact that
the set of logical truths is easier to study, as a mathematical object, than
the set of entailments.

4.4   Truth-Value Calculations

These definitions are all very well, but one needs to know how to actually compute in practice that a set entails a formula (or not), that another
set is consistent (or not), etc. There are a number of ways to accomplish
such calculations but we shall concentrate on the so-called *method of
counterexample*.

A counterexample, as we have already seen, is an assignment of a
certain kind, one which *refutes* the possibility of an entailment between
a certain set and a formula, by showing that it is possible (on the value
assignment in question) for the premises to be true while the conclusion
is false. The method charges us with trying to construct the specification
of one of these value assignments. If this turns out to be impossible;
if there cannot exist such a counterexample then the entailment holds.
Otherwise, if we succeed in specifying the value assignment, then the
entailment fails to obtain.

Since logical truth (and logical falsehood) as well as equivalence,
are all really variations on the theme of entailment, it will turn out that
the method can be used to compute whether or not these properties hold
also.

For semantic consistency, it will turn out that we need to turn the
method on its head, and to search for an *example* rather than a counterexample, but the two methods are entirely similar.

This is all very abstract, and it's time to descend to the level of concrete detail.

How does one specify an assignment? One constructs such a specification by saying which sentence letters get which truth-values.

The next question is: How do we know what sentence letters are
supposed to get which truth-values? The answer to this is that the truth-
functional definitions we use for the connectives always allow us to
work backwards from the specification of truth-values to compound for-

mulas, to the truth-values of the components. Sometimes, there will be more than one way to distribute truth-values to the components which will give the compound a certain value, but there will always be some (finite) number of possibilities. Eventually, we get down to the level of sentence letters.

So let's consider first our John and Mary example. We recall that the form is:

(P1) A

(P2) $A \supset B$

(C) $\therefore B$

A counterexample to this inference would be any value assignment on which the conclusion B is false and both premises A and $A \supset B$ are true. This distribution of T to the premises and F to the conclusion is called the *initial* distribution.

We construct another kind of table now which allows us to work out the consequences of the initial distribution of truth values. The table will have columns for each sentence letter and each formula and subformula which occurs in the inference. Here is an example:

A	B	$A \supset B$
T	F	T

It is customary to put all the sentence letters at the left of the table, which portion of the table is usually called the index of the table (for obvious reasons), and then more and more complex formulas from left to right until at the far right are the largest formulas.

In the next pass, the first consequences of the initial distribution are calculated. We have $A \supset B$ which has been marked T, and B which has been marked F. If we examine the table definition for $\supset$ (which we should memorize) we see that the only way a conditional with a false consequent can be true, is if the antecedent is also false. So we enter this *forced* distribution which gives us:

A	B	$A \supset B$
$T\ F$	F	T

But this is impossible! In this table, A has been assigned both T and F. This cannot be the specification of any truth-value assignment since no assignment can give one and the same sentence letter both truth-values. It would be a violation of the definition of truth-value assignment or, if we are feeling dramatic, a violation of the law of non-contradiction!

So we cannot specify, on pain of contradiction, a counterexample to the John and Mary inference. If there can be no counterexample then there is entailment between the premises and the conclusion, which is to say that the inference form must be valid.

Let's attempt to use this method of counterexample to show that the formula $(A \supset (B \supset C)) \supset ((A \supset B) \supset (A \supset C))$ is a logical truth. Since the definition of the term 'logical truth' requires that such a formula be true on every value assignment, a counterexample will be a value assignment on which the formula is false. We would specify such a (type of) value assignment by starting with the following table which represents our initial distribution.

A	B	C	$A \supset (B \supset C)$	$A \supset B$	$A \supset C$	$(A \supset B) \supset (A \supset C)$	X
							F

In this table we use the letter X to stand for the entire formula, so that we can fit the table on the page. Since our formula is a conditional, we know there is only one way that it can be false, so the following consequence of the initial distribution is forced on us:

A	B	C	$A \supset (B \supset C)$	$A \supset B$	$A \supset C$	$(A \supset B) \supset (A \supset C)$	X
			T			F	F

In entering these consequences of the initial distribution, we have made one conditional true, and another false. There is more than one way that the former could happen but only one way for the latter. We ignore the true conditional for the time being, and enter in the consequences of the false one:

A	B	C	$A \supset (B \supset C)$	$A \supset B$	$A \supset C$	$(A \supset B) \supset (A \supset C)$	X
			T	T	F	F	F

This has produced another pair of conditionals, one true and the other false. Once more we ignore the former and write in the consequences of the latter, which are forced on us by the fact that a conditional is false in only one case.

A	B	C	$A \supset (B \supset C)$	$A \supset B$	$A \supset C$	$(A \supset B) \supset (A \supset C)$	X
T		F	T	T	F	F	F

At this point we see that column 1 tells us that A is true and column 5 tells us that $A \supset B$ is true. But if B were false then, since A is true, $A \supset B$ would be false. From this it follows that B *must* be true. This gives us:

A	B	C	$A \supset (B \supset C)$	$A \supset B$	$A \supset C$	$(A \supset B) \supset (A \supset C)$	X
T	T	F	T	T	F	F	F

Next consider column 4. From this and column 1, we know that $B \supset C$ must be true, and since C is false, it must be the case that B is false as well (since if B were true, then $B \supset C$ would be false and so would $A \supset (B \supset C)$). So we must have as our specification:

A	B	C	$A \supset (B \supset C)$	$A \supset B$	$A \supset C$	$(A \supset B) \supset (A \supset C)$	X
T	F	F	T	T	F	F	F

But there couldn't be any such value assignment, since it would have to make the sentence letter B both true and false which is forbidden by the definition of value assignment. It follows that there can be no counterexample and hence that the formula $(A \supset (B \supset C)) \supset ((A \supset B) \supset (A \supset C))$, which was called X in the table, is a logical truth.

In the examples we have been given, the initial distribution of truth-values has forced us to assign truth-values to subformulas at each step of the way until we were forced, finally, to assign both T and F to some sentence letter. Since every move was forced we could carry out the whole calculation in just one row. It is not always possible to do that.

When we use the method of counterexample to test for semantic equivalence we often need at least two rows. An equivalence is defined to hold between two formulas, say P and Q if and only if there is no value assignment which makes one of them true and the other false. Suppose we try to specify an assignment which makes P true and Q false, and that turns out to be impossible, does it follow that there is no counterexample? No, it only follows that there isn't *that* kind of counterexample, let's call it a type 1 counterexample. There remains the possibility, until it too has been closed off, of an assignment on which P is false and Q is true, we call that a type 2 counterexample. So it won't be sufficient for equivalence that we show there can be no counterexample of just one type. We must show that both types are ruled out. Thus every demonstration that there is no counterexample to an equivalence, which is to say that P and Q *are* equivalent, must use at least 2 rows in the counterexample specification table.

We should hasten to add however that if even a single one of the cases does *not* generate an impossibility, then we can stop any further calculation having established a counterexample to the equivalence.

An example or two may aid our understanding of the process by which counterexamples are either discovered or shown to be impossible. Consider the pair of formulas $A \vee B$ and $\neg(\neg A \wedge \neg B)$. To see if there is a counterexample of type 1 we construct the table in which the initial distribution gives $A \vee B$ true and $\neg(\neg A \wedge \neg B)$ false.

type	A	B	$\neg A$	$\neg B$	$A \vee B$	$\neg A \wedge \neg B$	$\neg(\neg A \wedge \neg B)$
1					T		F

There are several ways for a disjunction to be true, so we ignore that and concentrate on the false negation. There is only one way for a negation to be false and that is for its negatum to be true.

type	A	B	$\neg A$	$\neg B$	$A \vee B$	$\neg A \wedge \neg B$	$\neg(\neg A \wedge \neg B)$
1					T	T	F

But the formula we have marked true is a conjunction and we know that the only true conjunctions are those which have both conjuncts true. We are then forced to mark in:

type	A	B	$\neg A$	$\neg B$	$A \vee B$	$\neg A \wedge \neg B$	$\neg(\neg A \wedge \neg B)$
1			T	T	T	T	F

But marking these two negations true, forces us by the definition of negation, to mark the two negata false.

type	A	B	$\neg A$	$\neg B$	$A \vee B$	$\neg A \wedge \neg B$	$\neg(\neg A \wedge \neg B)$
1	F	F	T	T	T	T	F

Strictly speaking what we ought to do now, is to introduce two rows under this type 1 attempt. In the first row, we mark A true in order to make $A \vee B$ true, and in the second row we mark B true in order to make that same disjunction true. In the first row we would have to make the sentence letter A both T and F, while in the second row we have to make the sentence letter B both T and F. Both are impossible and this would show the impossibility of a type 1 counterexample since no value assignment is allowed to make any sentence letter both true and false.

Such would be the completely rigorous way to do the example, but we will allow a shortcut. Since both A and B have been marked F, we shall mark the formula $A \vee B$ false, since we know that any disjunction with two false disjuncts is itself false. This will produce:

type	A	B	$\neg A$	$\neg B$	$A \vee B$	$\neg A \wedge \neg B$	$\neg(\neg A \wedge \neg B)$
1	F	F	T	T	T F	T	F

We claim that *this* table shows the impossibility of a type 1 counterexample even though we do not produce any sentence letter in the table which is marked as being both true and false. Given that we are using the definitions of the connectives that we are, the only way *any* formula in a truth-table can be both true and false, is relative to an assignment which makes one or more sentence letters true and false and all such value assignments are impossible.

Even after all this work we have not yet shown that the two formulas are equivalent—only that the equivalence cannot be refuted by a type 1 counterexample. To complete the demonstration we must now consider the possibility of a type 2 counterexample. The initial distribution for that would be:

type	A	B	$\neg A$	$\neg B$	$A \vee B$	$\neg A \wedge \neg B$	$\neg(\neg A \wedge \neg B)$
2					F		T

For the negation in the last column to be true the negatum must be false and for the disjunction to be false, both disjuncts must be false. This forces:

type	A	B	$\neg A$	$\neg B$	$A \vee B$	$\neg A \wedge \neg B$	$\neg(\neg A \wedge \neg B)$
2	F	F			F	F	T

There is more than one way for a conjunction to be false, so we leave
that and concentrate on the negations. Since the two negata are false,
the negations must be true. In other words we have:

type	A	B	$\neg A$	$\neg B$	$A \vee B$	$\neg A \wedge \neg B$	$\neg(\neg A \wedge \neg B)$
2	F	F	T	T	F	F	T

Now we can use the same kind of short-cut as we used for the last
case. Since both its conjuncts are true, the conjunction
$\neg A \wedge \neg B$ must be true. Hence we must have:

type	A	B	$\neg A$	$\neg B$	$A \vee B$	$\neg A \wedge \neg B$	$\neg(\neg A \wedge \neg B)$
2	F	F	T	T	F	$F\ T$	T

But now we have one formula which has been marked both T and
F and this is impossible. Thus there is no counterexample of type 2.
At last we have shown that the formulas $A \vee B$ and $\neg(\neg A \wedge \neg B)$ are
semantically equivalent.

We must use a variation of the method, which we might as well
call the *method of example*, when we have to show that a given set of
formulas is semantically consistent.

For a set to be consistent in that sense, there must be an assignment[20]
on which all of the members of the set are true. To use this method, we
start with an initial distribution of T to all the formulas in the set. We
then work out the consequences of this initial distribution in a series of
steps in exactly the same way as we did in the method of counterexamples. If some contradiction appears, which is to say some formula or
subformula to which we are *forced* to assign both T and F, then there
can be no value assignment which makes all the members of the set true,
and the set is not semantically consistent.

Consider the set $\{A \vee B, B \supset \bot, A \supset C\}$. The table which shows
all the formulas and subformulas is:

---

[20]It is part of the classical viewpoint that semantic consistency requires a *single* value assignment on which all the members of the set are true. There are paraconsistent approaches which
make this the most stringent account of consistency but which allow also less stringent ones e.g.
those which accept as consistent (in some qualified sense) those sets all the members of which are
true on at least one of several value assignments.

A	B	C	$A \vee B$	$A \supset C$	$B \supset \perp$

We put in the initial distribution like this:

A	B	C	$A \vee B$	$A \supset C$	$B \supset \perp$
			T	T	T

Now we work out the consequences of the initial assignment starting with $B \supset \perp$. We start there, because there is more than one way for the other two formulas to be true. But since $\perp$ is always F, in order for the conditional to be true, B must be F (since if it were true we would have true antecedent and false consequent). So we are forced to put in:

A	B	C	$A \vee B$	$A \supset C$	$B \supset \perp$
	F		T	T	T

Since B is F and $A \vee B$ is T we are forced to make A true since otherwise the disjunction would have two false disjuncts, which would make it false. This brings us to:

A	B	C	$A \vee B$	$A \supset C$	$B \supset \perp$
T	F		T	T	T

Finally, since A is true and $A \supset C$ is true, we are forced to mark C as true since otherwise the conditional would have a true antecedent and false consequent. We end with:

A	B	C	$A \vee B$	$A \supset C$	$B \supset \perp$
T	F	T	T	T	T

A quick check shows that we haven't been forced to make any formula both true and false. We have shown then that *any* value assignment that makes the sentence letters A and C true while making B false, will make all the sentences in our set true, and hence the set is semantically consistent.

Common Mistakes and Pitfalls

The method we have described is easy to use once the tables for the various connectives have been memorized. Without *knowing* that the only false conditional is one with a true antecedent and false consequent for example, the method will be not at all easy to apply. In fact it will be nearly impossible.

Apart from failure to get the connective definitions by heart, a frequent mistake made by beginners is to think that the method will produce some unique place in a table where a formula is marked both T and F. This is not at all true. Just where the contradiction appears is a matter of the order in which one does things. That order is not unique— in general there are several distinct ways of working through from an initial distribution to a final contradiction. So if you do it one way and the instructor does it another way, it doesn't follow that either of you is wrong.

Perhaps the most frequent error is in thinking that as soon as one and the same formula ends up being marked both true and false, then the task is finished. Of course, it *may* be finished, if there is no alternative to a contradiction, but it may not be. An example will illustrate this. Let's try to see if the formula $(A \vee B) \supset (A \wedge B)$ is a logical truth. To do this we construct a table showing the formula and all its subformulas, and we mark the formula F in this table. If no contradiction results from this initial distribution then we have specified a class of value assignments each of which is a counterexample to the logical truth of the formula. Here is the table with the initial distribution.

A	B	$A \vee B$	$A \wedge B$	$(A \vee B) \supset (A \wedge B)$
				F

Since the conditional is marked F, we know that $A \vee B$ must be true and that $A \wedge B$ must be false. Thus:

A	B	$A \vee B$	$A \wedge B$	$(A \vee B) \supset (A \wedge B)$
		T	F	F

Let us arrange for the falsity of the conjunction by making both A and B false. It is certainly true in that case that the conjunction must be false. This gives us:

A	B	$A \vee B$	$A \wedge B$	$(A \vee B) \supset (A \wedge B)$
F	F	T	F	F

But in this table, the disjunction $A \vee B$ can be seen to have two false disjuncts! We know that all such disjunctions are false, so we must have:

A	B	$A \vee B$	$A \wedge B$	$(A \vee B) \supset (A \wedge B)$
F	F	$T\ F$	F	F

Now an actual contradiction has appeared—a single formula which has been assigned both truth-values. It would be a *mistake* however, to think that we have shown the original formula to be logically true. We have not shown the impossibility of a counterexample even though we have produced a table containing a contradiction because *the contradiction was not forced.*

All that was required of us was to make the conjunction $A \wedge B$ false while we made the disjunction $A \vee B$ true. There are three ways to make the conjunction false: make A false, make B false, and make both A and B false. The third of these ways leads to a contradiction but what of the others? If we make the conjunction false by marking A false, that still gives us room to make the disjunction true by marking B true! Here is the table which does that:

A	B	$A \vee B$	$A \wedge B$	$(A \vee B) \supset (A \wedge B)$
F	T	T	F	F

In this table there is *no contradiction*. It specifies a counterexample to the logical truth of $(A \vee B) \supset (A \wedge B)$, namely any value assignment on which A is false and B is true. A little thought reveals that we can specify the class of counterexamples more generally as any value assignment on which one of A, B, is true (and thus the disjunction is true on the value assignment) and the other is false (which is sufficient for the conjunction to be false).

Remarks on truth-tables

The method which was presented above for doing semantic calculations, has been called the *shorter* truth-table method. There is in popular use an alternative which ought to be called the longer method, but which is usually referred to as the truth-table method without qualification.

The advantage of the truth-table method is that it can be presented in an entirely mechanical way so that it is much more difficult to make mistakes. The heart of the method is the construction of tables which detail every possible truth-value distribution to the formulas and sub-formulas under consideration. As an example, we shall consider the formula $A \supset (B \supset A)$. The (complete) truth-table for this formula is:

A	B	$B \supset A$	$A \supset (B \supset A)$
T	T	T	T
T	F	T	T
F	T	F	T
F	F	T	T

Here we can see at a glance what happens on all possible value assignments, since there are only four distinct assignments, given an index which contains only two sentence letters. So we see at once that the formula $A \supset (B \supset A)$ is true on every value assignment, since it has been marked T in every row of the table. Another way of describing this kind of table is that its rows list the set of truth-value assignments which *span* the index in question.

Similarly easy table-scanning will provide the answers to all other semantic questions. For every inference, we simply check every row in which the premises are all true. If the conclusion is also true in each of those rows, then the inference is semantically valid, otherwise invalid. For equivalence we check to see if the two formulas we are checking ever take on different truth values in any of the rows of their table. If so, then equivalence fails. For consistency we check to see if there are any rows in which all of the formulas in the set under consideration are marked true.

In each of these cases it is an entirely mechanical matter to construct the table of formulas and subformulas with a line for every truth-value assignment and then check to see if a row of the specified kind exists. No intellectual effort is required to generate the tables or to look for the rows. In other words, the truth-table method would seem to be noticeably *easier* than the method of counterexample. Such is certainly liable to be the opinion of a student who has already been exposed to the truth-table method in a previous class. Why not use this easy method?

The answer is that we prefer the method of counterexample because the truth-table method doesn't work. Or perhaps it would be more charitable to say that the method won't work once we get past the simplest cases. Consider the following formula which we wish to show is a logical falsehood:

$$A \wedge \neg A \wedge (B_1 \wedge B_2 \wedge \ldots \wedge B_{5999} \wedge B_{6000})$$

The method of counterexample has one row, and after assigning the whole formula T as the initial distribution, we soon work our way down to assigning the formula A both T and F or, if we work things out in a different order, the formula $\neg A$ would be the one to receive the two values. In either case we would have been forced into a contradiction, which would show that there is no counterexample to the logical falsehood.

The mechanical and supposedly easier truth-table method however would require that we construct a table having 2^{6002} rows. This is a large enough number that most students would be discouraged from even starting.

It gets worse than this. In real-world applications to computer hardware, it is not at all unusual to find a million or more elements (which correspond to formulas) on a single chip. $2^{1000000}$ is probably more than the number of protons in the universe.

We must take care not to leave the false impression that the shorter truth-table method is always shorter than the truth-table method. It is often shorter, as a look at the examples presented in this section show, but in the worst case, one would need to introduce as many rows as the truth-table method. By the worst case in this context we mean that an initial distribution assigns truth-values to formulas which require the consideration of more than one case. For instance, we might have assigned T to a conditional—which could be accomplished by making the antecedent F or the consequent T. This means we must consider at least two cases each of which is represented by a separate row. Now suppose that the antecedent is a conjunction, so that there are two ways for *it* to be false. That will require an additional two rows, and so on. We might have to keep introducing rows if we have 'bad' distributions, but the limit, the most we could ever be required to introduce, is the number of rows required by the truth-table method, which is to say 2^n where n is the number of sentence letters we use.

4.5   Exercises

1. Show that each of the following is logically true:

    a) $P_1 \vee P_2 \vee \ldots \vee P_{1000} \vee \neg P_1$

    b) $(P \supset (Q \supset R)) \supset ((P \supset Q) \supset (P \supset R))$

    c) $P \supset (Q \supset P)$

    d) $\neg P \supset (P \supset Q)$

2. Show that each of the following is logically false:

    a) $P_1 \wedge P2 \wedge \ldots \wedge P_{1000} \wedge \neg P_1$

    b) $\neg ((P \supset Q) \vee (Q \supset P))$

    c) $\neg (((P \supset BQ) \wedge (\neg P \supset Q)) \supset Q)$

3. Show that each of the following pairs are (semantically) equivalent:

    a) $P \wedge Q, \neg (\neg P \vee \neg Q)$

    b) $P \vee Q, \neg (\neg P \wedge \neg Q)$

    c) $P \supset Q, \neg (P \wedge \neg Q)$

    d) $\neg (P \supset Q), P \wedge \neg Q$

4. Show that in each of the following inferences, the premises entail the conclusion:

a) $P \supset (R \wedge S), Q \supset (\neg R \wedge \neg S) / \therefore \neg(P \wedge Q)$

b) $P \vee Q, P \supset R, Q \supset S / \therefore R \vee S$

c) $(P \supset \neg Q) \wedge (Q \supset \neg R), S \supset Q / \therefore S \supset (\neg P \wedge \neg R)$

d) $P \vee Q, (P \supset R) \wedge (\neg R \supset \neg Q) / \therefore R$

4.6 Inferences in Natural Language

We started this book by inquiring into the John and Mary inference. We seem to have wandered quite far from that humble beginning. In particular, we have introduced a formal language now, and then defined the connectives of this language in such a way that most of them seem quite remote from ordinary language. In that case, how can we say anything useful about inferences in their natural habitat?

Even though some of our definitions are at most inspired by ordinary language, that doesn't mean that our formal language is useless in the adjudication of natural language inferences and arguments. When we define a connective truth-functionally we may lose a lot of the phenomena which are present in its ordinary discourse inspiration, but we may not have lost anything at all of *logical* interest. There haven't yet been any cases in which it has been decisively shown that some inference which is intuitively correct (or not) in ordinary discourse is invalid (or valid) when formalized.

It's important to use the word 'decisively' in making this claim. There certainly *are* inferences the formal validity of which looks odd to put the matter charitably, but this can be explained away as the cost of the simplicity of the classical approach.

In general terms, when we want to determine whether some inference in natural language is correct we first formalize it, which is to say we *translate* the premises and the conclusion into our formal language. Once we have formulas to work with, we can use the method of counterexamples to determine whether or not the form is valid. If (and only if) it is, then the original natural language inference is correct.

The translation process is at best semi-mechanical but with a little practice, it becomes quite easy. There are some things to learn at first especially for translating conditional forms. Most of these are presented in table 4.1

Table 4.1: Natural Language Equivalents of $A \supset B$

$A \supset B$
If A then B
If A, B
B if A
A only if B
A is sufficient for B
B is necessary for A
A means B

Of all of these, the one which seems the most difficult or unnatural is translating A only if B by $A \supset B$. Beginners often think that the former expression should be translated by $B \supset A$ even though they don't hesitate to suggest the latter for A if B and if questioned, say that an 'if' expression means something different from an 'only if' expression. Worse, even the rankest beginner seems to have no trouble at all in understanding (and obeying) a prescription like 'Pass only if the center lane is clear.'[21] So it's a great mystery why this bit of translation confuses so many.

The explanation which works in the largest number of cases, although that may not be a very large number seems to be this. When we say 'John is happy only if Mary is happy.' we are saying something like 'John can't be happy without Mary being happy.' And this is to say something like John's happiness leads to Mary's. But it surely doesn't follow from this that Mary is restricted in her own happiness in any similar way, does it? We aren't required to say that Mary's happiness leads to John's. If you agree, then you must translate the only if expression as the table shows.

In the end, memorizing will get everybody over this particular bump.

---

[21]This example is due to Robert M. Martin

The only other trick, if that's what it should be called, is that the conjunctive use[22] of the ordinary language connective 'but' is always translated by $\wedge$. It is quite true that we often use 'but' when we think there is something surprising or unusual about the conjunction,[23] but this is an excellent example of something that might make a lot of psychological difference, without making any logical difference at all.

The last real difficulty which a beginner is likely to encounter is with the translation of 'unless.' Here there is no quick fix since there is room for a debate over how the translation should go.[24] Consider:

> There will be a picnic tomorrow, unless it rains.

What does this sentence mean?[25] At least this much: if there is rain tomorrow then the picnic is off. Sometimes, even much of the time, people are happy to take that as the translation. Let us use A to stand for 'There will be a picnic tomorrow' and B for 'It rains tomorrow.' Then the suggestion so far is:

> $B \supset \neg A$

Suppose now that there is no rain tomorrow. How would we feel if there were no picnic? Many would be annoyed perhaps. One (perhaps standard response) is to say that for such cases we should translate the unless as the disjunction:

> $A \vee B$

Since in this case, we won't have both no rain and no picnic, although we could still, under this disjunctive reading, have a rainy picnic.

This seems to suggest that the *proper* translation should be:

---

[22] We have already seen that there is also an ancient non-conjunctive sense which survives in 'It never rains but it pours.', and 'But for my instructor, I'd fail the course.'

[23] A not entirely happy example due to Paul Grice is: 'She was poor but honest.'

[24] Most introductions to logic tend not to highlight difficulties of this sort, preferring to present the view that translation is a nearly mechanical process. We can find scant support for such a view and consider it a major disservice

[25] This section has been rewritten after very useful discussions with Dorian Nicholson and Wayne Fenske.

$$(B \supset \neg A) \wedge (\neg B \supset A)$$

This expanded translation turns out to be equivalent (as is easy to check) to:

$$\neg A \equiv B$$

and also to the possibly more revealing:

$$A \underline{\vee} B$$

We might as well call this biconditional/exclusive disjunction the *strong* sense of unless and the previous translation the *weak* sense.

There is this to be said against translating in the strong way: When we use unless, we record a circumstance in which the conditioned event won't happen, only one such circumstance, and there may be others. A downpour will prevent the projected picnic, but so will the death of the host and, we may presume, many other acts of God and the King's enemies. So the most we are entitled to is the 'only if' translation earlier slandered as the weak sense.

There is this to be said in favor of the strong translation: We can certainly agree that were the host to drop dead, the prospects for the picnic taking place as planned are dim indeed. In fact, we might argue that such things may be counted as part of the background assumptions against which plans have been made. Of course when we announce the picnic, it goes without saying that we assume that the earth does not explode before the announced time and that all the other *standing conditions* are assumed to be in effect. The 'unless' conditions that we *do* trouble ourselves to record, in this case rain, are the ones that don't go without saying.[26]

---

[26]Dorian Nicholson has objected to the so-called strong sense of unless, by saying that a parallel argument might well eventuate in a similarly strong biconditional sense of only if'. In other words, when we announce the picnic by saying 'There will be a picnic tomorrow only if it doesn't rain.' haven't we left ourselves liable to complaints if on the morrow there is neither rain nor picnic? Perhaps not, since we used an explicitly conditional form, and had 'if and only if' available to us—we just decided, for some reason, not to use it.

4.7 Exercises

(A) Formalize the following arguments and determine which are semantically valid.

1. Sometimes it is relatively easy to deal with a negated compound as in this:

   > If I finish painting the fence (F), the neighbors will be pleased (P). Unfortunately I will miss the party (M)). It cannot both be true that the neighbors are pleased and I miss the party. So, I won't finish painting the fence.

2. Because of the classical truth-table for the conditional, the conjunction of the antecedent and the consequent must semantically entail the conditional. In most circumstances the reverse is not true, i.e. a conditional does not normally entail the conjunction of its antecedent with its consequent. Should this be 'all circumstances' rather then merely 'most?' Does 'If grass is green or not green, then grass is colored' entail 'Grass is green or not green, and grass is colored?' (G = Grass is green, C = Grass is colored)

3. Sometimes it's not so easy to deal with a negated compound. At least one philosopher seems to have been tempted by the following:

   > If either subjectivism or utilitarianism is correct, then ethical concepts are reducible to empirical concepts(R). However, neither of these ethical positions is correct. It follows that ethical concepts cannot be reduced to empirical concepts.

   (S Subjectivism is correct, U = Utilitarianism is correct, R)

4. Mary is sad. (M) So either John is happy or he isn't.

   (J = John is happy)

5. The preceding argument is a peculiar and apparently worthless argument. Why, then, should it have tested out as it did? Here is an explanation.

> The previous inference is valid if and only If it is logically impossible for its premise to be true while its conclusion Is false. It Is logically impossible for the conclusion of the previous inference to be false; and if this is so, then It is logically impossible for its premise to be true while its conclusion is false. Thus the previous inference is valid. (V)

(V, A = It is logically impossible for the premise of the previous inference to be true while its conclusion is false, B = It is logically impossible for the conclusion of the previous inference to be false)

6. Is our entire future determined by our genetic heritage? Here's an argument which claims not.

> If intelligence is wholly hereditary (H) and provided that identical twins have the same heredity, then being raised in separate households will not reduce the similarity of intelligence between two identical twins. But it does reduce the similarity. (R) Identical twins come from a common sperm and egg. (C) This means that they have identical heredity. Therefore Intelligence is not entirely hereditary.

(H, I = Identical twins have identical heredity, R, C)

7. One sometimes hears the phrase 'not everything can be explained.' If we think of defining as a kind of explaining, the following seems to put us in an uncomfortable position if we disagree with the earlier phrase.

> If some term in a theory is defined by means of a second term which has been previously defined with the

help of the first, then there is a circular chain of definitions. If no term in the theory is defined by means of a
second term which has been defined previously with the
aid of the first term, then all the terms In the theory are
defined only If there is an infinite regress of definitions.
Hence a necessary condition for defining all the terms in
a theory is having either an infinite regress of definitions
or a circular definitional chain.

(S = Some term in a theory is defined by means of a second term
which has been previously defined with the help of the first term,
C= There is a circular chain of definitions, A = All the terms in a
theory are defined, R = There is an infinite regress of definitions)

8. In the sixth Meditation, Descartes argues:

> Body is by nature divisible. (B) If so and if mind
> and body are one and the same (S), then mind is also
> divisible (M). However, the mind is entirely indivisible.
> It follows that the mind and body are not the same.

9. A perennial difficulty for beginning students is how to produce the
   form of 'A only if B.' For example, should S1 be translated as S2
   or S3?

   S1 You should pass only if the passing lane is clear.

   S2 If the passing lane if clear, you should pass.

   S3 If you pass then the passing lane should be clear.

   The following attempts to answer this question

   > S1 translates either as S2 or as S3 (but not both). If
   > the former, then the truth of S2 is both a necessary and
   > a sufficient condition for the truth of S1. S1 is true, but
   > S2 Is false. Therefore S1 translates as S3. (B)

   A = S1 translates as S2.

10. Pascal's famous wager is paraphrased by:

> If I believe in God, then (1) If he exists I gain, and
> (2) If he doesn't then (at least) I don't lose. If, on the
> other hand, I don't believe, then (1) if God exists I lose,
> and (2) If he doesn't I don't gain. From this it follows
> that if I believe I'll either gain or (at least) not lose,
> while if I don't believe I'll either lose or (at best) fail
> to gain.

(B = I believe in God, E = God exists, G = I gain, L = I lose)

11. (DIFFICULT) if any one of the three positions of hard determin-
    ism, soft determinism, and indeterminism is correct, then the other
    two are mistaken. So one of these three positions is correct, and
    the other two are incorrect.

    (H = Hard determinism is correct, S = Soft determinism is correct,
    I = Indeterminism is correct)

12. (DIFFICULT) The following puzzle appears in *101 Puzzles in
    Thought and Logic*, by C. R. Wylie, Jr.

    The personnel director of a firm in speaking of three men the com-
    pany was thinking of hiring said,

    > 'We need Brown and if we need Jones then we need
    > Smith, if and only if we need either Brown or Jones and
    > don't need Smith.'

    If the company actually needed more than one of the men, which
    ones were they?

(B) Determine whether or not the following sets of sentences are
semantically consistent).

1. $\{A_1, A_2 \wedge \neg A_1, A_3 \wedge \neg A_2 \wedge \neg A_1, A_4 \wedge \neg A_1 \wedge \neg A_2 \wedge \neg A_3, \ldots\}$
   (notice that this an infinite set)

2. $\{\neg(P \supset Q), \neg(Q \supset P)\}$

3. $\{P \lor Q, P \supset R, Q \supset R, \neg R\}$

4. $\{(P \supset (Q \supset R)) \supset ((P \supset Q) \supset (P \supset R)), P \land \neg R, Q \lor \neg R\}$

4.8 Truth-tables Quick Reference

$P \wedge Q$	T	F
T	T	F
F	F	F

$P \vee Q$	T	F
T	T	T
F	T	F

$P \underline{\vee} Q$	T	F
T	F	T
F	T	F

$P \supset Q$	T	F
T	T	F
F	T	T

P	$\neg P$
T	F
F	T

The symbol $\perp$ always takes the truth-value F.

$P \equiv Q$	T	F
T	T	F
F	F	T

4.9 Key Definitions Quick Reference

If Γ is the set of formulas $\{P_1, P_2, \ldots\}$ then $\models_v \Gamma$ (*Gamma is true relative to* v) if and only if $\models_v P_1, \models_v P_2, \ldots$.

The set Γ *semantically entails* the formula P (written $\Gamma \models P$) if and only if for every truth-value assignment v, $\models_v \Gamma \implies \models_v P$

The inference from premises Γ to conclusion P is *semantically valid* if and only if $\Gamma \models P$.

A formula P is a *logical truth* (written $\models P$) if and only if for every truth-value assignment v, $\models_v P$.

A set Γ of formulas is said to be semantically *consistent* if and only if there is at least one truth-value assignment v on which $\models_v \Gamma$. If a set is not semantically consistent, it is said to be semantically *inconsistent*.

Two formulas P and Q are *semantically equivalent* written $P :: Q$, if and only if for every truth-value assignment v, $\models_v P \iff \models_v Q$.

Chapter 5

Metalogic of Classical Sentence Logic

5.1 Overview

Meta-something is, (or has come to be), the something *of* something. So, for example, meta-beliefs are beliefs about beliefs.

A metalanguage, for a language L, is a language in which we talk about L, a particular language, as opposed to talking about language in general (which is usually reckoned *linguistics* rather than metalanguage).

Thus metalogic must be logic applied to itself, and so it is. We study the classical logic of sentences, by applying the very principles of reasoning which we earlier used on formulas of the language of classical sentence logic. But not *just* those principles. It turns out that our metalogic contains other forms of reasoning besides those licensed by the rules of inference of CSL.

What kinds of things fall under the heading of metalogic? There really aren't any limits. Any time we reason about derivability or semantic entailment in general, as opposed to this or that particular derivation or entailment issue, we are doing metalogic.

5.2   Notational Preliminaries

We continue with the convention of using (for the most part) capital Greek letters like Γ, Δ, etc. to represent sets of formulas. To say that a formula P is a *member of* the set Γ, we write $P \in \Gamma$.

In the object language we use $\supset$, $\equiv$, $\wedge$, $\vee$, $\neg$, and $\bot$ for the conditional, biconditional, conjunction, disjunction, negation, and falsum (or 'the false') respectively. Although we have a separate piece of notation for the biconditional, we don't normally regard it as 'primitive,' i.e. we usually regard it as an abbreviation for the conjunction of two conditionals.

In the metalanguage we use $\implies$, $\iff$, and $\&$, for the conditional, biconditional, and conjunction, and various sorts of 'strikethrough' for negation, along with the word 'not.' For the syntactical consequence relation we normally use $\vdash$ (usually read 'proves'). When it becomes necessary to indicate different notions of proof, we often use the 'turnstile' notation with superscripts or subscripts. For the semantic consequence relation we use the 'double-bar turnstile' $\models$ (usually read 'entails') with subscripts and superscripts again providing the means to distinguish different flavors of these, one from the other.

When a formula contains no formula as a proper part or, alternatively, contains no operators, we say that it is an *atomic* formula or a *sentence letter*. The set of such formulas will be referred to by means of At.

We use the standard 'set brace' notation, with $\{A, B, C\}$ representing the set containing as members just the formulas A, B and C, while $\{A\}$ is the unit-set of A, and, letting x be a variable which ranges over set elements, $\{x \mid F(x)\}$ is an *abstract*, in this case the set of all items x, such that x has the property F.

Definition 5.2.1. $\varnothing$ is the *empty* or *null* set, which is defined
$\varnothing = \{x \mid x \neq x\}$

Since every object is self-identical, there can be no such x's and hence the empty set is bereft of members.   The operators $\cup$, and $\cap$

stand for set union and intersection respectively which we may define in the following schemes:

Definition 5.2.2. The *union* of two sets Γ and Δ, indicated by $\Gamma \cup \Delta$ is defined:
$P \in \Gamma \cup \Delta \iff P \in \Gamma$ or $P \in \Delta$

Definition 5.2.3. The *intersection* of two sets Γ and Δ, indicated by $\Gamma \cap \Delta$ is defined:
$P \in \Gamma \cap \Delta \iff P \in \Gamma \,\&\, P \in \Delta$

Definition 5.2.4. The relation of *inclusion* defined between sets Γ and Δ, indicated by $\Gamma \subseteq \Delta$ is said to hold if and only if:
$(x \in \Gamma \implies x \in \Delta)$ for every element x

---

while $\subset$ represents proper inclusion.

Definition 5.2.5. The relation of *proper inclusion* defined between sets Γ and Δ, indicated by $\Gamma \subset \Delta$ is said to hold if and only if:
$(\Gamma \subseteq \Delta \,\&\, (x \in \Delta \,\&\, x \notin \Gamma))$ for at least one element x.

5.3   An Important Technique

In order to carry out our metalogical investigations we are going to need some more logic than we have already acquired. This often strikes beginners as very strange. If you need some or other logical principles to get the job done, why not put them in the object level—which we might as well call the *object logic*, instead of hiding them away in the metalogic. Are they perhaps not entirely respectable?

The answer is that they are entirely in keeping with the classical viewpoint but that they cannot be *expressed* in the object language. That

is certainly true of the technique which we are about to introduce—
mathematical induction.

We have already had a brush with a near relative of induction, in the
form of recursive (or *inductive*) definitions, like our definition of 'formula' (of this or that language). Whenever we define a class recursively,
there are two parts to the definition The initial part is called the *basis* and
the elements of the defined class which are introduced by this part are
called the *basis elements.* The second, the *recursive* (or *inductive*) part,
introduces a way of generating further elements using those which have
already been defined.

For any recursively defined class C, of elements, it must be the case
that the following kind of reasoning is correct:

(α) Every basis element has the property $\mathcal{P}rop$.

(β) Every way of generating new elements from already defined
elements preserves the property $\mathcal{P}rop$.

Therefore every element of C has the property $\mathcal{P}rop$.

This kind of reasoning about recursively defined classes is usually
called *natural induction.* We would be using it if we wished to argue
that all formulas of SL have a certain property by means of:

(α) All sentence letters have the property $\mathcal{P}rop$.

(β) If P and Q have the property $\mathcal{P}rop$, then so do $P \wedge Q$, $P \vee Q$,
$P \supset Q$, $P \equiv Q$, and $\neg P$.

Therefore every formula of SL has the property $\mathcal{P}rop$.

There is also an alternative form, one that we shall find ourselves
using more often than not, called *strong induction.* The difference be-

tween strong and natural induction is that in the latter we reason from the immediate predecessors of an element while in the former we reason from the whole class of all *earlier* elements. In talking about earlier elements and predecessors, we must have in hand some principle for ordering the elements. To take our formula example, we usually define the *length* of a formula P, written $\ell(P)$, to be the number of connectives in P, and this provides a way of ordering. Then the pattern for strong induction would be:

(α) Every atomic formula has the property $\mathcal{P}rop$.

(β) If every formula of length less than $\ell(P)$ has the property $\mathcal{P}rop$, then so does P.

Therefore all formulas have the property $\mathcal{P}rop$.

In a case of this sort, $\ell(P)$ is said to be the quantity *on which* the induction takes place. In other words, the result that every formula P has $\mathcal{P}rop$, is said to be established by induction on $\ell(P)$. The antecedent of the conditional in step β is called the *hypothesis of induction*.

We now use this new technique to establish a result which we assumed in the last chapter—the result that justifies our use of replacement rules.

Theorem 5.3.1. *Suppose that the formula P' is like the formula P except for having an occurrence of the formula Q' at zero or more places where P has an occurrence of the formula Q then:*
$$Q \dashv\vdash Q' \implies P \dashv\vdash P'$$

Proof. We prove this by strong induction on $\ell(P)$.

(α) $\ell(P) = 0$. In this case P must be a sentence letter, say A. Now if P' contains Q' at zero or more places where P contains Q, then since A is the only formula contained by P, Q must be A. Suppose that Q' is B. If P' contains Q' in the one place that P contains Q, then we must establish that $A \dashv\vdash B \implies A \dashv\vdash B$ which is obvious. If, on the other hand, P' has zero occurrences of Q' where P has Q, then P' is P and since $A \dashv\vdash A$, the result obtains trivially again.

(β) Assume the hypothesis (i.e. assume that the result holds for all formulas of length less than $\ell(P)$—which is greater than 0). We wish to show on this assumption that the result holds for P. We now proceed by cases according to the possible forms that P might have. In other words we consider

($\wedge$) $P = R \wedge S$

($\vee$) $P = R \vee S$

($\supset$) $P = R \supset S$

($\equiv$) $P = R \equiv S$

($\neg$) $P = \neg R$

In each of the cases the hypothesis of induction (HI) is that the result holds for both R and S individually (since their length is less than that of P).

(case $\wedge$)
We have two possible cases, P' has Q' where P has Q at zero or more places in only one of the conjuncts, or in both. Suppose that the replacement is in R alone. Then we have by HI that $Q \dashv\vdash Q' \implies R \dashv\vdash R'$ (where R' is like R except for containing Q' at zero or more places where R contains Q). We must show that from this we can get that $Q \dashv\vdash Q' \implies R \wedge S \dashv\vdash R' \wedge S$. This follows at once from the general principle: $P \dashv\vdash Q \implies P \wedge R \dashv\vdash Q \wedge R$. Evidently then the result holds if either conjunct receives the substitution and hence when they both do.

(case $\vee$)
We know that either the substitution takes place in both disjuncts or it takes place in only one. Let us suppose the weaker, which is that only one disjunct, say R has Q replaced by Q' in zero or more places (to give R', as before). Now we must prove that $Q \dashv\vdash Q' \implies R \vee S \dashv\vdash R' \vee S$ given that $Q \dashv\vdash Q' \implies R \dashv\vdash R'$ (which follows from HI). But this follows at once from the principle $P \dashv\vdash Q \implies P \vee R \dashv\vdash$

$Q \vee R$. And if only one disjunct is sufficient for the result then so will two disjuncts be.

We leave the remaining cases as an exercise. No great ingenuity is required. □

5.4 Some Important Sets

The main work of this chapter will involve showing that the relation '$\models$' is the same as the relation '$\vdash$' in the sense that both are comprised of the same pairs (Γ, P) (which is usually called *having the same extension*). This must involve some similar connection between the formal concepts of truth and provability, since entailment is defined in terms of truth.

At first blush it seems that 'true' and 'proved' are quite different predicates. At least as we have defined these ideas formally, the concept of 'true on truth-value assignment v' ($\models_v$) would seem to be quite different from 'proved by the set Γ' ($\Gamma \vdash$). In fact the two agree only on the treatment of conjunction. In other words, we can see that both

$$\Gamma \vdash A \wedge B \iff \Gamma \vdash A \,\&\, \Gamma \vdash B$$

$$\models_v A \wedge B \iff \models_v A \,\&\, \models_v B$$

This property was referred to simply as [∧] when it formed part of the definition of truth relative to a truth-value assignment, but now that we need it also to refer to a property of provability we shall coin the name *conjunctivity* . Alas it is the only point of contact between truth and proof, so to speak.

We mustn't give up quite yet though. Even though we cannot hope to match provability by *arbitrary* sets, to truth on a truth-value assignment, we *can* hope to find a narrower notion of proof—provability by a special *kind* of set, which does match. In pursuit of this, we shall first consider a special kind of set known as a *theory*.

Before we look at definitions, we require a slightly different approach to the rules we have earlier caller *structural*. When we were doing derivations, we simply rolled two such rules into one, which we called [R]. Now that we are talking about provability, we find it more convenient to disentangle the two, and add a third. First the unbundling:

[R] $P \in \Gamma \implies \Gamma \vdash P$

Although the name [R] is maintained, we now think of it as a mnemonic for *reflexivity* rather than reiteration. The other half of what was reiteration is now called [M] (to suggest *monotonicity*):[1]

[M] $\Gamma \vdash P \implies \Gamma \cup \Sigma \vdash P$

It is also convenient to add to our stock of structural rules the following one which represents a kind of conditional elimination without mentioning a conditional.

[T] $[\Gamma, P \vdash Q \ \& \ \Gamma \vdash P] \implies \Gamma \vdash Q$

Obviously we can derive [T], which is named to suggest *transitivity*,[2] by using conditional introduction on the first conjunct of the rules's antecedent, followed by conditional elimination on the second.

It might strike us that a transitivity rule, in order to conform more closely to the property of relations as it is usually defined,[3] should be more like:

[TRAN] $[\Gamma \vdash P \text{ for every } P \in \Delta \ \& \ \Delta \vdash Q] \implies \Gamma \vdash Q$

It takes a certain amount of effort to see that we can derive [TRAN] from [T] (using also [M]), but such effort is not at all misplaced.

Proposition 5.4.1. [TRAN] *may be derived from the other structural rules.*

Proof. Suppose that Γ proves every member of the set Δ and that Δ, in it's turn proves Q. We wish to show, given this assumption, that $\Gamma \vdash Q$. Since derivations are required to be of finite length, there can only be finitely many members of Δ which participate in the derivation

---

[1]This rule is sometimes referred to by the name Thinning or Dilution, which is (a translation of) the name first given to a rule of this form by the German logician Gentzen.

[2]Gentzen referred to a rule of this sort, i.e. one which eliminates a formula which appears on both sides of the $\vdash$, by a name which translates as 'cut.'

[3]We encounter this idea in the logic of relations. A rough version of the definition is: a relation $>$ is transitive provided that for any three objects, x, y, z, if $x > y$ and $y > z$ then $x > z$.

of Q. Let the set of these actually used formulas be $\{P_1, \ldots, P_n\}$. So $\{P_1, \ldots, P_n\} \vdash Q$ and by [M] we have $\Gamma, P_1, \ldots, P_n \vdash Q$, where the expression to the left of $\vdash$ abbreviates $\Gamma \cup \{P_1, \ldots, P_n\}$. But now we see, from the assumption, that since $\Gamma \vdash P_n$, so also $\Gamma, P_1, \ldots, P_{n-1} \vdash P_n$ by [M]. One use of [T] now produces $\Gamma, P_1, \ldots, P_{n-1} \vdash Q$. And we simply repeat this $n-1$ more times eliminating P_{n-1} and then P_{n-2} and so on until at the last iteration, we have proved that $\Gamma \vdash Q$, as required.

$\square$

We already have a connection between set membership and provability, through the structural rule [R]. On account of that rule, every set of formulas must prove all of its members. The concept of a *theory* adds the converse, thus entirely collapsing the distinction between 'proved by' and 'member of.'

Definition 5.4.2. A set of formulas Δ is a *theory*, indicated by THEORY(Δ), if and only if $\Delta \vdash P \implies P \in \Delta$, for every formula P.

Everything such a set proves is a member and every member is proved. We may think of this as a way of *reducing* the concept of set-membership to the concept of provability by a set.

Although this is certainly a technical term, it is actually quite close to our ordinary use of the term theory to represent something like 'an organized body of data.'[4]

Every theory contains everything it proves by definition, but only one theory contains every formula. It is usually called the *improper* theory. We usually confine our attention to the consistent theories, which we now show are the same as the proper ones. First let us formally define the terms:

---

[4]There is also a pejorative use of the word theory in which it contrasts unfavorably with fact. Needless to say, there is absolutely nothing of this use in our term.

Definition 5.4.3. A theory Δ, which contains every formula, is said to *improper*, otherwise Δ is said to be *proper* which is indicated by PROP(Δ).

Though we have already defined consistency for arbitrary sets, we shall re-define it now for theories.[5]

Definition 5.4.4. A theory Δ is said to be consistent, indicated by CON(Δ), if and only if $\Delta \nvdash \bot$.

Proposition 5.4.5. *For every theory* Δ, PROP(Δ) $\iff$ CON(Δ).

Proof. The proof is left as an exercise.   □

So the largest theory contains every formula; what formulas does the smallest theory contain?[6]

Theories are interesting and useful kinds of sets, but how do we *make* them? This turns out to be easy: All you have to do to make a (proper) theory is to start with any consistent set of formulas, and throw in all the consequences. Let's say this more precisely.

Definition 5.4.6. The deductive closure operator $\mathbb{C}_\vdash$ is defined for every set of formulas Δ as:
$$\mathbb{C}_\vdash(\Delta) = \{P \mid \Delta \vdash P\}$$

Proposition 5.4.7. *For every set* Δ, THEORY($\mathbb{C}_\vdash(\Delta)$)

Proof. The proof is left as an exercise.   □

---

[5]The original definition, due to E.L. Post, is more like the definition of propriety.

[6]This is an exercise question. Hint: the smallest theory is *not* the empty set—why not?

Definition 5.4.8. A set Δ of formulas, is said to be *deductively closed* if and only if $\mathbb{C}_{\vdash}(\Delta) = \Delta$

Proposition 5.4.9. *Every theory is deductively closed.*

Proof. This proof is an exercise. □

5.5 Specialized Kinds of Theory

We have hinted above that in order to connect the predicates 'proved by Δ' and 'true on the assignment v' we must define the right kind of Δ. This is because the properties:

$$[\text{PRIME}(\Delta)]\ \Delta \vdash P \vee Q \iff (\Delta \vdash P \text{ or } \Delta \vdash Q)$$

$$[\text{IMPLIC}(\Delta)]\ \Delta \vdash P \supset Q \iff (\Delta \vdash P \implies \Delta \vdash Q)$$

$$[\text{COMP}(\Delta)]\ \Delta \vdash \neg P \iff \Delta \nvdash P$$

all fail for arbitrary sets Δ.
Of course we *do* have the property

$$[\text{CONJ}(\Delta)]\ \Delta \vdash P \wedge Q \iff (\Delta \vdash P \ \& \ \Delta \vdash Q)$$

If we think about it for a moment, corresponding properties for the concept of truth relative to an assignment might fail as well, were it not for restrictions we place on truth-value assignments. Not just any way of assigning truth-values will do, it is required that every atomic formula receive exactly one truth-value. This is just to say that assignments are functions, as has been previously mentioned.

In order that our usage not outrun our inferential practice by too large a margin, we pause to consider something a bit more manageable than a language based on an infinite set of atomic formulas.

When we actually use CSL to work on a problem, we rarely use more than finitely many atomic formulas. Certainly textbook problems are normally of this character and so we provide a refinement of our notion of a language for sentence logic. This refinement is called an *indexed language for sentence logic.* First we give a formal definition of the concept we introduced informally on page 127:

Definition 5.5.1. An *index I for a language* SL is a subset of **At**—the set of all atomic formulas (sometimes called sentence letters).

Definition 5.5.2. The set of formulas of SL_I is the same as the set of formulas of SL except that only members of I count as atomic formulas.

Given an index I and the corresponding language SL_I we define both a semantic, and a syntactical class of objects as follows.

Definition 5.5.3. The *class* $\mathbb{V}_I$ *of indexed truth-value assignments for* SL_I is defined:
$$\mathbb{V}_I = \{v_i | i \subseteq I \;\&\; v_i(A) = T \iff A \in i\}$$

Definition 5.5.4. The *diagram of* $i \subseteq I$, indicated by $\mathbb{D}_i$, is defined:
$$\mathbb{D}_i = \{A \in i\} \cup \{\neg B | B \in I \;\&\; B \notin i\}$$

Informally, the diagram of a set $i \subseteq I$ is a set which 'says' that all of the atomic formulas in i are provable (by virtue of rule [R]) and that for every other atomic formula in the index I, that negation of that formula is provable. One sometimes says that a set like $\mathbb{D}_i$ *decides* $i \subseteq I$. We shall refer to the class of all diagrams spanning the index I by means of $\mathbb{D}_I$. We shall refer to $i \subseteq I$ as the *positive component* of the diagram $\mathbb{D}_i$. The set of negated atomic formulas which ensures that the diagram spans all of I will be referred to as the *negative component* of $\mathbb{D}_i$.

We shall refer to the deductive closure $\mathbb{C}_\vdash(\mathbb{D}_i)$ by T_i.

Definition 5.5.5. $\mathbf{T}_I$, the *indexed class of theories spanning SL_I*, is defined:
$$\mathbf{T}_I = \{T_i | i \subseteq I\}$$

The first thing to notice is that we can assure ourselves that for every index $i \subseteq I$, $\mathbb{D}_i$ is consistent. What we need in this case is a new principle—a rule which is unlike any of the others in that it doesn't really center on forms, but rather on the inferential role of atomic formulas. In his famous *Tractatus Logico Philosophicus*, Wittgenstein gave as a general principle that there could be no logical relations between atomic sentences, and in fact this property was constitutive of the concept of atomic sentence.

We make this insight into a rule by specifying that if we have a set of atomic formulas and they *do* enter into logical relations with some batch of (distinct) sentences, at least some of the latter sentences must not be atomic.

First some precision:

Definition 5.5.6. A formula A is said to be *distinct from* the formulas $B_1, \ldots, B_n$ if and only if A is not a subformula of any of the B's.

Notice that this rules out the possibility of A being one of the B's (a non-proper subformula).

Here is the rule in question, which we name [W]:

[W] If $A_1, \ldots, A_m$ are all atomic, and distinct from $B_1, \ldots, B_n$, then:
$(\{A_1, \ldots, A_m\} \vdash B_1 \vee \ldots \vee B_n) \implies (B_1 \notin \mathbf{At} \text{ or } \ldots \text{ or } B_n \notin \mathbf{At})$

We shall refer to this rule as Wittgenstein's Law (of Atomicity) and with it's aid it is easy to see the diagram of any i must be consistent, for otherwise:

$\{A|A \in i\} \cup \{\neg B|B \notin i \& B \in I\} \vdash \bot$

Since derivations are of finite length there must be some finite number of the B formulas which suffice to prove $\bot$. Say there are n of them,

$\{A|A \in i\} \cup \{\neg B_1, \ldots, \neg B_n\} \vdash \bot$

by classical reasoning then

$\{A|A \in i\} \vdash (\neg B_1 \wedge \ldots \wedge \neg B_n) \supset \bot$ and

$\{A|A \in i\} \vdash \neg(\neg B_1 \wedge \ldots \wedge \neg B_n)$ which is to say that

$\{A|A \in i\} \vdash B_1 \vee \ldots \vee B_n)$

But in this case since the A's are distinct from the B's (no atomic formula can both belong and not belong to i) [W] assures us that some of the B formulas must be non-atomic, which is impossible.

Given the consistency of $\mathbb{D}_i$, the consistency of T_i follows right away. If $\bot$ can be deduced from the *consequences* of some set (in this case the diagram of i) the structural rule [T] assures us that $\bot$ can be deduced from that same set.

It will turn out that T_i has the properties after which we hankered above, namely primeness, completeness, and implicativity. Let's start with completeness. We wish to show that

[COM] $T_i \vdash \neg P \iff T_i \nvdash P$

The $\implies$ direction of this we have at once from the propriety (consistency) of T_i, so we need only provide a proof of the right-to-left ($\impliedby$) direction.

Lemma 5.5.7. *For every index I and $i \subseteq I$: $T_i \nvdash P \implies T_i \vdash \neg P$*

Proof. We see at once[7] that the completeness property must hold for the atomic formulas of I on the definition of $\mathbb{D}_i$. Suppose now for reductio that there is a formula P, of SL_I such that $T_i \nvdash P$ and $T_i \nvdash \neg P$. We shall say in this case that T_i *fails to decide* P. We now proceed by cases.

---

[7]This argument was pointed out to me by Gillman Payette

[$P = Q \wedge R$] If $T_i \nvdash Q \wedge R$ then it must be the case that either $T_i \nvdash Q$ or $T_i \nvdash R$ (otherwise T_i would prove the conjunction after all). On the other hand, since $T_i \nvdash \neg(Q \wedge R)$ it must be the case that $T_i \nvdash \neg Q \vee \neg R$ but that can only happen in case $T_i \nvdash \neg Q$ and $T_i \nvdash \neg R$. From all of this it follows that if T_i fails decide a conjunction then it must fail to decide a conjunct.

[$P = Q \vee R$] This case is left as an exercise

[$P = Q \supset R$] This case is left as an exercise

[$P = \neg Q$] This case is left as an exercise.

In each case then, the failure of T_i to decide a formula P results in a similar failure for a (proper) subformula of P. Since all formulas are of finite length, it follows that if there were any formula which is not decided by T_i, there would be an atomic formula which is not decided by T_i. But since T_i is defined to be the closure of a diagram, it must decide every atomic formula in I. □

Corollary 5.5.8. [T_i is complete] *For every index I and $i \subseteq I$*
$$T_i \vdash \neg P \iff T_i \nvdash P$$

From completeness, the other properties follow at once. For instance:

Lemma 5.5.9. [T_i is Prime] *For every index I and $i \subseteq I$,*
$$T_i \vdash P \vee Q \iff T_i \vdash P \text{ or } T_i \vdash Q$$

Proof. We have the $\impliedby$ direction as a consequence of the rule of disjunction introduction. For the $\implies$ direction, we argue indirectly. Suppose that $T_i \nvdash P$ and also that $T_i \nvdash Q$. It follows by completeness that $T_i \vdash \neg P$ and $T_i \vdash \neg Q$. But then $T_i \vdash \neg P \wedge \neg Q)$ which is to say that $T_i \vdash \neg(P \vee Q)$. By consistency then, $T_i \nvdash P \vee Q$. □

Lemma 5.5.10. [T_i is Implicative] *For every index I and $i \subseteq I$,*
$$T_i \vdash Q \supset R \iff T_i \vdash Q \implies T_i \vdash R$$

Proof. The proof is left as an exercise. □

5.6   Exercises

Apart from those proofs which have been left as exercises, show that not only do primeness and implicativity follow from completeness of the theories T_i, but indeed all three are equivalent. In other words, show

Theorem 5.6.1. *The following are equivalent for any index I and i $\subseteq$ I*

COMP(T_i)

PRIME(T_i)

IMPLIC(T_i)

Hint. The most efficient way to carry out a proof that a number of assertions are equivalent is prove implications between them in a circle. In other words one might prove, e.g. that

COMP(T_i) $\implies$ PRIME(T_i)

PRIME(T_i) $\implies$ IMPLIC(T_i)

IMPLIC(T_i) $\implies$ COMP(T_i)

$\square$

5.7   Putting it Together Part 1

What we mean to do in this chapter is to study the relations between the semantic and the proof-theoretic accounts of inference. As a start to that worthy enterprize we should ask exactly what the semantics is doing. Once we have answered that to our satisfaction we can begin asking how the same thing might be accomplished using syntactical elements.

So what exactly is it that the semantics does? The answer to this would seem to have two parts: First, the semantics provides a means for assigning, in a functional way, truth values to atomic formulas. The means in question are the truth-value assignment functions we have been referring to by v, with or without subscripts. The second thing the semantics does is to extend, in a unique way, the assignment represented by v_i, to an evaluation of all formulas (of an indexed language

SL$_I$). The latter is accomplished by the definition of truth relative to an assignment v_i.

Perhaps the most important feature of $\models_{v_i}$ is that it extends v_i to all formulas of SL$_I$ *uniquely*. To make this assertion precise, assume that $X_i(P)$ is a predicate which extends v_i and obeys the truth-conditions. In other words:

$$X_i(A) \iff v_i(A) = T \text{ for all } A \in I$$

$$X_i(P \wedge Q) \iff X_i(P) \,\&\, X_i(Q)$$

$$X_i(P \vee Q) \iff X_i(P) \text{ or } X_i(Q)$$

and similarly for the other conditions, then X_i is said to be a (classical) *truth-functional extension* of v_i. Evidently $\models_{v_i}$ is such an extension, and it is in fact the only one.

Theorem 5.7.1 (Uniqueness of truth-functional extensions). *Let X_i be any truth-functional extension of v_i, for every formula P of* SL$_I$,
$$X_i(P) \iff \models_{v_i} P$$

Proof. Suppose, for reductio, that for some formula P,
$X_i(P)$) but $\not\models_{v_i} P$.
We shall say in this case that the two extensions *disagree over P*. We proceed by cases to show that the disagreement in question must also involve a sub-formula of P. But since formulas are of finite length, a disagreement over a formula must amount to a disagreement over an atomic formula. Since both are extensions of $i \subseteq I$, this is impossible. We do only the case in which P is of the form $Q \supset R$, the rest being left as exercises.

$[P = Q \supset R]$ If $X_i(Q \supset R)$ then either $X_i(R)$ or not-$X_i(Q)$. Similarly if $\not\models_{v_i} Q \supset R$ then $\models_{v_i} Q$ and $\not\models_{v_i} R$. So the disagreement descends to the the level of subformulas. QED

$\square$

We can now show that, in an important sense, $T_i \vdash$ and $\models_{v_i}$ are the same predicate.

Theorem 5.7.2 (Correspondence Theorem for CSL**).** *For every index* I *and* $i \subseteq I$ *and for every formula* P *of* SL$_I$, $\models_{v_i} P \iff T_i \vdash P$

Proof. The proof follows from the uniqueness of truth-functional extensions together with the observation that $T_i \vdash$ *is* a truth-functional extension of v_i. □

We can also see that there is a sense in which the underlying notions—truth-value assignments (relative to i) and diagrams spanning I are the same.

Definition 5.7.3. The sets X and Y are said to be *isomorphic*, written $X \rightleftharpoons Y$ if and only if there are two functions $f : X \longrightarrow Y$ and $g : Y \longrightarrow X$ such that $g(f(x)) = x$ for every $x \in X$ and $f(g(y)) = y$ for every $y \in Y$.

Theorem 5.7.4. $\mathbb{V}_I \rightleftharpoons \mathbb{D}_I$

Proof. Define $f : \mathbb{V}_I \longrightarrow \mathbb{D}_I$ to be the function which takes v_i to $\mathbb{D}_i$, and $g : \mathbb{D}_I \longrightarrow \mathbb{V}_I$ to be the inverse function which takes $\mathbb{D}_i \longrightarrow v_i$. □

5.8   Putting it Together Part 2

What we need to do now is to connect our syntactical reconstruction of the semantics with the relation between provability and semantic entailment. The latter is defined for arbitrary pairs $<\Gamma, P>$ using the notion of truth relative to to an assignment v_i, in the familiar way. The former also defines a relation for arbitrary pairs, but our syntactical equivalent of truth relative to v_i is $T_i \vdash$, where T_i is not at all arbitrary.

There must be some way to connect the theories T_i with arbitrary sets of formulas of SL$_I$.

An obvious place to start is with the question of whether we can embed an arbitrary (consistent) set of formulas of SL$_I$ into some T_i.

To carry out this *extension* we need to be able to find a 'compatible' diagram. The following construction[8] takes care of that. We first define:

Definition 5.8.1. Let Γ be and arbitrary consistent set of formulas of SL_I and suppose all the members of I have been placed in an urn.[9] We can now build up a sequence of sets: $\Sigma_0, \Sigma_1, \ldots$, in the following way

$$\Sigma_0 = \Gamma$$

$$\vdots$$

$$\Sigma_k = \begin{cases} \Sigma_{k-1} \cup \{A_k\} & \text{if this is consistent,} \\ \Sigma_{k-1} \cup \{\neg A_k\} & \text{otherwise.} \end{cases}$$

$$\vdots$$

In this construction A_k is the kth member of I which is drawn from the urn. After the kth stage, that atomic sentence is not returned to the urn. The sequence continues until the urn is empty.[10]

Σ^+ is defined to be the union of all the stages, or alternatively, if the sequence is finite, the last member.

$$i_\Gamma = \{A \in I \,|\, A \in \Sigma^+\}$$

It is important to notice here that if

$B \in I$ does not belong to i_Γ, it must be the case that $\Sigma^+, B \vdash \bot$ and hence,

by $[\neg I]$ $\Sigma^+ \vdash \neg B$.

This means that when we form the diagram of i_Γ we take the union of two sets:

---

[8]This construction was suggested by Luke Fraser
[9]This is a familiar thought experiment from probability and statistics.
[10]This construction is inspired by the work of Leon Henkin. See especially his Henkin (1949)

i_Γ which is consistent with Γ by definition, and

$\{\neg B | B \in I \ \& \ B \notin i_\Gamma\}$, all the members of which are proved by $\Gamma \cup i_\Gamma$.

Lemma 5.8.2. $\Gamma \cup \mathbb{D}_{i_\Gamma} \nvdash \bot$

Proof. Suppose, for reductio, that the set is inconsistent after all.

Then there must be n and m such that

$\Gamma, A_1, \ldots, A_n, \neg B_1, \ldots, \neg B_m \vdash \bot$

where the A formulas are from i_Γ and the $\neg B$ formulas are all from the other half of $\mathbb{D}_{i_\Gamma}$.

By [Mon] then $\Gamma \cup i_\Gamma, \neg B_1, \ldots, \neg B_m \vdash \bot$

But $\Gamma \cup i_\Gamma \vdash \neg B_k$ for $1 \leq k \leq m$, as noted above.

Now an m-fold application of the rule [T] gives us the result:

$\Gamma \cup i_\Gamma \vdash \bot$, which is impossible by the definition of i_Γ.

□

We make a stylistic variation to avoid double subscripting

Definition 5.8.3. $T_\Gamma = \mathbb{C}_\vdash(\mathbb{D}_{i_\Gamma})$

We would like to show now that $\Gamma \subseteq T_\Gamma$. But to do that we need to appeal to a general property of the theories T_i. That property is:

The property of *maximality* is defined

Definition 5.8.4. max$(\Delta) \iff [P \notin \Delta \implies \Delta, P \vdash \bot]$

Lemma 5.8.5. *For every index I and $i \subseteq I$ **max**(T_i)*

Proof. The lemma is an obvious consequence of the the completeness property of the theories T_i.

□

With this behind us we can show that T_Γ contains Γ.

Lemma 5.8.6 (Little Lindenbaum Lemma). *For every index I, every consistent set Γ, of formulas of* SL$_I$ *can be extended to T_i for some $i \subseteq I$.*

Proof. We should notice first that

$T_\Gamma \cup \Gamma \not\vdash \bot$ else, by an application of [M] Γ would be inconsistent with $\mathbb{D}_{i_\Gamma}$, which we know to be impossible from lemma 5.8.2.

But we know from lemma 5.8.5 that $\mathbf{max}(T_\Gamma)$ so that if any member of Γ were not a member of T_Γ, $T_\Gamma \cup \Gamma \vdash \bot$.

So every member of Γ must be a member of T_Γ which is to say

$\Gamma \subseteq T_\Gamma$

$\square$

5.9 Exercises

It is easy to see that the above construction of i_Γ is not unique. In fact the chances are that if we construct the Σ sequence again, we shall obtain a distinct result since the members of I are chosen at random.

Construct a method for generating all the $i \subseteq I$ such that $\mathbb{D}_i$ is consistent with a given consistent set Γ of formulas of SL$_I$.

5.10 Overview of the Main Result of this Chapter

In the central investigation of this chapter we shall take up the question of the relationship between four propositions. In order to state these more economically, we introduce some notation.

Notation . $\Gamma \vdash^i P$ abbreviates $T_i \vdash \Gamma \implies T_i \vdash P$ for every index I and $i \subseteq I$.

Notation . $\Gamma \models^i P$ abbreviates $\models_{v_i} \Gamma \implies \models_{v_i} P$ for every index I and $i \subseteq I$.

We shall take the core result for the metalogic of CSL to be the demonstration that certain assertions are all equivalent. For ease of presentation, the four assertions in question are laid out in the *Equivalence Diagram for* CSL.

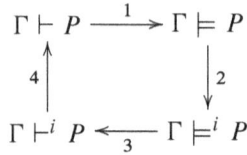

$$\begin{array}{ccc}
\Gamma \vdash P & \xrightarrow{\;\;1\;\;} & \Gamma \models P \\
{\scriptstyle 4}\big\uparrow & & \big\downarrow{\scriptstyle 2} \\
\Gamma \vdash^i P & \xleftarrow[\;\;3\;\;]{} & \Gamma \models^i P
\end{array}$$

Figure 5.1: The Equivalence Diagram for CSL

If each of the arrows in this picture represents an implication relation ($\Longrightarrow$), then obviously all the four corners are equivalent. What we might call the standard way of presenting the metalogic of CSL is a bit like that. We shall present some comments on the matter later in this section and the next.

Our approach will be rather different. We notice that the arrow labelled 2 stands for $\Longleftrightarrow$ in virtue of the fact that entailment is defined to be the relation $\models^i$.

It also seems that the arrow 3 likewise represents a metalanguage biconditional as a consequence of the correspondence theorem. We shall prove this.

Finally, the arrow 4 clearly holds from top to bottom by appeal to monotonicity. We shall show that the other direction holds as well, as a consequence of the so-called Little Lindenbaum Lemma.

But if any three arrows in the diagram represent the $\Longleftrightarrow$ relation, then so must the forth (by 'diagram chasing'). Here are the bits laid out in a more official-looking form.

Theorem 5.10.1 (Equivalence Theorem for CSL**).** *The following are all equivalent to one another:*

[truth-preservation] $\Gamma \models^i P$
[proof-preservation] $\Gamma \vdash^i P$

[provability] $\Gamma \vdash P$
[entailment] $\Gamma \models P$

Proof. The result follows from the following two results and the fact that entailment is defined as $\models^i$.

□

Theorem 5.10.2 (Proof-Preservation Theorem for CSL**).** *For every index I, $i \subseteq I$, and pair Γ, P*

$$\Gamma \vdash P \iff \Gamma \vdash^i P$$

Proof. For the left to right direction ($\Longrightarrow$), since the T_i are all theories, if any should prove all the members of Γ, they must also contain Γ as a subset. Thus [M] shows that whatever Γ proves, the theories which contain Γ must likewise prove. For the right-to-left direction ($\Longleftarrow$) we shall show that when $\Gamma \nvdash P$ there will be at least one T_i which satisfies the condition of the theorem such that $T_i \vdash \neg P$ (which obviously implies that $T_i \nvdash P$). Consider the set $\Gamma \cup \{\neg P\}$. This must be consistent or else $\Gamma \vdash P$ by [¬E], contrary to the hypothesis that $\Gamma \nvdash P$. But if the set is consistent we know from the Little Lindenbaum Lemma that there is a T_i, namely T_Γ which contains Γ and which proves $\neg P$). Thus, by indirect proof, if $\Gamma \vdash^i P$ then $\Gamma \vdash P$, which is just what we wanted.

□

Theorem 5.10.3 (Equivalence of preservation for CSL**).** *For every index I, $i \subseteq I$, and pair Γ, P*

$$\Gamma \vdash^i P \iff \Gamma \models^i P$$

Proof. Assume that $\Gamma \vdash^i P$. Hence by definition of that relation, this will hold if and only if for every $i \subseteq I$, if $T_i \vdash \Gamma$ then $T_i \vdash P$. But from the Correspondence Theorem for CLS (Theorem 5.7.2) this can hold if and only if $\models_{v_i} \Gamma$ implies $\models_{v_i} P$ for all $i \subseteq I$.

□

5.11   Essay and Discussion Topics and Questions

1. The equivalence diagram with the four arrows taken to represent implication only, shows that the four assertions are equivalent but also that one could not take truth-preservation to be merely necessary for entailment, and not also sufficient. Why is that? Why would anyone be interested in the latter project?

2. The equivalence theorem encodes a lot of information including both the so-called *soundness* and *completeness* of classical sentence logic. These are the generally accepted names for the two directions of biconditional which corresponds to the arrow labeled 1 in the equivalence diagram. However one uses these terms after the fashion ⊢ is sound provided that every derivation has a matching entailment. and ⊢ is complete if for every entailment, there is a corresponding derivation. This terminology would seem to suggest that it is provability which must measure up to the standard provided by entailment.

3. The top row of the equivalence diagram is clearly the most important because it shows that ⊢ = ⊨—that the semantic characterization of 'follows from' is the same relation as the syntactic version, at least in the realm of (classical) sentence logic.[11]

4. The discovery of the equivalence result belongs to the 20th Century. Perhaps this is because only in the 20th Century were logicians rigorous enough and careful enough to see that this kind of result needed to be proved. In the past it was often assumed that provability and logical truth were just two ways of looking at the same thing. At least the legitimacy of equivocating between the two was seldom called into question. On the other hand, is this a somewhat overly brisk condemnation of ancient and medieval logic? It's not clear that the Stoic logicians, for instance, didn't have at least the consistency part of this result. And it isn't

---

[11]This is an extremely important proviso. One of the most significant events of 20th Century logic was the proof in 1932 of Gödel's result that the two versions are not the same, and *cannot* be the same, for any logic which is expressive enough to represent elementary arithmetic.

really true that the logical theorists of the middle ages were careless about the relation between their syntax and their truth-value
semantics—they had no such semantics (on theological grounds).

5. Once we are careful in our definitions, the temptation to equivo-
cate between the semantical and the syntactical is not so intense.
There would seem to be a very important distinction between $\models$
and $\vdash$ which involves infinity. A proof is defined to be a *finitary*
object—a derivation in CSL is defined to be a finite sequence, for
instance. It follows at once from this definition that if $\Gamma \vdash P$
there must be some finite subset of Γ, Γ' such that $\Gamma' \vdash P$. In
other words there cannot be any proof which is essentially infini-
tary. But the definition of entailment makes no such requirement.
There is no part of the definition of $\Delta \models Q$ which requires that
some finite set also entails Q. Of course if we could show that entailment and provability were the same relation, *that* would show
that entailment must also have this finitary property.[12]

5.12 Brief Historical Notes

The first to show that provability and entailment are the same, was the
American logician E.L. Post in his doctoral thesis in 1920 (see Post
(1994)). Post's proof, in common with many of those up until the late
1940's, was confined to the special case of logical truth and theoremhood. In other words Post (and others after him) showed that entailment
and provability were identical when the premise set was empty. Such
a proof contains less information than we might wish, since it fails to
show that entailment is compact.

On the other hand, all of these earlier proofs work by showing how
to convert a demonstration that P is logically true into an actual categor-
ical derivation of P. Such a technique is usually said to be *constructive*.
The Henkin technique (see Henkin (1949) and Henkin (1996)) a variation of which we use, by contrast, shows that if P is logically true then

---

[12]This property of relations such that if the relation holds between an infinite set and some
object, it also holds between some finite subset and that object, is usually called *compactness* .

there must be a derivation of P, but it doesn't point to some particular derivation. For this reason it is said to be *non-constructive*.

5.13   Yes, but what does it all mean?

Struggling through a mass of theorems, lemmata, definitions, propositions, and, corollaries, it is more than easy to lose sight of the significance of all these results. Why should we care about the equivalence theorem, especially when so many people already think that it is true before we even begin?

One of the answers has been given already. When we think carefully about the difference between semantics and proof theory, it isn't all that obvious that the two approaches converge. It certainly isn't something that can be simply assumed. What is required is a proof and the fact that the proof is more than routine, simply reinforces its necessity.

The other answer, also courtesy of 20th Century logic, is that the equivalence theorem is important because it isn't always provable. Once our language gets descriptively rich enough, we won't be able to prove equivalence any more. This is not because we aren't clever enough to discover the proof, in fact we can *prove* that proof theory and semantics are *not* equivalent in general.

Another facet of our presentation of the equivalence result is that our approach to the proof, a bit roundabout though it might be, managed without using induction. This is not true of many of the standard accounts. It is of interest since induction, in effect, presumes arithmetic[13] As is well known, the second of Gödel's famous theorems of 1932 shows that the consistency of arithmetic cannot be proved using finitary resources. In other words, to prove the consistency of arithmetic one must use a system stronger (logically speaking) than arithmetic. But how do we know that this stronger system is itself consistent? In fact, it seems clear that the more principles of proof we adopt the higher the probability (in no very exact sense of that term) that we have lapsed into inconsistency.

---

[13]more particularly it requires the structure $<\omega, \leqq>$ in which structure the arithmetic operations can be defined in the usual way.

All of this reflects not only upon arithmetic, but also on simple little CSL once we are committed to the use of induction proofs in order to demonstrate consistency. To put it most bluntly, we are then using a system, the consistency of which we cannot prove (in any absolute sense) to prove the consistency of CSL. To say the least, there would seem to be a certain amount of tension in this situation.

5.14 Essay and Discussion Topics and Questions

1. To say that we need to demonstrate the consistency of arithmetic is akin to saying that we need to reassure ourselves that the so-called standard meter in Paris, is indeed 1 meter in length.[14] We cannot hold the standard up to itself and so the whole issue of reassurance being needed simply dissolves. What we use to detect a certain property cannot be used as a detector of that property in itself. Arithmetic is what we use to judge the consistency of other systems—CSL for one. The idea that arithmetic itself now stands in need of a proof of consistency is simply a mistake.

---

[14]This example belongs to an earlier era since now the meter is defined in terms of so many wavelengths of a certain kind of light. It is a telling example nevertheless.

5.15   Rules Quick Reference

[R] $P \in \Gamma \implies \Gamma \vdash P$

[M] $\Gamma \vdash P \implies \Gamma \cup \Sigma \vdash P$

[T] $[\Gamma, P \vdash Q \,\&\, \Gamma \vdash P] \implies \Gamma \vdash Q$

[W] If $A_1, \ldots, A_m$ are all atomic, and distinct from $B_1, \ldots, B_n$, then:
$(\{A_1, \ldots, A_m\} \vdash B_1 \vee \ldots \vee B_n) \implies (B_1 \notin \mathbf{At}$ or $\ldots$ or $B_n \notin \mathbf{At})$

Chapter 6

Philosophy of Logic

6.1 Introduction

Philosophy of logic is the study of philosophical issues to which logic gives rise. Quite a few of these have already come up[1] but many of them would require too much of a digression from the main matter of a chapter. In the two previous chapters for instance, the student is already being challenged by so many new concepts that any distraction is liable to be unwelcome. For that reason we gather together some of the main questions in a chapter of their own. A few of the topics have been alluded to earlier but for the most part, they are new.

6.2 The Nature of the Beast

The most central question of all is probably this one: Given that deductive logic is the theory of deductive reasoning, what kind of theory is it? Those who pose this question generally have in mind the distinction, familiar from social science, between a *descriptive* theory and a *normative* theory—the distinction between the way things are and the way they ought to be. Decision theory serves as a useful example.

It might seem obvious that the best way to make decisions is to maximize some quantity (pleasure or happiness or utility) which we'd like to

---

[1]One prominent example of such a question is the connection between reasoning and rationality, which arose in the first chapter.

see more of, perhaps subject to certain intuitively reasonable constraints (the happiness of the few, however intense, cannot be at the expense of the many). When empirical studies show, as they often seem to, that people don't use this 'best' way when they actually make decisions, we have a choice. We can say 'Well if those whom we take to be the most successful or able decision-makers don't do what we would count as maximizing (perhaps constrained maximizing) then we must have got the theory wrong.' Taking this tack amounts to saying that decision theory is, on our understanding, descriptive in the sense that it describes what good decision makers do. The alternative is to say 'If actual decision makers don't maximize then so much the worse for actual decision makers—they certainly *ought* to maximize.'

To say that, is to say that decision theory is normative—a theory not of the way actual (good) decisions are made, but rather the way any decision ought to be made in order that it be considered good. In the first case, the theory has to measure up to the world, and in the second it is the world that must measure up.

So is (deductive) logic, a normative or descriptive theory? This is not an easy question to answer, as it turns out. Partly, that's because it is *never* an easy question to answer—even in the case of our supposedly clear example of decision theory.

This is usually taken to be a normative account since the empirical studies, almost without exception, diverge from the theory. But it won't be enough to say, with a sigh, 'Well I guess the theory must be normative then.' Calling a theory normative by no means exempts it from having to bear some connection to what actually happens, in this case to the way good decision makers actually make decisions. Or at least the output of the theory can't always be at odds with the practice.

At first it might seem a bit strange to say this, since the whole point of norms is to point *away* from the down-and-dirty world of practice, to a more refined (perhaps ideal) world. But we must be careful of setting the bar too high, of putting the ideal entirely out of reach. A normative theory is supposed to be action-guiding (for the most part, although one cannot rule out more punitive uses entirely). So the usual examples of normative theories, a theory of rationality (of which we might take decision theory to be a proper part) for instance, or a theory of morality, shouldn't, on this view, have the consequence that *everybody* is irrational, or immoral.

If you offer for my subscription, a theory of rationality according to which not just me, but also you, and everybody else who ever lived and who ever will live, is irrational, that feature of your theory will give me pause. How could anybody possibly *live up* to a theory like that? And this is just a way of saying that such a harsh theory can't really be a serious candidate for guiding my actions.

So how high can the bar be set before the label 'normative' can no-longer save the theory? This is a matter of degree and the answer is certainly context-relative. But it would seem that the classical account of deduction, and many of the non-classical variants as well, are above that crucial height. If we observe people at their everyday reasoning tasks (performed unconsciously, or nearly so, for the most part) we shall see a multitude of diversions from the canon. People make mistakes—in reasoning, as in other things. Even good reasoners make mistakes.

And, it is my contention, there are enough of these mistakes made by enough actual reasoners, that we should hesitate to say that the (classical) theory of deduction is normative, though we wouldn't hesitate to say that it isn't descriptive. Perhaps it would be better to say that the normative—descriptive distinction isn't very useful in this case.

None of this is to say that there aren't normative features to logic. Suppose you and your friend are arguing:

> If Mary is happy then John is sad—wouldn't you agree?
> Oh yes, they're quite a pair, they are.
> And would you say that Mary is happy, or not?
> Oh happy, I'd definitely say happy.
> Well then, you'd have to admit that John is sad, wouldn't you?
> I admit no such thing!

If there isn't something like a joke or deliberate provocation here then your friend just did not 'get' the move from 'If P then Q' and 'P' to 'Q'. They have agreed that the conditional is true and also agreed to the truth of the antecedent. But they balk at the last move. You are liable to be a little angry at this point, and more than a little frustrated. Your opponent, you will feel, has made an illegal move. It's as if she had moved her king off the board in order to avoid checkmate.

But isn't this simply to say that deductive logic *is* normative in the sense just floated? There are rules, we are saying, and anybody who doesn't recognize them is a rule-breaker. This is a bad thing. The whole point of a rule is its imperative nature: to say that something is a rule is to say that following the rule is at worst not-blameworthy and may be praiseworthy and that breaking the rule is at best not-praiseworthy and in all other cases, blameworthy.[2] What prevents being able to pass from this one case (or any and all of the several others that one might produce here) to the normativity of the classical theory of deduction, is that the theory goes very far beyond these simple cases.

This is not the occasion of distress. It is, after all, the *function* of a theory to carry us beyond our immediate intuitions. If we intended always to stay within sight of our intuitions, we would have no need for theory. When one says classical logic, one might have in mind inferential moves like harvesting the consequent of a conditional for which one has the antecedent, but there are a myriad other forms which nobody has in mind. Think of all those which we have already characterized as indirect. A great many of those will cause the untutored to balk in just the way depicted above, and even the experts may find reason to question the validity[3] of certain moves. The history of logic is littered with balkers of all sorts.

But the question 'What kind of theory is classical logic?' hasn't yet been answered. Let's try the boring answer. There is nothing at all special about classical logic. It is a theory just like any other, and it is to be judged by the same standards as we judge any theory. Those standards are represented by the usual suite of virtues.[4]

Given a set of observations or phenomena which are to be explained, and future phenomena to be predicted, the successful theory must win

---

[2]The invocation of the notion of a rule here is not intended to count as an analysis of that concept. The latter project is difficult and vexed on every side.

[3]Here we use the term 'validity' in an extended rather informal way.

[4]See Quine and Ullian (1970) Chapter 6.

out over its competitors in the arena of modesty, generality, simplicity and perhaps a few others. But this won't typically be an easy matter to adjudicate. In many, if not most cases, it will be a matter of more or less, without very precise measurements.

We have a problem right away: What are the phenomena which we are trying to explain? Some people have naively assumed that the logical truths, or valid inferences play this role. So any theory which correctly captures exactly the valid inferences, for example, must be adequate (sometimes the term *empirically adequate* is used). The difficulty here is obvious if we think about it. In order that we may compare two candidate theories, we must have a way of generating the class of valid inferences. But this can only be done by using a theory of exactly the kind we claim to be looking for.

The class of valid inferences, or at least a proposal for the characterization of such, is the candidate theory, not the phenomena which such a theory must save. So the answer to what are the phenomena, must be whatever it is we use to judge whether or not a formal characterization of validity is adequate. We can't compare the class given formally with the 'real' class, as we have just noticed, so we must be judging the formalism on some other basis. We needn't travel very far to find that basis.

Let us ask ourselves how we would view a theory on which there was no rule of conditional elimination. It seems pretty clear that we would scornfully reject such a theory out of hand. No matter what other advantages the theory might display in terms of simplicity or generality, we are certain to feel that it fails to be adequate. This is transparently a case of some vital phenomenon not being preserved. So it isn't some entire class of inferences that we have in mind but it *is* a (presumably much smaller) class of *basic logical intuitions* as represented by such rules as conditional elimination—*those* must be the phenomena.

This characterization is not the kind of rock upon which one might prefer to found the science of logic—on some views the science on which all the other sciences depend. For one thing, there would appear to be a, not-very-subtle, element of relativity. Everything comes down to basic intuitions concerning which inferences are correct, and there is no guarantee that such intuitions are uniform among all reasoners. Indeed, from what has been said above, there is every reason to believe that there is divergence from unanimity on the basic intuitions. Where does that leave logic?

It would seem to leave logic without its position of privilege among the sciences. It might be worse than not being privileged, logic might turn out to be *underprivileged*. The phenomena of physics, the observations let's call them, seem virtually indisputable. At least there doesn't seem to be any dispute that *this* is an observation which must be explained by physical theory, and *that* isn't.

Deduction on the other hand, would seem to seethe with dissention concerning the core logical intuitions, which must at all cost be respected by the theory. So isn't physics superior to logic, in this area at least? This is not quite so cut and dried as it might first appear. The history of physics contains many cases in which observations have been discounted because they tended to embarrass an established theory even though the circumstances in which the observations were obtained satisfied the most stringent conditions of suitability. The other side of this tarnished coin is that other observations, ones which were obtained in far more suspicious circumstances, have been accepted because they bolstered established theory.

In fact the whole notion that there is a class of objects, observations, which are entirely distinct from theory, at least from the theory for which they are supposed to be observations, has been called into question by a number of philosophers of science.[5]

Leaving that issue, which threatens to overwhelm us, at least for now, let us confront the *mutability* of logic. What is to prevent us all (or many) from waking up tomorrow with entirely different logical intuitions? We'd have to change the theory in that case. Far worse perhaps, suppose we each woke up with wildly different intuitions from those of anybody else. In that circumstance, there would be no logic, according to the view we are now considering.

There are many philosophers who would find this view repugnant. For instance anybody who holds something akin to the view expressed

---

[5]Most notably by Imre Lakatos. See Worrall and Come (1978).

by George Boole in the 19th Century, that logic codifies the *laws of thought*, won't like the idea that such laws can be overturned as the result of a mere shift in the winds of intuition.

But if we are honest with ourselves, we shall see that in this, the theory of deduction is no worse off than any other theory. In physics, for instance, there is no guarantee that the observations won't suddenly change radically. If that were to happen, many or most of what we took to be the laws of nature could fall by the wayside. And the same can be said about virtually any other kind of theory.

Some authors, perhaps a majority of them, would find a distinction here between empirical theories like physics (is said to be) and formal theories like logic, and especially like mathematics. If the view we are now considering is correct and if logic and mathematics are alike in the sort of theories that they constitute, then that distinction is unsupportable. But if logic and mathematics are not alike, if there is a realm of mathematical objects containing the numbers at least, and perhaps other kinds of object as well, then we could be *pragmatic*[6] about logic but maintain the distinction between formal and empirical theories.

Those who maintain the existence of a special realm of mathematical objects are usually referred to as *Platonist*, since Plato seems to be one of the first to popularize the idea that there are abstract or ideal objects which lie beyond the everyday world of sensible qualities. Sometimes the view that there are mathematical objects distinct from physical objects, is called mathematical *realism*. A Platonist is obviously a realist, but the converse might not be true.[7]

---

[6] It isn't clear that the label 'pragmatic' applies to the view that we have constructed, since it would seem that most of the philosophers who are regarded as members of the later school, Pierce, James, and Dewey for three, would not find it congenial. On the other hand, W.V.O. Quine, who was counted as a pragmatist by some, would.

[7] It seems to be part and parcel of Platonism that the realm of mathematical (and perhaps other ideal objects) must be eternal and independent of (mere) human existence. This should be contrasted to the views of certain French mathematicians and philosophers of mathematics on which there is a realm of mathematical objects all right but mathematicians *construct* these objects. A Platonist mathematician, on the other hand, would say that she *discovered* the object in question, but that it had to be there (in advance and independent of her efforts) in order for there to be a discovery.

Essay or Discussion Questions and Topics

1. If I add two volumes of alcohol to two volumes of water, I discover that the result is less than four volumes. What effect does physical additivity have on arithmetic? Have I refuted $2 + 2 = 4$. Does a Platonist have to give a different answer from a non-Platonist? Does a realist have to answer differently from a non-realist?

2. Logic is Seinfeldian. Logic is different from other kinds of theory in that it isn't about anything. There are no phenomena to explain except in a very limited sense. To say that some inference is deductively correct is to record our determination to use words (or symbols) in a certain way and nothing else. It is in this sense (only) that logic is prior to the other sciences.

3. Just as mathematics has its own subject matter, the universe of mathematical objects, so logic has its own subject matter, the universe of *propositions*, where a proposition is an abstract object of the sort which is expressed by an indicative sentence (sometimes called a *meaning* or a *content*). Logic is the study of relations between propositions.

4. Logic has just as much of a problem with the distinction between theory and observation as any other science. For consider: once you have studied inference for a time (which may be surprisingly short) you train up your intuitions as much as your inferential skills. You may begin your study finding *Modus Tollens* puzzling and unconvincing and end by claiming it as part of the intuitive basis of any logic. So the question is: *Which* basic logical intuitions are we talking about as the supposed phenomena of logic? The intuitions of the beginner? The intuitions of the expert logician? Is there any reason to prefer one to the other?

6.3 Which Comes First: Syntax or Semantics?

As we have seen in earlier chapters, the deducibility relation comes in two flavors: semantic (or model-theoretic) and syntactic (or proof-theoretic). Let us raise the question now of which of the two is *prior*, or indeed if it makes sense to divide the issue in this way. After all, why couldn't the two approaches have been born simultaneously, each springing from a different part of Zeus' head?

To ask this, is to misunderstand the question. It is not a matter of primogeniture, but rather of *conceptual* priority. And the latter is worth a look, since there are many who seem to give the semantic picture the nod without much, if any, argument. For instance, some experts say 'The syntactical presentation tells us what the rules are, and the semantic one tells us why.'[8] It doesn't seem very controversial to say that if semantics does indeed justify syntax, then the former is clearly (conceptually) prior to the latter.

But we don't have to think either long or hard to find the problem with this assertion. What justifies semantics? In order for either semantics or syntax to have priority, it will have to terminate the justification issue.[9] So suppose we now try that tack. The (classical) truth-condition for the conditional justifies the rule of conditional elimination[10] and nothing in turn justifies the truth-condition. This would seem to be less than satisfactory.

One of the reasons for thinking of semantics as primary, was its explanatory role—it explains why certain rules command our allegiance, by showing them to be truth-preserving. But if there is nothing to explain the truth-condition, then we are left with the feeling that a trick has been played on us. Except of course, there *is* something to explain or justify the truth-condition at least in part. This condition is the one that makes conditional elimination truth-preserving.[11] It is precisely this kind of justification which is used by Rosser and Turquette in a

---

[8]This is, as close as I can recall, a remark made in conversation by Max Cresswell.

[9] Lewis Carrol in (Lewis Carroll, 'What the Tortoise Said to Achilles', Mind, n.s. 4 [1895], pp. 278-80), gives an amusing example of what happens when an attempt is made to justify conditional elimination by semantic means, and then to justify the justification ...

[10]Notice that this is far from unique. *Plenty* of other truth-conditions would also justify that rule.

[11]We are entitled to use 'the' in this claim because of all the possible candidates for the truth-condition, i.e. all the possible truth-functions see p. 120 we could use here, it is the only one to make conditional elimination truth-preserving without, at the same time making biconditional elimination truth-preserving.

non-classical context.[12] In that context there are syntactical elements, given in advance, which serve as so-called plausibility conditions for proposed truth-conditions. But of course, if we take a similar stance, then so much for the priority of the semantic perspective.

Are there any other considerations which might break this log-jam? Perhaps so. How do we *know* that the rule of conditional elimination preserves truth? For some people perhaps, it is a matter of just seeing. However for others, the rest of us, it takes more work. Suppose you have to convince me. You might say something like:

> Let's say that the premises are true. Now all we have to do is show that the conclusion has to be true in that circumstance. But the antecedent of the conditional premise is true, since it is one of the premises. So if the conclusion is false, then since the conclusion is the consequent of that premise, we would have a true antecedent and false consequent. But then the conditional premise would have to be false which would be impossible since we have already said all the premises are true. So it must be the case that the conclusion is true. Since we have been considering only the case in which the premises are true without any other restriction, we have just demonstrated that every time the premises are true, so must be the conclusion.

That does the job all right, but what is the job that it does? It would seem to *prove* that the rule of conditional elimination is truth-preserving. In fact we can easily recognize most of the moves as licensed by the classical proof theory and those which we don't recognize, we shall by the end of our studies.

Very well, but let's continue to ask about knowledge. How do we know that conditional elimination is correct? Here we might think to break out of the circle. Instead of saying that we know it's correct because we know it preserves truth, we might say instead, perhaps a little defiantly, that *we just know*.[13] To say this is to say that a basic logi-

---

[12] see Rosser and Turquette (1952)

[13] This response was mooted earlier, see page 191.

cal intuition is like a pain. If you tell me that you're in pain and I ask you how you know that, my response will be thought bizarre at best—perhaps as an odd way of making some sort of joke. To have a pain is, for most of us, to know that we have a pain. We don't suddenly notice that we are in pain after it has been going on for a long time. The connection is more direct than that.

Essay or Discussion Questions and Topics

1. If one defines basic logical intuitions as the intuition that certain basic inference rules are correct, this seems to give priority to syntax. Can a plausible account of such intuitions be given which inclines toward the semantic?

2. Making an analogy between pain and basic logical intuitions might misfire if one is hoping for something like *incorrigibility*. Some authors, A.J. Ayer for instance, have argued that one might have the feeling normally associated with having a pain and yet some other (hypothetical) element might be missing. In such a case, one might be unsure. But won't any such misgiving destroy the foundation of logic?

3. According to the text (see page 51) many reasoners, especially those who have not yet had their intuitions pummelled into shape by an introductory class in formal logic, have a basic logical intuition to the effect that you shouldn't use the classical negation rules unless the premises are consistent before one adds the formula that is to be 'reduced'. How can classical logic get away with ignoring this intuition?

6.4 Which Comes First: Inference or Logical Truth?

In the following we agree to use the terms 'logical truth' and 'valid' as applying equally well to the syntactical or the semantical picture of deductive inference. In ancient times, logic was the science of argument as much as, or more than it was the science of reasoning. For that reason the earliest sustained work, the famed *organon* of Aristotle, treats only inference.

Before long, however, by the time of the Stoic approach to logic, something like the notion of logical truth had appeared. But this notion remained in the background until the 19th Century. At that time the mathematical analysis of logic began with the work of Boole. It was at this point that the 'laws of thought' approach begins, in its modern incarnation at least.[14]From a mathematical perspective, the logical truths are a nicer class of object to study. This point of view continues to prevail among mathematicians, and even among many philosophers, to this very day.

One might think that this preference could never stand a chance for anybody who thinks of logic the way we do, as the theory of reasoning. But in classical logic, there is a way to recover exactly the classical theory of inference, from an account of logical truth.

One simply *defines* the inference from set of premises Γ to conclusion C to be valid if and only if there is some natural number n such that $P_1, \ldots, P_n$ are all members of Γ and

$$\vdash (P_1 \wedge \ldots \wedge P_n) \supset C$$

In words: if and only if some conditional (sometimes called the *corresponding* conditional) formed by taking the conjunction of finitely many premises as antecedent and the conclusion as consequent, is logically true. In this way all the valid inferences can be coded up as logical truths, and it really makes no difference which notion we take as primary since, as we noticed earlier on page 131, we can easily define logical truth in terms of inference.

On the laws of thought view then, the goal of deduction is to identify the class of logical truths. This kind of project, we should notice, is very familiar from abstract algebra. The correct theory of inference then falls out of this identification as a kind of bonus.

In spite of the fact that the laws of thought tradition in formal logic continues to be, if not the majority, then at least an extremely vigorous

---

[14]It seems clear that the Stoics had the equivalent of logical truths, although their account of inference is very different from the classical one.

minority, it seems to get the order wrong. Unless we want to think that formal logic is a part of abstract algebra, then nothing could be clearer than that logic is *primarily* about inference and only secondarily about logical truth. To put the matter another way, the laws of thought tradition gets the psychology wrong.

Beginning students, even at the earliest possible stage of their career, *get* the notion of inference. Many of these same students don't understand the notion of logical truth. Even more of them understand the notion in the abstract, but cannot think of a single example. When the latter group are shown examples of logical truths they are disappointed. 'Is that all?' they are likely to say, 'But those are just silly!' Every teacher of introductory logic has seen this reaction.

There are perhaps more telling arguments to be made in favor of the primacy of inference over logical truth, but these arguments require an excursion into non-classical logic.[15]

Essay or Discussion Questions and Topics

1. The fact that one can derive the correct theory of inference from the correct theory of logical truth is no mere bonus for classical logic, it is a deep part of the very meaning of inference. For consider: what on earth can it mean for an inference to be valid except that if the premises are all true then so must be the conclusion. And this in turn must mean that every circumstance in which the premises are true is one in which the conclusion is true. But that is exactly to say that some corresponding conditional is logically true! So properly understood, it's clear that any account of logical truth (which need not necessarily be the classical account) *must* also capture a theory of inference.

2. Whatever else we might wish to say about the connection between logical truth and valid inference in classical logic, it is undeniably *nice*. Can you think of a circumstance in which we might nevertheless be willing to give up the connection?

---

[15]For instance, it is easy to construct a three-valued logic which has *no logical truths* but has plenty of valid inferences. See Schotch (2004), especially the chapter on many-valued logic.

3. Call the definition of valid inference given above in terms of the
   logical truth of a corresponding conditional $\vdash_L$. Show that $\Gamma \vdash$
   P if and only if $\Gamma \vdash_L P$. Notice that you have to be able to
   demonstrate this in order to see that $\vdash_L$ is genuinely equivalent to
   the classical notion of valid inference.

6.5   Where Does Logic Fit in Philosophy?

Just now, we were considering (and by implication, rejecting) the view
that deductive logic is a branch of abstract algebra. Perhaps it might be
better to say that deductive logic isn't *just* a branch of abstract algebra.
Whatever we might wish, there can be no real debate over whether or
not it is possible to treat much of logic, especially deduction, by mathematical techniques. The fact is that the mathematization of deduction
was successfully demonstrated in the 19th Century, and that program
has been thriving ever since.

This looks pretty suspicious to lots of philosophers. There don't
seem to be other sub-disciplines of philosophy which are also branches
of some other science. So maybe logic isn't really part of philosophy.
There are many examples of subjects which got their start in philosophy,
all of natural science was once called natural philosophy, and then broke
off into an independent area. Isn't that exactly what has happened to
logic? Isn't it true that the study of logic began in an informal (non-
mathematical) way as a way of attempting to adjudicate arguments, and
since that time it has become something else entirely, something quite
outside of philosophy?

To say such a thing (and many philosophers *do* say such a thing),
is not to say that there is no longer anything of philosophical interest
in the science of logic. The philosophy of logic makes just as much
sense as the philosophy of science or of mathematics. In this way does
philosophy maintain a civilizing influence on her rowdy children.

There would seem to be a significant difference however between
the cases. There are plenty of what we might term mathematically
interesting questions which are also philosophically interesting. It is far
from clear however, that the converse is true. Far from clear, that is,

that there are questions which arise in some area other than logic and the philosophy of mathematics, which turn out to be mathematically interesting questions. In this logic is different. There are questions which arise in other areas of philosophy which are also questions of logic.

We shall consider ethics, but it is by no means the only example, nor even the easiest one to come by. It seems to be part of our ordinary moral experience that we can find ourselves in a dilemma, which is to say a situation in which the demands of morality cannot (all) be heeded. Let us suppose that such situations might extend beyond the world of everyday all the way into philosophy.[16]

Let us next ask the question of whether or not obligations[17] are closed under logical consequence, which is simply a way of asking whether or not the logical consequences of obligations are themselves obligations. This might be seen as an example of a question which is both of interest to ethical theory, and also to logic. Some philosophers, even some ethicists, might object that the question is one that only a logician could love, and that they, as ethicists, have not the slightest interest in it. Such a position betrays a lack of thought.

The issue is really quite deep. If you deny that the logical consequences of obligations are also obligations, then you are saying that moral argument, at least moral argument of a certain standard kind, is impossible. When you and I enter into a moral dispute, a dispute over whether or not you ought to bring it about that P say, then what often, perhaps usually, happens is that I try to demonstrate that P follows from something, some general moral principle, to which you subscribe. In stage one then, we obtain the subscription.

> Don't you think that we ought to help those who cannot help themselves?
> Not in every case, suppose somebody is both helpless and

---

[16]Such a supposition is by no means beyond the bounds of controversy. There are moral philosophers who argue that such conflicts of obligation are merely apparent.

[17]We are sacrificing rigor in the cause of clarity in this example. Strictly speaking we are not talking about obligations at all, since those are typically *actions*. We should be talking rather about 'sentences which ought to be true'. This is a much more awkward form of words however and it would interfere with the flow without adding very much to what we are saying.

not in need of help?

Very well, we ought to help those in need who cannot help themselves?

Wonderfully high minded, but impossible I'm afraid.

Why impossible?

We are overwhelmed by the numbers don't you see?

The numbers of what? Those in need?

Precisely! We would spend all our resources helping the needy only to join their ranks before long.

Ah, well how about this modification then: We ought to help those in need who cannot help themselves, but not to the point of harming ourselves or even seriously inconveniencing ourselves?

Yes, it doesn't sound so high-minded, but now it's something I can support.

Having obtained agreement with a general principle, we now attempt to use it to generate a specific 'ought.'

Would you say that Jones is in need of help?

Yes, not much doubt about that, poor bloke he.

We should pass the hat, don't you think? Everybody could put in what they can easily spare.

I don't see the point in that.

Do you imagine then that Jones can pull himself up by the bootstraps, that all he needs is sufficient willpower?

No, I wouldn't say that, not in his present state at least.

Then, we ought to help him, wouldn't you say?

Well somebody needs to help him if he's going to be helped, but I don't see how that got to be my problem.

What has been shown is that 'We help Jones' is a logical consequence of 'We help those in need who cannot help themselves and whose help is not a significant burden to us.' This much is non-controversial. Having first agreed upon 'We ought to help those in need ...'. But the remaining step, the step from the forgoing to 'We ought to help Jones' will only follow if the logical consequences of obligations are themselves obligations. It is just crazy to say that the issue is of no interest to ethicists, unless the ethicists in question have no interest in arguments like our sample.

Nor can the relevance of logic to ethics be exhausted by this one issue. Suppose that in exasperation, our stubborn ethicist agrees that the issue is of interest after all. But the interest is over once we see that we must answer 'yes' to the question of whether or not the consequences of obligations are themselves obligations, isn't it? Not at all. Recall how this got started.

We were wondering about moral dilemma, about *conflict of obligations*. In view of what we just said about obligations and logical consequences, we now have a problem. Suppose I am in a moral dilemma, that there are two sentences P and Q which I believe should both be true (I believe that each, individually, *ought* to be true). But the two cannot be true together—hence the dilemma.

This is bad enough, but it gets worse. One of the consequences of the set of sentences which we say ought to be the case, the set of obligations, is the sentence $P \wedge Q$. But since the two sentences cannot both be true at the same time, this consequence is equivalent to $\perp$. Since the consequences are also obligations, $\perp$ is an obligation. But *everything* follows from $\perp$ as we have seen (see page 132) so in the case of a moral dilemma, one is obliged to do *everything*. This seems a bit harsh. It also seems a matter of some interest to ethics. It is certainly of interest to logic.

Essay or Discussion Questions and Topics

1. Give an example of an issue which is of interest to both logic and epistemology.

2. There may be more examples of areas of philosophy which overlap other disciplines. It seems clear that applied ethics is part of ethics, and hence of philosophy. But is bioethics also part of health-science? Is business ethics part of management? How does either answer affect the status of logic in philosophy?

3. The only way to deal with the problem of moral dilemma is to use a non-classical account of logical consequence.

4. The problem of conflict of obligations is just a particular instance of the more general problem of reasoning from (classically) in-consistent sets of premises. Give other examples of this problem.

6.6   Is Classical Logic Two-Valued?

As we noticed in Chapter 4, the prevailing view is that classical logic and two-valued logic are pretty much the same, or more accurately that it is part of the classical perspective that logic is two-valued. In consid-ering the status of the so-called law of excluded middle in that chapter, we noticed that when threatened by the possibility of counterexamples to the 'law' more than one author has proposed simply *defining* the term declarative sentence to be any sentence which is either true or false (i.e. which satisfies excluded middle).

But we need to answer a prior question before we worry about the number of truth-values. What exactly do we mean by the expression 'classical logic?' Notice that if we answer this question by saying 'Clas-sical logic is whatever logic is characterized by the classical truth defini-tions.', we have taken the definitional route once more. So it seems that anyone who takes this kind of semantic picture as basic, might well be stuck with blunt force, in order to fend off 'deviant'[18] logical intuitions. We are not required to characterize classical logic in this way however, even if we have semantic leanings. We can say instead that classical logic is the set of pairs $<\Gamma, P>$ such that the inference from Γ to P, is (classically) valid.

Interestingly enough, classical logic in this sense can also be recov-ered with more than two truth-values. In order to see this, we need a couple of definitions.

---

[18]This derogatory term is usually associated with Quine, see Quine (1970).

Definition 6.6.1. Define the *product* of two truth-value assignments:

$$v_1 \otimes v_2(A) = <v_1(A), v_2(A)>$$

In words, the product of the truth-value assignments v_1 and v_2 assigns to each atomic sentence A the pair of truth-values formed by first taking the truth-value assigned by v_1 and then the value assigned by v_2.

Next we define the product truth-values assigned by connectives. We shall produce only the tables for $\wedge_\otimes$ and $\neg_\otimes$, but it should be clear how the tables for the other connectives go.

Definition 6.6.2. The definition of $\wedge_\otimes$ in terms of product truth-values:

$P \wedge_\otimes Q$	$<T,T>$	$<T,F>$	$<F,T>$	$<F,F>$
$<T,T>$	$<T,T>$	$<T,F>$	$<F,T>$	$<F,F>$
$<T,F>$	$<T,F>$	$<T,F>$	$<F,F>$	$<F,F>$
$<F,T>$	$<F,T>$	$<F,F>$	$<F,T>$	$<F,F>$
$<F,F>$	$<F,F>$	$<F,F>$	$<F,F>$	$<F,F>$

Definition 6.6.3. The definition of $\neg_\otimes$ in terms of product truth-values:

P	$\neg_\otimes P$
$<T,T>$	$<F,F>$
$<T,F>$	$<F,T>$
$<F,T>$	$<T,F>$
$<F,F>$	$<T,T>$

In these tables we compute the compound value by forming the pair of the simple truth-value calculations. So, for example, when we wish to know the product value of $P \wedge_{\otimes} Q$ when P takes the product value $<T, T>$ and Q takes the value $<F, F>$, we simply form the pair $<\wedge(T, F), \wedge(T, F)>$, where $\wedge(T, F)$ is the result of looking up in the table for (the non-product) $\wedge$, the entry for P takes T and Q takes F.[19]

Although it might be relatively easy to understand the principle for computing product values, the tables are not easy to read. In aid of improving the readability, we shall make some abbreviations.

  1 for $<T, T>$

  2 for $<T, F>$

  3 for $<F, T>$

  4 for $<F, F>$

In terms of these abbreviations, our two tables may be rewritten:

$P \wedge_{\otimes} Q$	1	2	3	4
1	1	2	3	4
2	2	2	4	4
3	3	4	3	4
4	4	4	4	4

[19]In algebra, one would say that the values of $\wedge_{\otimes}$ are defined *componentwise* from the values of $\wedge$.

P	$\neg_\otimes P$
1	4
2	3
3	2
4	1

Let us now take the plunge and define a logic—the *classical product logic*, in semantic terms.

Definition 6.6.4. The relation of semantic entailment for the classical product logic, indicated by $\Gamma \models_\otimes P$ is defined
$\Gamma \models_\otimes P$ if and only if for every product truth-value assignment $v_\otimes$, if every member of the set Γ takes $<T, T>$ (the value 1) on $v_\otimes$, so does P.

Now for the *really* interesting part:

Lemma 6.6.5. $\Gamma \not\models_\otimes P \implies \Gamma \not\models P$

Proof. If $\Gamma \not\models_\otimes P$, there must be some product $v_\otimes = v_i \otimes v_j$, such that $\models_\otimes \Gamma$, where this means as usual that every member of Γ takes the value $<T, T>$ relative to $v_\otimes$, but P takes one of the product values $< T, F>$, $<F, T>$, or $<F, F>$. But in the first case v_j is a counterexample to the validity of $\Gamma \models P$, in the second case v_i is such a counterexample, and in the last case, both of v_i and v_j are counterexamples. □

Corollary 6.6.6. $\Gamma \models P \implies \Gamma \models_\otimes P$

Lemma 6.6.7. $\Gamma \not\models P \implies \Gamma \not\models_\otimes P$

Proof. If $\Gamma \not\models P$ then there must be a counterexample, i.e. a truth-value assignment v such that every member of Γ takes the value true relative to v while P takes the value false. But then $v \otimes v$ must likewise be a counterexample to $\Gamma \models_\otimes P$. □

Corollary 6.6.8. $\Gamma \models_\otimes P \implies \Gamma \models P$

And if we put these results together, we get:

Theorem 6.6.9. $\Gamma \models P \iff \Gamma \models_\otimes P$

Proof. The proof is trivial given the two corollaries.   □

But this shows that classical product logic is *the same logic* as classical logic, provided that we agree to identify a logic (semantically) as the set of pairs (Γ, P) such that the inference from Γ to P is valid. To put the matter even more emphatically:

> *Classical logic is two-valued, but it is also four-valued.*

Exercises

Use the methods employed in the proofs of the last theorem to prove that classical logic is also 8-valued, 16-valued, ... 2^N-valued ...

Part Two:
The Classical Logic of Elements

Chapter 7

Introducing The Logic of Elements

7.1 Overview

It is easy to see that the *quantifiers*, words and phrases embedding 'all' or 'some,' are what we earlier called *logical words*. It's easy to see that, because it's easy to see that inferences like the famous:

Table 7.1: A Famous Example

(P1) All humans are mortal.
(P2) Socrates is a human.
(C) Therefore Socrates is mortal.

are correct *because* of the way 'all' is used. The theory of inference which we have constructed up to this point, fails to reflect that correctness, a deficiency which we must now repair.

The difference between the above inference and one of the 'John and Mary' kind, is that in the latter *whole sentences* are at issue, while in the former it is parts like 'mortal' and 'is a human,' parts which are not themselves sentences, which are crucial. For this reason, the logic of the quantifiers is sometimes called 'the logic of *analyzed* sentences.'

Another way to make the distinction, from the semantic view, is to say that sentence logic is a matter of truth-values but that the logic in our example must take into account also *things*. What kinds of things? In the first instance at least, the things which interest us are *individuals* (as opposed to more exotic kinds of things).

In ordinary speech we often use the term 'individual' to mean 'individual person' and in our technical use of the term we shall comprehend persons too—Socrates, in our example, but we are not restricting ourselves to people. When we say 'individual' we have in mind the distinction between individuals and *classes* or *sets*. To make this even clearer, the kind of logic we shall now study is sometimes called *elementary*. Such usage is not intended to convey that the logical principles are basic, though they do indeed fall under that description, but rather that we focus on elements as opposed to sets. Elements are the things that *belong* to sets, but might not themselves be sets.

With which of the many possible sets of elements should we be concerned? The glib answer is 'The largest one—the set of *all* individuals.' However, if we think about it a bit, we will see that we are not at all sure which exactly *is* that set.

This is, in fact, a metaphysical question and one that has engaged philosophers from antiquity. It will likewise engage us, from time to time, but for now we can at least agree that there exist some individuals rather than none.[1] But if this is the extent of our metaphysical urgings, then we should allow ourselves the liberty of adopting different sets of elements for different projects. Sometimes we want to talk about people and other times we are more interested in numbers or in negatively charged particles. For any given application, the set of individuals of interest is called the *universe* or *domain of discourse*. When we are talking in the abstract we mostly fail to specify any particular universe, but we always reserve to right to be as particular as we need to be.

---

[1] And even this is not entirely beyond the bounds of controversy.

7.2 Expanding our Formal Language

In order to analyze this new class of reasoning, we must expand our existing formal language to make it more expressive. To accomplish this we shall construct a new language called EL.

To deal with inferences like the 'Socrates' example, we need something like *names* in the new language—that is, we need a way to refer specifically to an individual or element. Such names have often been called *singular referring terms* or often just singular terms. The contrast is with *general* or *mass* terms, which are intended to refer to collections, e.g. 'dogs' and 'water.'

To represent singular terms, the names for our elements, we shall use what are usually called *individual constants*. In our formal language these will be indicated by the members of an (infinite) list:

$$a_1, b_1, c_1, a_2, b_2, \ldots$$

of lower case Roman letters, with subscripts. These will usually be drawn from the beginning of the alphabet, although we shall also feel free to use 'j' for 'John' and to drop the subscripts when no confusion will result from our taking that liberty.

We must also have something that plays the role of verb phrases like 'is a human' and 'is mortal.' We shall use a part of speech (in this case of formal speech) which is usually called a *predicate* for this. Linguistically speaking, a predicate is what is left over after you take out the subject, or subjects. For instance in 'Socrates is seated,' the predicate is 'is seated' while in 'John loves Mary' it is 'loves.'

The second case is a bit of stretch, since one would normally count John as the subject while Mary is the *object*, however unwelcome such usage may be in certain quarters. We are using 'subject' in an extended sense then, one which is captured by the (informal) definition: 'what the sentence is about.' 'John loves Mary' is clearly about both John and Mary, so for us the sentence has two subjects (in this extended sense of the term).

In the second half of the 19th Century, a number of philosophers and mathematicians had begun to notice that there is a very strong analogy between the way predicates, in our sense, combine with their subjects, and the way that mathematical *functions* combine with their *arguments* to produce a value. For example, the function − combines with the argument 3 to produce the value −3 and the function + combines with the numbers 3 and 2 to produce the number 5.

That value, in the case of predicates, is a sentence. In other words: if you combine the predicate 'loves' (which is not a sentence) with the singular terms 'John' and 'Mary' (neither of which are sentences) in that order, you get 'John loves Mary,' a palpable sentence. This led to what we have been calling predicates, being termed *propositional functions* by many authors. Since that time, the word 'proposition' has come to be used mainly to denote abstract objects like *meanings*, i.e., what sentences *express*, rather than sentences.

We use capital Roman letters, mostly from the middle of the alphabet, with and without subscripts, to stand for predicates. We give ourselves infinitely many of these, but rather than use a single list we have a separate list for each *degree*.

What is meant by this term is the number of singular terms that a given predicate takes in order to make a sentence. For example, 'is happy' is degree 1 since it takes a single term, e.g. 'John' to make the sentence 'John is happy.' 'Loves' is degree 2 since it requires a pair of terms like 'John' and 'Mary' to make the sentence 'John loves Mary.' 'Between' is degree 3, requiring three terms like 'Henry,' 'James' and 'Scott' to make the sentence 'Henry is between Scott and James.' After degree 4, it is quite difficult to produce ordinary language examples of those predicates but, just as we go beyond our intuitions when we allow conjunctions of any finite length, so we allow ourselves predicates of all finite degrees.

So for each degree n, we shall allow ourselves infinitely many predicates of that degree. This means that we shall give ourselves infinitely many lists in the manner of:

$F^1, G^1, H^1, F_2{}^1, \ldots$

$\vdots$

$F^n, G^n, H^n, F_2{}^n, \ldots$

$\vdots$

Here the superscript tells us the degree of the predicate.

Often, when no confusion will result, we allow ourselves to drop the super or sub-scripts (or both). It is normal to distinguish between the initial list of this sequence, the first degree or *one-place* or *monadic* (or even *unary*, for all of its manifest barbarity) predicates and the remaining lists of *n-place* or *n-ary relational* predicates (we often simply say *relations*).

Since the quantifiers are at the center of things, in the 'Socrates' inference, and a great many others, we must have some vocabulary to represent 'all' and 'some.' We shall use the standard symbols ∀ and ∃ for that purpose. The first is always called the *universal* quantifier while the second is called, not the particular as one might expect, but rather the *existential* quantifier. Although we use these notions every day in ordinary language, fitting them into a theoretical framework is no easy task.

Quantifiers seem to occupy the same grammatical position as names when we first examine them. We say 'Socrates is seated' and also 'Somebody is seated,' but there is no individual person named by 'somebody' or 'everybody' in the way that a term like 'Socrates' names some one individual. Fortunately, there is another way to explain the grammatical type of quantifiers, one which will rescue us from assigning them to the same class as terms.

We have already explained predicates by their function, which is to convert singular terms into sentences. We may think of quantifiers as a device for turning predicates themselves into sentences, in the first instance at least. We shall shortly encounter another property of quantifiers.

This much of the new language might be extrapolated from ordinary speech but the remaining ingredient does not fall into the same category. It is, to the contrary, quite remote from our ordinary linguistic experi-

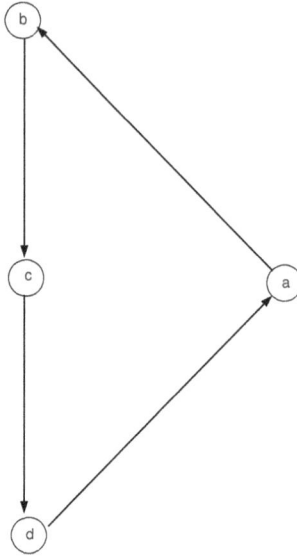

Figure 7.1: Everybody loves somebody—the normal reading

ence. There turns out to be a large problem which pretty much dictates our use of an exotic device.

The problem concerns the representation of quantifiers in combination with relational predicates like 'loves.' It might be put this way: A sentence like 'Everybody loves somebody' is ambiguous, in that there are two distinct *readings*, or perhaps meanings that the sentence might have. The first, and what we might well call, the *normal* reading might be diagrammed as in figure 7.1. In these diagrams the small circles represent the elements of our universe. For purposes of illustration, we are using a universe consisting of four individual people, which we have labeled 'a,' 'b,' 'c,' and 'd.'[2] The arrows represent the relation, in this case 'loves,' in such a manner that 'a loves b' is represented by an arrow going from a to b (the arrow's direction is indicated by the head)

What is depicted is the situation in which each and every individual

---

[2]If this is too abstract, think of the people as Bob and Carol and Ted and Alice.

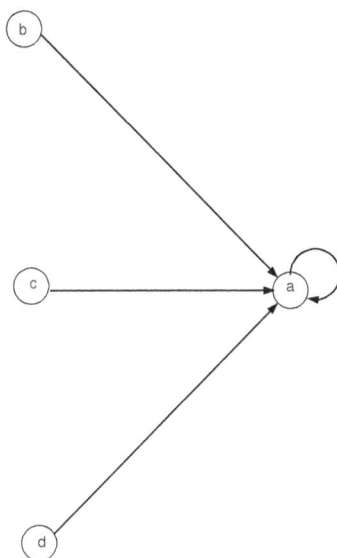

Figure 7.2: Everybody loves somebody—the abnormal reading

has an arrow 'leaving' that individual. We might call this the *dependent* reading, since, in this diagram, we can determine which individual is loved only after we have selected a lover. The person loved *depends upon* the person doing the loving. On the other hand consider the situation diagrammed in figure 7.2, in which an arrow leaves every individual (so everybody really does love somebody) but all the arrows arrive at precisely one individual, *b* in this case. We might term this the *independent* reading since *b* is the individual loved independently of our choice of lover.

Such a reading is bizarre and unlikely but it is *possible*. It's possible for everyone to love some one *particular* person and if that were true it would indeed be true that everybody loved somebody. And so we must require of our formal language that it be able to represent both the normal and the abnormal readings of 'everybody loves somebody.' It turns out to be hard to do—so hard, that it took until the end of the 19th Century to work out an adequate formalization.

What is absolutely required is the ability to distinguish the different *places* in a relation, and to be able to attach a quantifier to a place in some clear way. In our example, we need to distinguish between the lover and the lovee, so to speak, and to indicate which quantifier goes with which. The device which makes this possible is the use of *variables*.

We have already encountered variables in our metalanguage, variables for formulas, but we shall now use them also in the object language. In that venue, we shall introduce *individual* variables, variables which *range over* the elements of our universe of discourse. This concept is one which people are supposed to just get, and for sure it is difficult to explain. The thing is that variables 'refer' to elements, but not in the way that singular terms refer which is why we use the quotes around the word refer just now. A singular term refers to its target and that is pretty much that[3] but a variable varies. It 'refers' to an element, but not to any one element in particular. We are reduced to uttering oxymorons like 'ambiguous name.'[4]

However mysterious the notion of a variable may be, we shall compound the mystery when we combine their use with quantifiers. Consider the two readings of 'everybody loves somebody' one last time: We shall use L to stand for the relation 'loves.' The way we translate a sentence like 'John loves Mary' into our new formal language will echo the function-argument usage which inspired the treatment we are pursuing. So, if a and b represent John and Mary respectively, then Lab is what we write in translating, rather than aLb. But for the quantified version, we build up to the final translation in stages.

First we have the expression Lxy in which x and y are individual variables. This is not a sentence, but it *is* rather sentence-like. Such an expression is often called an *open sentence* but one should resist the temptation to think that it is a kind of sentence.[5] The best we might do in the way of interpretation is to say '(an unspecified individual) x loves (an unspecified individual) y,' which isn't terribly informative. But the

---

[3] which is emphatically *not* to say that there is no mystery involved with singular reference.

[4] This particular oxymoron seems to have been invented by P. Suppes.

[5] An open sentence is no more a type of sentence than an alleged criminal is a type of criminal.

point of all this is to label the places in the relation, and that we have plainly done. x marks the lover, while y marks the lovee.

To attach the quantifiers to the places, we shall use the variables once more. We shall write '$\forall x$' and '$\exists y$' to show which quantifier goes with which place in the relation. So the final translation reads: '$(\forall x)(\exists y)Lxy$.' This bit of formal language can be interpreted along the lines of 'For any individual x, there exists some individual y, such that x loves y.' Now it will take a bit of practice to see this, but the later is another way of saying (with variables) that everyone loves someone. Furthermore, we can see that this represents what we earlier called the dependent or normal reading.

If we ask 'Who is the one who is loved?,' the answer is 'the individual y,' but we don't *get* to that individual *until* we first select an individual x. The y which is loved *depends upon* the x which is doing the loving.

If there really are, in some sense, variables embedded in the quantified expression, what happened to them? How is it that we don't *see* them in ordinary language? The answer to this important question is that variables are destroyed by quantification. The way we say this in technical language is to say that quantifiers *bind* variables. The x and y, wherever they occur in the translation, are said to be bound by the quantifiers which are marked with the same variable. This usage is as misleading as our previous use of the term open sentence. The hard truth of the matter is that a bound variable is not a variable at all—it has been *quantified away*. Of course if we start to take off the quantifiers to bring back the variables, we get something, e.g. 'Everyone loves y', which is not a sentence and so not a part of ordinary language.

This is the *other* defining property of quantifiers which was alluded to earlier. Quantifiers make sentences (out of predicates) and they also bind variables. So quantifiers are wildly different from the sentence connectives we have been studying and it would be quite a stretch to refer to former as connectives. In spite of this, we are sometimes able to stretch that far, when our convenience is at issue. In other circumstances, when we are casting about for a category which comprehends both connectives and quantifiers, we shall use the term *operators* mentioned earlier.

Perhaps it would be best to think of variables as analogous to some exotic sub-atomic particle, the existence of which is required by our best theory but the observation of which is extremely problematic. To show the utility of variables even without being able to find examples of them in ordinary speech, consider the problem of the two readings of 'everybody loves somebody.'

As we have already said, the example translation represents the dependent or normal reading. How then shall we represent the independent or abnormal reading? In that reading, the somebody that everybody loves is independent of whatever lover we pick. In other words when we ask the question 'Who is the one who is loved?' about the independent reading, we shall once again say the individual y, but we don't, on the abnormal reading, have to first select some lover x *before* we can specify y. It should be clear that the way to represent that is to put the '$\exists$' first, as in: $(\exists y)(\forall x)(Lxy)$

We may finally give a precise account of the language EL.

First, we have the alphabet of EL:

The infinite list $A, B, C, A_1, B_1, \ldots$ of *sentence letters*

the infinite list of infinite lists

$$F^1, G^1, H^1, F_2{}^1, \ldots$$

$\vdots$

$$F^n, G^n, H^n, F_2{}^n, \ldots$$

$\vdots$

of predicates

the two infinite lists of *individual terms*

the list $a_1, b_1, c_1, a_2, \ldots$ of individual constants the list $x_1, y_1, z_1, x_2, \ldots$ of individual variables

the list $\wedge, \vee, \supset, \equiv, \neg, \forall, \exists$ of truth-functional connective and quantifier symbols

the punctuation symbols (,)

Next, the definition of the notion of a *formula* of EL:

Definition 7.2.1. Any sentence letter of SL and any predicate of EL followed by the appropriate number of individual terms is a formula of EL, known as an *atomic* formula (of EL).

If P and Q are formulas of EL then so are

$(P \wedge Q)$

$(P \vee Q)$

$(P \supset Q)$

$(P \equiv Q)$

$(\neg P)$.

If P is a formula of EL and v is an individual variable which occurs in P then:

$(\forall v)P$ is a formula

$(\exists v)P$ is a formula.

Nothing else is a formula of EL except as defined by the above clauses.

We need a way of talking about just which variables are bound by a given quantifier. This is codified in the following.

Definition 7.2.2. We define the *scope* of a quantifier as follows:
In either of '$(\forall v)P$' or '$(\exists v)P$,' where v is an individual variable and P is a formula, each occurrence of the variable v lies within the scope of the initial quantifier including, we stipulate, the v which is part of $\forall v$ and $\exists v$.

Each occurrence of an individual variable within the scope of a quantifier is said to be *bound* by that quantifier, or to be a bound occurrence. If the variable is not within the scope of any quantifier, it is said to be *free*, or to be a free occurrence of the variable.

Definition 7.2.3. We define a *sentence* of EL to be a formula of EL in which there are no free occurrences of any variable.

In case the formula in question is an atomic formula, the sentence will be called an *atomic sentence*. We shall mostly be concerned with sentences.

7.3   Essay or Discussion Questions and Topics

1. We can indeed see a part of speech in ordinary language which does what variables do in the language of elementary logic, namely *pronouns*. Pronouns exhibit what are called *anaphoric* relationships with other bits of an utterance, to use a more common idiom, they 'refer back,' and this is exactly what variables do.

2. Much of what we say every day doesn't use relations at all. If we restrict ourselves to this mode, do we really need variables? Couldn't we use expressions like $\forall(F \supset G)$ to say that all F's are G's?

3. There is absolutely no reason to think of individual variables as mysterious entities. They are in fact nothing other than singular referring expressions, the reference of which has not (yet) been

fixed. In this they are no different from other referring expressions like names. The name 'John' is a referring expression but we have no idea what the actual reference is until it is fixed by the context of utterance.

7.4 Translation Issues

We know from our previous exposure to these matters that one of the things we wish to be able to do is to translate, at least some, bits of natural (and technical) discourse into our new language. Even when we were dealing only with whole sentences, there were things that caused us to wonder, and now that we also have individuals and predicates to worry about, the translation enterprize has become even less mechanical.

But though things have become more complex in one way they have become easier in another. When we introduced the connectives of sentence logic it was seldom done without an apology for their failure to conform to ordinary speech. Even when we used phrases like 'approximation' and 'inspired by,' there was usually something of which to complain. When we talk about all and some, there isn't going to be any kind of gap between the formal uses of the terms and their ordinary uses. There isn't, for example, some technical use of 'all' which would be entirely unfamiliar to speakers of ordinary discourse. Nor will we find some colloquial use of 'some' which we cannot represent.

The major difference between the formal use of quantifiers and their ordinary use, is the size of the universe of discourse. We often either fail to specify a universe, or take the universe to be *everything* in our formal musings. In ordinary speech it is very rare (though not unknown) to utter 'all' or 'some' without qualification. We usually say 'all people' or 'some pigs' and the like.

Though it is not possible to present an *algorithm*, in the strict sense, for translating natural language into the language of elementary logic, there are two rules of thumb which will resolve a great many translation puzzles.

Universal-Conditional Rule of Thumb

If the main operator within the scope of the quantifier is the conditional then the quantification is universal and if the quantifier is universal then the main operator within the scope of that quantifier is the conditional.

Notice that the rule takes us from the quantifier to the connective *and vice versa*.

Example 7.4.1. Translate the sentence 'All professors are self-absorbed' into the language of elementary logic.

We use Px to stand for x is a professor and Sx to stand for x is self-absorbed. Since the quantifier is universal we know from the rule of thumb that the connective between the two predicates must be the conditional. This gives as the solution:

$$(\forall x)(Px \supset Sx)$$

In this example we started the translation by giving a kind of dictionary which matched verb phrases to predicates. In doing this, we also used a variable; we said that 'Px' represents 'x is a professor.' Beginning students often find this confusing especially when, in the translation, the variable is changed to y or some other variable different from x. If we begin by saying Px indicates that x is a professor, how is it that we can later translate 'All professors ...' by means of '$(\forall y)(Py ...)$?'

The answer is that which variable appears in the dictionary is not significant since the unquantified variable is merely a place holder. Once the variable is quantified, it is quantified away—it no longer exists. There is no x in 'All professors drive used cars.'

This is just another way of saying that it doesn't matter which symbol we use for a *bound* variable, and that $(\forall x)(Px ...)$ is equivalent to $(\forall y)(Py ...)$.

Example 7.4.2. Translate the sentence 'A stitch in time, saves nine' into the language of elementary logic.

We use Tx to represent that x is a timely stitch and Sx to represent that x saves nine stitches. The burden of the saying would seem to be that *if* one applies a timely stitch, *then* one will thereby save oneself later effort. This makes the connective between the predicates the conditional. The rule of thumb now tells us that the quantification must be universal even though the word 'all' does not appear explicitly. In other words the correct translation is:

$$(\forall x)(Tx \supset Sx)$$

It is not at all unusual for a sentence in ordinary speech to be quantified implicitly rather than using words like 'all' and 'some.' We have just seen the indefinite article 'a' do duty for the universal quantifier. Exactly the same article can also serve to indicate the existential quantifier, as in 'A man came to the door.' However 'A man is only as good as his word.' is obviously universal again. How can we tell? We have to be sensitive to nuances of meaning. We have to ask ourselves 'Does this really mean "some particular person?" or does it mean people in general?' We usually have the resources to answer questions like this, if we think carefully.

Existential-Conjunction Rule of Thumb

If the main connective within the scope of the quantifier is conjunction then the quantification is existential and if the quantifier is existential then the main connective within the scope of that quantifier is conjunction.

Example 7.4.3. Translate 'Some people swim.' into the language of elementary logic.

We use Px for x is a person and Sx for x swims. Since the existential quantifier is used, the rule of thumb tells us that the connective must be conjunction. In other words the correct translation is:

$$(\exists x)(Px \wedge Sx)$$

Example 7.4.4. Translate 'A panhandler asked for money.' into the language of elementary logic.

We use Px to represent x is a panhandler and Ax for x asked for money. Here we can see the description of the person must be that x is a panhandler *and* x asked for money. In any such case, the rule of thumb tells us that the quantifier is existential. So the translation must be:

$$(\exists x)(Px \wedge Ax)$$

Some of these translation problems require us to stop and think. There can be quite deep subtleties in even relatively simple natural language examples. Consider:

Example 7.4.5. Translate 'Every rose has its thorn.' into the language of elementary logic.

We use Rx for x is a rose, Tx for x is a thorn, and Hxy for x has y. We can see that the leading quantifier is universal which means that the main connective within the scope of that quantifier must be the conditional. In other words we have as a partial translation:

$$(\forall x)(Rx \supset Ty \text{ and } Hxy)$$

This might be easy after all. Since the connective in the consequent is conjunction, the rule of thumb tells us that the quantifier binding the y must be existential. In other words this would seem to be the correct translation:

$$(\forall x)(Rx \supset (\exists y)(Ty \wedge Hxy))$$

Alas it is mere seeming. It's usually a good idea to pause for a moment after a translation has been completed and ask whether *all* of the natural language has been processed. In this case honesty would compel the answer 'No.' The translation has it that every rose has a thorn, some thorn or other. But the sentence being translated says rather that every rose has *its* thorn, its own thorn which is unique to that rose. This is actually a trick question since we can't really represent the uniqueness of each rose's thorn without extending our formal language. What we need is the notion of *identity* which we shall introduce in the next chapter.

The rules of thumb are useful but sometimes their correct application requires care. Consider the sentence:

If anybody is tall, John is.

Here 'anybody' sounds as if it should be translated by the universal quantifier on two grounds. In the first place the 'any' part sounds more like 'all' than like 'some,' and in the second place the overall construction is conditional which seems to bring the first rule of thumb into play. When we look closely though, we see that the rule in question applies only to sentences in which the conditional is the main connective *within the scope of the quantifier*. If we agree to use Tx for x is tall and j for John, then the antecedent of the conditional would be represented by Tj. There is no x in this formula, and so the conditional must be the main connective of the whole sentence, which is to say that it is *not* within the scope of the quantifier.

Finally, if we ask ourselves if the universally quantified formula would make sense as the translation, we would have to answer that it didn't. This is because the universally quantified formula would say 'If *everybody* is tall, then John is.' which, though clearly true, is quite a different sentence. So the correct translation must be:

$$(\exists x)Tx \supset Tj$$

These same considerations would apply to the sentence

If anything is attractive and some attractive things hurt, then something hurts.

There is nothing in this to indicate that the conditional lies within the scope of a quantifier. This would lead us to once again translate the 'anything' by the existential quantifier. Letting Ax represent that x is attractive and Hx that x hurts we should translate the sentence by means of

$$(\exists x)(Ax \wedge (\exists y)(Ay \wedge Hy)) \supset (\exists z)Hz$$

Notice that the phrase 'some attractive things hurt' is translated by means of the second rule of thumb since we have the clearly existential 'some,' but it would still be translated that way if it read 'any attractive things hurt.' This is because we would continue to distinguish between 'any' and 'every' and we would soon come to see that it must be conjunction which connects the hurting and the attractiveness.

Is there any mutation of our sentence which would require the universal quantifier? There is only one such change: put the conditional inside the scope of the first quantifier. We can arrange that without making any change at all in the natural language quantifier phrase by simply replacing the final 'something' with 'it.' In the sentence:

If anything is attractive and some attractive things hurt, then it hurts.

the pronoun 'it' obviously refers to the same thing as the initial attractive thing in the antecedent of the conditional.

This puts the conditional inside the scope of 'anything' which must now be translated by the universal quantifier even though in the previous example the same phrase was translated by the existential quantifier. In other words, by putting the conditional inside the scope of the quantifier we have forced the first 'any' to mean 'every' as in the translation:

$$(\forall x)(Ax \land (\exists y)(Ay \land Hy) \supset Hx)$$

There are plenty of other translation problems which require extraordinary attention to nuance. For example, there are many problems associated with the so-called *intensional* predicates like 'searches for' and 'wants.' One of the problems involves non-existence. It turns out that some sentences can be true even though they would seem to embed reference to things that don't exist. For instance we can imagine that

Victor is searching for a unicorn.

is true, Victor being the unsophisticated person that he is. But we could never translate that as

$$(\exists x)(Ux \wedge Svx)$$

where Ux means x is a unicorn and Svx means Victor is searching for x. This cannot be the translation because it is false (if there are no unicorns). The usual way to solve this is to make up a predicate SUx meaning x is searching for a unicorn. Then the correct translation would be SUv.

Another problem with these predicates is a kind of inverse to the uniqueness problem we mentioned earlier. Suppose we say:

Leslie wants a girlfriend.

Our first inclination is to translate this using l for Leslie, Wxy for x wants y for a friend, and Gx for x is a female person, as:

$$(\exists x)(Gx \wedge Wlx)$$

But this actually says *more* than the sentence being translated. It says that there is some female person and Leslie wants *that specific* person as a friend. Now of course, that *might* be true. It might be that Mary is in fact the one that Leslie wants. But the sentence doesn't say that there is some specific person. Tired of being alone, Leslie wants an *unspecified* somebody, is just as likely, isn't it? For that kind of translation we must have recourse to another big predicate and use WGx for x wants a girlfriend. Then the correct translation would be WGl.

We said at the start of this section that the universal and existential quantifiers are not in any way remote from their counterparts in everyday speech. Although this is true, it requires two qualifications.

The unfortunate fact of the matter is that we frequently use a construction for negated quantification which is at odds with what we would (and should) take as a translation. To put the matter plainly, we ignore rules of syntax in the pursuit of smooth discourse. There are many examples of such a thing in ordinary speech, examples in which we use bad grammar even though we know better. We split infinitives and dangle participles and end sentences with prepositions even though we know that we aren't supposed to do these things. We do it because, quite frankly, always speaking in accord with all the rules makes us sound pedantic.

So it goes with negated universally quantified predicates. Somebody says to you 'Everybody is happy, aren't they?' and you wish to assert the contrary since you yourself are definitely not happy. To emphasize your disagreement you are more liable to say 'Everybody is *not* happy!' even though your disagreement entitles you to assert only 'Not everybody is happy!', assuming that you know for certain only that you personally are unhappy.

In such a case we should translate using $\neg(\forall x)(Px \supset Hx)$ rather than the literal $(\forall x)(Px \supset \neg Hx)$ where 'Px' indicates that x is a person and Hx that x is happy.

However natural is the formal treatment of quantification, the *language* of elementary logic is quite remote from any natural language. Translation normally produces a (formal) *paraphrase* rather than any direct account of the meaning of the sentence being translated. In many cases the best paraphrase that we can construct, given the resources of the language of elementary logic, will be awkward and extremely unnatural.

One of the differences between translating into the language of sentence logic and elementary logic is that we must have either a long or complicated formula of SL before we have something that is unlikely to serve as the translation of an actual natural language sentence. In EL quite simple formulas can be very unlikely to be the translations of any sentence in ordinary language.

A striking example of such a thing is the almost logically true

$$(\exists x)(Fx \supset Gx)$$

This does *not* say that some Fs are Gs. To say that, one would replace the $\supset$ with $\wedge$. If we try the word-for-word approach we would obtain 'There is something such that if it is an F, then it is a G.' But what does that mean? Perhaps something like 'There exists at least one thing which cannot be F without also being G' is the closest we can get. Although this may not be quite correct either.

Consider how to *falsify* the sentence. At first blush it sounds as if it requires all the *F*s in the world to be not-*G*s. But that won't do it. What is required is for *everything* in the world to be both an *F* and a not-*G*. And *this* is probably the only way to get the precise effect of the formula, to say 'If everything in the world were both *F* and not-*G* then this sentence would be false.' Put in that way, it seems that we are unlikely to require that formula to translate any sentence except for textbook examples.

As can now be seen more clearly, translation of natural language into the language of elementary logic, requires the application of *skill*. This, like other skills the logic student must somehow acquire, requires practice—the more the better. In aid of this:

7.5 Exercises

Translate each of the following sentences into the language of elementary logic.

1. Anyone who deliberates about alternative courses of action believes he is free.

    (Universe of discourse: persons; Dx = x deliberates about alternative courses of action, Bx = x believes himself to be free)

2. Some human behavior is rule following.

3. Rule-following behavior cannot be explained adequately in terms of causes.

    (Universe of discourse: human behavior; Rx = x is rule following, Cx = x can be adequately explained causally)

4. There are people who publicly praise law and order while privately encouraging defiance of law.

(Universe of discourse: persons; Px = x praises law and order publicly, Ex = x encourages defiance of law privately.)

5. If any men are lovers, they all are.

6. If a person is still young or attractive, then if all men are lovers that person is social success.

7. If an attractive man is intelligent but no longer young, then if some lovers are men he's a social success if he's a good cook.

(Universe of discourse: persons; Ax = x is a attractive, Lx = x is a lover, Mx = x is a man, Yx = x is still young, Sx = x is a social success, Ix = x is intelligent, Cx = x is a good cook)

8. There is a book which has been read by every person who has read any books.

9. Everybody has read at least one book.

(Bx = x is a book , Px = x is a person, Rxy = x has read y)

10. People like anything liked by anyone they like.

11. Not everybody dislikes everybody.

12. People like those who like them.

(Px = x is a person, Lxy = x likes y)

13. Everybody wants whatever anybody has.

14. A person has whatever is given to him.

(Px = x is a person, Wxy = x wants y, Hxy = x has y, Gxyz = x gives y to z)

15. All that glitters is not gold.

(Px = x glitters, Gx = x is gold)

7.6   Properties of Relations

In mathematics and the other sciences, relations, especially binary relations, are part of the daily diet. It is of interest in these areas (and others as well) that a standard classification scheme is adopted, and we now present a brief survey.

Definition 7.6.1. A binary relation is said to be *reflexive* when every element bears the relation to itself. In other words:

$$R \text{ is reflexive if and only if } (\forall x)Rxx$$

In graphical terms, we represent a binary relation by means of a so-called *directed graph* the way we did above in figure 7.1. On that kind of graph, a binary reflexive relation is represented by a graph in which each node has a loop as for example in figure 7.3.

As concrete examples of a reflexive binary relation, 'as good as' will serve since every element is as good as itself, and likewise the relation of similarity.

The two ways in which a binary relation might fail to be reflexive are catalogued as follows:

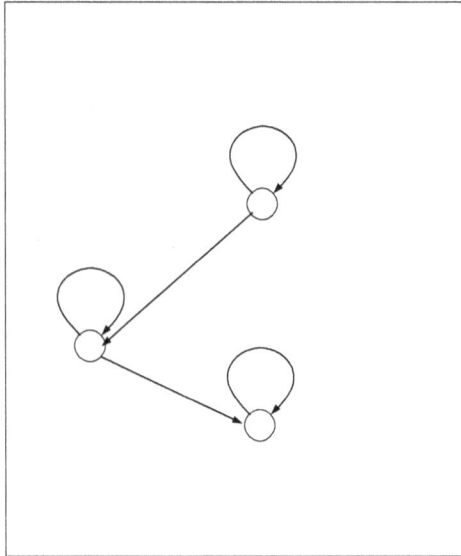

Figure 7.3: A Reflexive Binary Relation

Definition 7.6.2. A binary relation is said to be *non-reflexive* if and only if there is at least one element which does not bear the relation to itself.
A binary relation is said to be *irreflexive* if and only if no element bears the relation to itself.

The 'employs' relation in the domain of people is non-reflexive in the usual case in which not everybody is self-employed, without also being irreflexive since (normally) some people *are* self-employed. An arithmetic example with the same character is 'equals the square of.' The relations 'is better than' and 'is greater than' are both irreflexive.

Reflexivity is one of the properties which generalizes painlessly beyond the binary to the case of n-ary relations.

R^n is reflexive if and only if $(\forall x)R^n x...x$

Thus, for example, a reflexive ternary relation would satisfy:

$$(\forall x)R^3 xxx.$$

Definition 7.6.3. A binary relation is said to be *transitive* when the relation can be composed i.e. whenever the relation holds between elements x and y and between elements y and z, it also holds between x and z. In other words:

R is transitive if and only if
$$(\forall x)(\forall y)(\forall z)[Rxy \ \& \ Ryz \implies Rxz]$$

This is another of those cases in which what might look complicated or mysterious looks entirely comprehensible when presented in graphical form. In figure 7.4 the 'dashed' arrow represents the relation which is required by the definition of transitivity (i.e. the relationship mentioned in the consequent of the definition).

Two concrete examples of a transitive binary relation are 'greater than' in the domain of numbers, and "taller than" in the domain of people.

Two of the negative versions of transitivity are:

Definition 7.6.4. A binary relation is said to be *intransitive* if and only if for every triple of (not necessarily distinct) elements, if the relation holds between the first and the second and between the second and third, it does not hold between the first and third.

A binary relation is said to be *non-transitive* if and only if there are three elements (not necessarily distinct) such that the relation

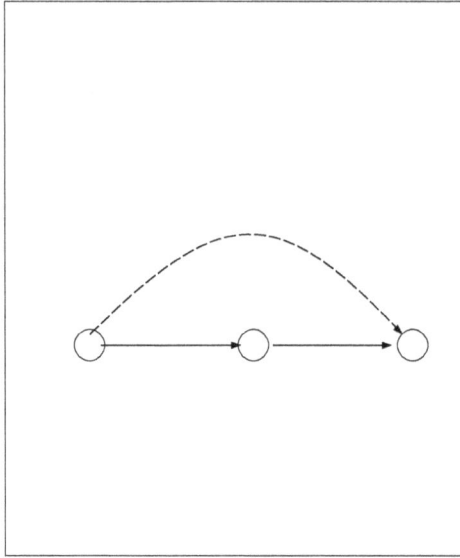

Figure 7.4: A Transitive Binary Relation

holds between the first and the second, the second and the third, but not between the first and the third.

For example, 'comes just before' in the domain of natural numbers is intransitive, as is 'comes just after.'

'Is similar to' is an example of a non-transitive relation since a might be similar to b in a certain respect while b is similar to c in a different respect and there is no respect in which a is similar to c. On the other hand, the respects might be the same ones for another triple d,e,f, in which case we would say that d is similar to f and so the relation is not also intransitive.

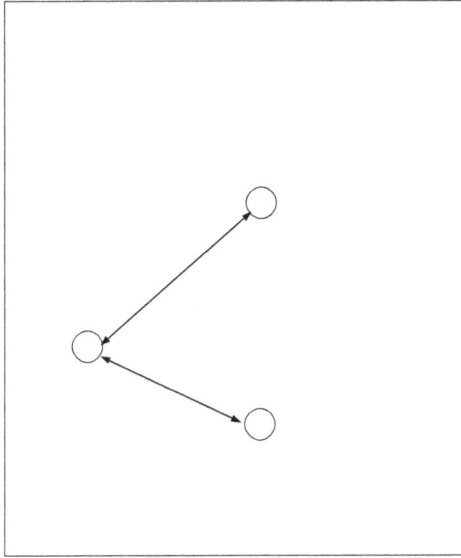

Figure 7.5: A Symmetric Binary Relation

Definition 7.6.5. A binary relation is said to be *symmetric* if whenever the relation holds between elements x and y, it holds in the reverse direction between elements y and x. In other words:

R is symmetric if and only if $(\forall x)(\forall y)[Rxy \implies Ryx]$

The graph of a symmetric relation would have only double-headed arrows between distinct nodes, as in figure 7.5.

'Is near to' is an example of a symmetric relation.

Two of the ways to negate the property of symmetry are the following:

Definition 7.6.6. A binary relation is said to be *asymmetric* if and only if whenever it holds between two (not necessarily distinct) elements x and y, it does not hold between y and x.
A binary relation is said to be *non-symmetric* if and only if there are a pair of (not necessarily distinct) elements x and y such that the relation holds between x and y but not between y and x.

'Is a parent of' in the domain of human beings, is an example of an asymmetric relation while 'is a subset of' in the domain of sets is an example of a non-symmetric relation which is not also asymmetric.

The important notion of an *equivalence relation* is defined:

Definition 7.6.7. A binary relation is an equivalence relation if and only if it has all of the properties: reflexivity, transitivity, and symmetry.

Having seen something of the workings of the language of elementary logic, we shall now go on to construct an expanded logic, one which builds upon but goes beyond CSL. We call the new logic CEL for *Classical Elementary Logic*.

7.7 Definitions and Rules of Thumb Quick Reference

We define the alphabet of EL to be:

The infinite list $A, B, C, A_1, B_1, \ldots$ of *sentence letters*

the infinite list of infinite lists

$F^1, G^1, H^1, F_2{}^1, \ldots$

$\vdots$

$F^n, G^n, H^n, F_2{}^n, \ldots$

$\vdots$

of predicates

the two infinite lists of *individual terms*

the list $a_1, b_1, c_1 \ldots$ of individual constants

the list $x_1, y_1, z_1, \ldots$ of individual variables

the list $\wedge, \vee, \supset, \equiv, \neg, \forall, \exists$ of connective and quantifier symbols

the punctuation symbols (,)

The concept of a formula of EL is defined recursively as follows:

Any sentence letter of SL and any predicate of EL followed by the appropriate number of individual terms is a formula of EL, known as an *atomic* formula (of EL)

If P and Q are formulas of EL then so are

$(P \wedge Q)$

$(P \vee Q)$

$(P \supset Q)$

$(P \equiv Q)$

$(\neg P)$

If P is a formula of EL and v is an individual variable which occurs in P then:

$(\forall v) P$ is a formula

$(\exists v) P$ is a formula

Nothing else is a formula of EL except as defined by the above clauses.

Universal-Conditional Rule of Thumb

If the main operator within the scope of the quantifier is the conditional then the quantification is universal and if the quantifier is universal then the main operator within the scope of that quantifier is the conditional.

Existential-Conjunction Rule of Thumb

If the main operator within the scope of the quantifier is conjunction then the quantification is existential and if the quantifier is existential then the main operator within the scope of that quantifier is conjunction.

Chapter 8

Proof Theory of Elementary Logic

8.1 Introduction to the New Rules

In this chapter we encounter the rules of our new logic CEL. There are only four *new* rules, at first, as we shall carry over the rules of CSL. Since we have added two new connectives to the language, we expect that there will be a pair of rules for each which introduce and eliminate ∀ and ∃. Our expectations are well founded, but there are significant differences between the new rules and the rules that deal with whole sentences in CSL.

We start by considering actual patterns of inference in ordinary or technical discourse. We sometimes (although not very often) assert a sentence about some individual, say John, because we have previously accepted an assertion about all individuals. Thus we might say that John is happy, given that everyone is happy. The only problem with such an inference is that it is too obvious. Similarly we would accept that somebody is happy, given that we have previously accepted that John is happy. This too is clearly correct reasoning, but we should notice that in passing from the premise to the conclusion, we lose information, in the same fashion that we lose information when we reason from a disjunct to a disjunction.[1]

---

[1]In fact, the situation is even worse in the quantifier case. We can think of an existentially quantified sentence, say $(\exists x)Fx$ as asserting the, possibly infinite, 'disjunction' $Fa_1 \vee \ldots \vee Fa_j \vee \ldots$ which is a much weaker claim than any real disjunction, i.e., one with only finitely

This gives us the two (nearly trivial) rules:

Universal Quantifier Elimination ([∀E])

$$(\forall v)P$$
$$\vdots$$
$$P(a/v)$$

Terminology . If v is an individual variable, $P(a/v)$ is the formula which is like P except that it has a everywhere that P has v. The formula $P(a/v)$ is called an *instance* of $(\forall v)P$.

This rule is often called *universal instantiation* abbreviated UI.

Existential Quantifier Introduction ([∃I])

$$P(a/v)$$
$$\vdots$$
$$(\exists v)P$$

This rule is sometimes called *existential generalization* abbreviated EG, even if such an expression trembles on the brink of being an oxymoron. Notice that while the use of $P(a/v)$ in the rule [∀E] implies that a replaces v wherever the variable occurs, there is no such 'everywhere' assumption for the rule [∃I] in which we go the other way. For example, the move from '$a = a$' to '$(\exists x)(x = a)$' is justified by the rule.

There can be no doubt that we *need* the rule [∃I], since it is so obviously correct and since, without it, we would be unable to demonstrate the theoremhood of sentences like
'$F(a/x) \supset (\exists x)Fx$.'
We ought to be very wary of this rule however, for the same reason that we are wary of [∨I]. We move from the stronger to the weaker, when we

---

many disjuncts

move from 'John loves Mary' to 'Somebody loves Mary.' In both cases
we know that somebody loves Mary but in the first we can actually put
a name to at least one Mary-lover. That isn't true of the second. This
leads to another rule of thumb.

Don't use the rule [∃I] *on the main scope line of a derivation.*

In fact both of these rules are so unsurprising, that one might not
expect them to be as useful or as powerful as the other rules and in this,
one would be correct. The remaining two rules are, generally speaking,
more useful, but they are of a rather different character from the first
two.

Consider, for a moment, how we actually argue that such and such
is true of *every* object in a certain class. If the class is finite we can
simply go through all the cases, at least in principle. For an infinite class
however, it is not possible to survey each of the members individually.
Suppose, for an example, that we are trying to show that the interior
angles of *every* triangle add up to two right angles. We cannot examine
all the triangles, so instead we consider a single triangle, say ABC. We
then reason about ABC *in a general way* showing that its interior angles
add up to two right angles. We end the proof by saying something like:
'Since ABC was *arbitrary*, the result holds for all triangles.'

Other phrases that one hears in similar situations are: 'arbitrarily
selected' or even 'randomly selected.' What we mean to express by
phrases like these is that nowhere in our proof do we use anything about
the particular triangle ABC. Had we appealed to a measurement with a
protractor of the angles of our depiction of the triangle ABC, this would
have been a violation of the stricture requiring the arbitrariness of ABC.

So much is clear enough that it has been used as a method for proving something in general, for thousands of years. What we need to know
is how to translate this requirement into a rule of inference to introduce
the universal quantifier in CEL. It is probably not obvious that the following formulation accomplishes the correct translation.

Universal Quantifier Introduction ([∀I])

$$\begin{array}{|l} P(a/v) \\ \vdots \\ (\forall v)P \end{array}$$

Provided

(i) *a* does not occur in any assumption of the line on which $P(a/v)$ is derived (which includes the case in which $P(a/v)$ is itself, an assumption)[2] , and

(ii) *a* does not occur in $(\forall v)P$

This is also known as *universal generalization* [UG], even if that sounds a bit redundant. *a*, in this formulation, is often called the constant upon which one *generalizes*.

The provisos to the rule, sometimes called *side conditions*, do indeed capture the notion of the constant *a* being arbitrarily selected, or that we are reasoning about *a*, in a general way. We cannot prove this at the moment, but we shall be able to prove it later, once we take up metalogical issues. What we can show right now is that if one ignores the conditions, one can utter a patently mistaken inference.

For instance, if we assume that $a < 7$ we could then derive that every number is less than 7, if we ignored the first proviso. On the other hand we could reason from the fact that $2 = 2$ to the 'fact' that every number equals 2 by ignoring the second.

These little cautionary demonstrations are usually called *counterexamples*[3] to the proposed forms of inference. To amplify what we said earlier, we can see that there are counterexamples to the versions of the rule [∀I] which omit either of the side conditions. What we don't (yet) know is whether or not there remain counterexamples to the rule we have given, which is to say we haven't yet proved that we don't require further conditions.

---

[2]The need for this point of clarification was pointed out to me by Darren Abramson.

[3]What we earlier called by this name were *value assignments* but it should be clear that this usage is closely related to the previous one.

For certain types of reasoning with existentially quantified sentences, we find ourselves with a similar need for an arbitrarily selected individual. When, for instance we say, 'Given the existence of a certain type of individual, let's call it Fred, ...' and then go on to argue *in a general way* about Fred, we can arrive at an acceptable conclusion. What we need to do is spell out what conditions must be met for us to reliably use this 'let's call it such-and-such' kind of reasoning. We give the conditions as the provisos to the rule:

Existential Quantifier Elimination ($[\exists E]$)

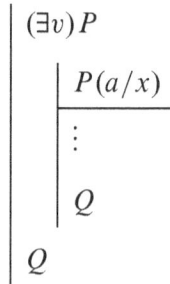

$$
\begin{array}{|l}
(\exists v)\,P \\
\quad \begin{array}{|l}
P(a/x) \\
\hline
\quad \vdots \\
Q
\end{array} \\
Q
\end{array}
$$

Provided

  (i) a does not occur in any assumption of the line on which $P(a/x)$ is derived, and

 (ii) a does not occur in $(\exists v)\,P$ and

(iii) a does not occur in Q

The rule is also called *existential instantiation* [EI], and a in this formulation is sometimes called the *instantiating constant*, or *witness*.

That these are the conditions that match only 'arbitrarily selected' constants as witnesses must be taken on faith until we are in a position to prove it later. For now, it is easy to manufacture arithmetic counterexamples to inferences which violate the conditions.[4]

---

[4]It turns out to be no accident that for every incorrect inference of elementary logic there is an arithmetic counterexample, as was proved by Georg Kreisel

It is worth mentioning that even though we call this rule existential quantifier elimination, more often than not we find ourselves using the rule to derive an existentially quantified sentence (different from the one we started with of course).

8.2   How to use the new rules

The new rules fit quite smoothly with the old rules, even though we have side conditions now that we never had previously. In general terms our counsel to new provers remains unchanged: Work backwards as far as you can. Avoid using disjunction introduction on the main scope line (except that we now add: and that goes for existential quantifier introduction as well). We do have some advice tailored specifically to quantificational reasoning and it deals with the order of subderivations.

> Always do existential quantifier elimination subderivations as early as possible in any derivation.

The reason: existential quantifier elimination imposes three conditions on the constant of instantiation. The earlier in the derivation you do this, the less likely are you to infringe one of the three—especially the proviso that forbids the use of any constant that is mentioned in an active assumption (since the earlier a subderivation occurs, the fewer will be its active assumptions).

This rule of thumb may cut against the 'work backwards!' directive from time to time, since if there are any premises which have the form of existentially quantified sentences, the natural assumption is that their use will involve existential quantifier elimination, and those should be the first subderivations to be introduced.

8.3   Common Errors

The most common sort of error committed by beginners is shown in the following:

1	$A \supset (\forall x) F x$
2	$\neg F a$
3	$A \supset F a \;\; x \to a \; (MISTAKE!)$ $\qquad$ [$\forall$E], 1
4	$\neg A$ $\qquad$ [MT], 2, 3

Here, in a mad rush to use the new rule of universal quantifier elimination, the novice prover has forgotten that the form of the rule requires
that the quantifier in question be the main operator. In the premise, the
main operator is the conditional and so the rule [$\forall$E] is not available.

8.4 Exercises

In each of the following construct a derivation in CEL of the conclusion
from the premises.

1. $\{Ga \supset (\forall x) F x, (\exists x) F x \supset Ga\}/ \therefore (\forall x)(Ga \equiv F x)$

2. $(\exists x)(\exists y) F xy \vee (\forall x)(\forall y) Gyx/ \therefore (\exists x)(\exists y)(F xy \vee Gxy)$

3. $\{(\forall x)(\neg F x \supset Gx), (\forall x)[(\neg Gx \vee F x) \equiv \neg Gx)], (\exists x)(Hx \equiv F x)\}$
   $/ \therefore \neg(\forall x)(Hx \equiv Gx)$

4. $\{(\forall x)(F x \equiv Gx), (\forall x)(Hx \equiv Ix), (\exists x)[Ix \wedge (\forall y)(Fy \supset Jy)]\}$
   $/ \therefore \exists x)[Hx \wedge (\forall y)(Jy \vee \neg Gy)]$

5. $(\forall x)(F xa \supset F xb)/ \therefore (\forall x)[(\exists y)(Gxy \wedge Fya) \supset (\exists y)(Gxy \wedge Fyb)]$

6. $\{(\forall x)(\forall y)[(F x \wedge Gy) \supset Hxy], (\exists x)(\exists y)[F x \wedge \neg Fy) \wedge \neg Hxy]\}$
   $/ \therefore (\exists x)(\neg F x \wedge \neg Gx)$

7. $\{(\forall x)(F x \supset Gx), Fa\}/ \therefore Ha \supset Ga$

8. $\{(\forall x)(Fx \supset \neg Gx), (\forall x)(Fx \wedge Hx)\}/ \therefore (\exists x)\neg Gx$

9. $(\exists x)Fx \supset (\forall x)Gx/ \therefore (\forall x)(\neg Gx \supset \neg Fx)$

10. $\{(\exists x)Fxb \supset (\forall x)Gx), (\forall x)Fax\}/ \therefore (\forall x)(Fxc \supset Gx)$

11. $\neg(\forall x)\neg Fx/ \therefore (\exists x)Fx$

12. $(\exists x)Fx \supset (\forall x)Gx/ \therefore (\forall x)(\forall y)(Fx \supset Gy)$

13. $(\exists x)Fx \wedge (\forall x)Gx/ \therefore (\exists x)(Fx \wedge Gx)$

14. $\{(\exists x)Fx, (\exists x)Gx\}/ \therefore (\exists x)[(\exists y)Fy \wedge Gx]$

15. $(\exists x)[Fx \supset (\exists y)Gy]/ \therefore (\forall x)Fx \supset (\exists x)Gx$

16. $\{(\forall x)(Fx \supset Gx), (\forall x)[(\exists y)(Gy \wedge Ixy) \supset Hx], (\exists x)[Jx \wedge (\exists y)(Fy \wedge Ixy)]\}$
$/ \therefore (\exists x)(Jx \wedge Hx)$

Selected Solutions for Exercises 8.4

1. $\{Ga \supset (\forall x)Fx, (\exists x)Fx \supset Ga\}/ \therefore (\forall x)(Ga \equiv Fx)$

This looks easy and it is, except that you have to realize that the premises are *not* quantified sentences. So we start in the usual way:

$$
\begin{array}{c|l}
1 & Ga \supset (\forall x)Fx \\
2 & (\exists x)(Fx) \supset Ga \\
\vdots & \vdots \\
n & (\forall x)(Ga \equiv Fx)
\end{array}
$$

Working backwards from the conclusion we expect it to follow from an instance by universal quantification introduction. Keeping in mind the side conditions on that rule we know that the constant upon which we generalize cannot be a since that occurs in an active assumption (in this case both premises). For that reason we pick the constant b. So the derivation, we now think, is going to look like:

$$
\begin{array}{c|l}
1 & Ga \supset (\forall x)Fx \\
2 & (\exists x)(Fx) \supset Ga \\
\vdots & \vdots \\
n-1 & Ga \equiv Fb \\
n & (\forall x)(Ga \equiv Fx) \qquad [\forall\mathrm{I}], n-1
\end{array}
$$

At this point our CSL skills come into play since what we have to derive is a biconditional. We know that we do that by doing two sub-derivations, one above the other just above where we want to conclude the biconditional. One of the subderivations starts with Fb and concludes with Ga and the other starts with Ga and concludes with Fb. So what we have is this:

1	$Ga \supset (\forall x)Fx$	
2	$(\exists x)(Fx) \supset Ga$	
3	$\quad Ga$	
$\vdots$	$\quad \vdots$	
k	$\quad Fb$	
$k+1$	$\quad Fb$	
$\vdots$	$\quad \vdots$	
$n-2$	$\quad Ga$	
$n-1$	$Ga \equiv Fb$	$[\equiv I],\ 3\text{--}k,\ k+1\text{--}n-2$
n	$(\forall x)(Ga \equiv Fx)$	$[\forall I],\ n-1$

At this point it ought to be pretty easy to fill in the blanks. First the upper subderivation.

1	$Ga \supset (\forall x)Fx$	
2	$(\exists x)(Fx) \supset Ga)$	
3	Ga	
4	$(\forall x)Fx$	[$\supset$E], 1, 3
5	Fb	[$\forall$E], 4
6	Fb	
$\vdots$	$\vdots$	
$n-2$	Ga	
$n-1$	$Ga \equiv Fb$	[$\equiv$I], 3–5, 6–$n-2$
n	$(\forall x)(Ga \equiv Fx)$	[$\forall$I], $n-1$

And the lower subderivation is similarly easy:

1	$Ga \supset (\forall x)Fx$	
2	$(\exists x)(Fx) \supset Ga$	
3	$\quad Ga$	
4	$\quad (\forall x)Fx$	[$\supset$E], 1, 3
5	$\quad Fb$	[$\forall$E], 4
6	$\quad Fb$	
7	$\quad (\exists x)(Fx)$	[$\exists$I], 6
8	$\quad Ga$	[$\supset$E], 2, 7
9	$Ga \equiv Fb$	[$\equiv$I], 3–5, 6–8
10	$(\forall x)(Ga \equiv Fx)$	[$\forall$I], 9

3. $\{(\forall x)(\neg Fx \supset Gx), (\forall x)[(\neg Gx \vee Fx) \equiv \neg Gx)], (\exists x)(Hx \equiv Fx)\}$
$/ \therefore \neg(\forall x)(Hx \equiv Gx)$

This one looks a little trickier because it's always more difficult to work with equivalences and we also see that we have an existentially quantified premise. First the bare bones:

1	$(\forall x)(\neg Fx \supset Gx)$
2	$(\forall x)((\neg Gx \vee Fx) \equiv \neg Gx)$
3	$(\exists x)(Hx \equiv Fx)$
$\vdots$	$\vdots$
n	$\neg(\forall x)(Hx \equiv Gx)$

At this point we need to restrain our enthusiasm to use the quantifier rules. Notice that the conclusion is a *negation* which we presumably derive by means of the rule of negation introduction. In other words our derivation develops like this:

1	$(\forall x)(\neg F x \supset G x)$
2	$(\forall x)((\neg G x \vee F x) \equiv \neg G x)$
3	$(\exists x)(H x \equiv F x)$
4	$(\forall x)(H x \equiv G x)$
⋮	⋮
$n - 1$	$\bot$
n	$\neg(\forall x)(H x \equiv G x)$ [¬E], 4–$n - 1$

But now we see there is another rule we should apply, namely the one which says to do the existential quantifier elimination early. We already know what we want to conclude, so we are now saying that we think the derivation will look like this:

1	$(\forall x)(\neg F x \supset G x)$	
2	$(\forall x)((\neg G x \vee F x) \equiv \neg G x)$	
3	$(\exists x)(H x \equiv F x)$	
4	$(\forall x)(H x \equiv G x)$	
5	$H a \equiv F a$	
$\vdots$	$\vdots$	
$n - 2$	$\bot$	
$n - 1$	$\bot$	$[\exists E]$, 3, 5–$n - 2$
n	$\neg(\forall x)(H x \equiv G x)$	$[\neg I]$, 4–n

Notice that the three side conditions on the rule [∃E] have been met. Now we have to decide which formula and its negation we shall derive. This is the tricky bit—we look to see what negations we can get and there are two: $\neg F$ and $\neg G$. Now we try to judge how difficult it would be to get either of them, and having got them, how difficult it would be to get the un-negated formula as well. As a preliminary to this we shall instantiate the two universally quantified premises and the universally quantified assumption at line 3, in order to see more clearly what we have to work with. It ought to be clear that we should use the same constant as we used for the witness in assumption 5.

1	$(\forall x)(\neg F x \supset G x)$	
2	$(\forall x)((\neg G x \vee F x) \equiv \neg G x)$	
3	$(\exists x)(H x \equiv F x)$	
4	$\quad (\forall x)(H x \equiv G x)$	
5	$\quad\quad H a \equiv F a$	
6	$\quad\quad \neg F a \supset G a$	[$\forall$E], 1
7	$\quad\quad (\neg G a \vee F a) \equiv \neg G a$	[$\forall$E], 2
8	$\quad\quad H a \equiv G a$	[$\forall$E], 5
⋮	$\quad\quad$ ⋮	
$n-2$	$\quad\quad \bot$	
$n-1$	$\quad \bot$	[$\exists$E], 3, 5–$n - 2$
n	$\neg(\forall x)(H x \equiv G x)$	[$\neg$I], 4–$n - 1$

This is an awful lot to work with and there is probably more than one contradiction to be got here. If we scan the resources it seems that if we assume Fa we can easily derive a contradiction which means that $\neg Fa$ would follow. That would make the derivation look like this:

1	$(\forall x)(\neg Fx \supset Gx)$	
2	$(\forall x)((\neg Gx \vee Fx) \equiv \neg Gx)$	
3	$(\exists x)(Hx \equiv Fx)$	
4	$(\forall x)(Hx \equiv Gx)$	
5	$Ha \equiv Fa$	
6	$\neg Fa \supset Ga$	[$\forall$E], 1
7	$(\neg Ga \vee Fa) \equiv \neg Ga$	[$\forall$E], 2
8	$Ha \equiv Ga$	[$\forall$E], 5
9	Fa	
10	Ha	[$\equiv$E], 5, 9
11	Ga	[$\equiv$E], 8, 10
12	$\neg Ga \vee Fa$	[$\vee$I], 9
13	$\neg Ga$	[$\equiv$E], 7, 12
14	$\perp$	[$\perp$I], 11, 13
15	$\neg Fa$	[$\neg$E], 9–14
$\vdots$	$\vdots$	
$n-2$	$\perp$	
$n-1$	$\perp$	[$\exists$E], 3, 5–$n-2$
n	$\neg(\forall x)(Hx \equiv Gx)$	[$\neg$E], 4–$n-1$

But once we have $\neg Fa$ we get Ga by conditional elimination and then we have Ha form biconditional elimination and finally Fa by means of another biconditional elimination, and the thing is done. Here it is all nicely written out:

1	$(\forall x)(\neg Fx \supset Gx)$	
2	$(\forall x)((\neg Gx \vee Fx) \equiv \neg Gx)$	
3	$(\exists x)(Hx \equiv Fx)$	
4	$(\forall x)(Hx \equiv Gx)$	
5	$Ha \equiv Fa$	
6	$\neg Fa \supset Ga$	[$\forall$E], 1
7	$(\neg Ga \vee Fa) \equiv \neg Ga$	[$\forall$E], 2
8	$Ha \equiv Ga$	[$\forall$E], 5
9	Fa	
10	Ha	[$\equiv$E], 5, 9
11	Ga	[$\equiv$E], 8, 10
12	$\neg Ga \vee Fa$	[$\vee$I], 9
13	$\neg Ga$	[$\equiv$E], 7, 12
14	$\perp$	[$\perp$I], 11, 13
15	$\neg Fa$	[$\neg$E], 9–14
16	Ga	[$\supset$E], 6, 15
17	Ha	[$\equiv$E], 8, 16
18	Fa	[$\equiv$E], 5, 17
19	$\perp$	[$\perp$I], 15, 18
20	$\perp$	[$\exists$E], 3, 5–19
21	$\neg(\forall x)(Hx \equiv Gx)$	[$\neg$E], 4–20

8.5 Key Definitions

We need not take a great deal of trouble to produce definitions of derivation, proves, (syntactically) consistent, and the rest, even though we have extended our earlier sentential logic by a large margin. This is because we can take over the earlier definitions in terms of CSL simply replacing the latter name by CEL in every case.

For example:

Definition 8.5.1. $\Gamma \vdash P$ in CEL if and only if there is a derivation in CEL of P from Γ.

Similarly:

Definition 8.5.2. The logic CEL is defined as the set of all pairs Γ, P such that $\Gamma \vdash P$ in CEL.

---

and so on for the other definitions.

8.6 Derivable Rules in CEL

We have already encountered the notion of *duality* when we spoke of the relationship between the semantic definitions of $\vee$ and $\wedge$. This is in fact the relationship which is exposed by the replacement rules named [DeM], and which we might define more generally:

Definition 8.6.1. Two n-place connectives represented by $f(p_1, \ldots, p_n)$ and $g(p_1, \ldots, p_n)$ are said to be *dual* to each other if and only if:

$g(p_1, \ldots, p_n)$ is equivalent to $\neg f(\neg p_1, \ldots, \neg p_n)$ and

$f(p_1, \ldots, p_n)$ is equivalent to $\neg g(\neg p_1, \ldots, \neg p_n)$

It turns out that $\forall$ and $\exists$ are dual in exactly this sense, which we signal by producing the following rule of replacement called *Quantifier Negation* [QN]:

$$\neg(\forall v)P \longleftrightarrow (\exists v)\neg P$$

$$\neg(\exists v)P \longleftrightarrow (\forall v)\neg P$$

8.7 Exercises

In each of the following, construct a derivation of the conclusion from the premises. The use of derived rules is allowed.

1. $\{(\forall x)(Fx \supset (\forall y)(Gy \supset Hxy)), (\forall x)(Dx \supset (\forall y)(Hxy \supset Cy))\}$
   $/ \therefore (\exists x)(Fx \wedge Dx) \supset (\forall y)(Gy \supset Cy)$

2. $\{(\forall x)((Fx \lor Hx) \supset (Gx \land Kx)), \neg(\forall x)(Kx \land Gx)\}/ \therefore (\exists x)\neg Hx$

3. $(\exists x)(Fx \land (\forall y)(Gy \supset Hxy))/ \therefore (\exists x)(Fx \land (Ga \supset Hxa))$

4. $\{(\forall x)(\forall y)(Gxy \equiv (Fy \supset Hx)), (\forall z)Gaz\}/ \therefore (\exists x)Fx \supset (\exists x)Hx$

5. $\{(\forall x)(Mx \supset Hx), (\exists x)(\exists y)((Fx \land Mx) \land (Gy \land Jyx)), (\exists x)Hx \supset (\forall y)(\forall z)(\neg Hy \supset \neg Jyz)\}/ \therefore (\exists x(Gx \land Hx)$

6. $\{(\forall x)[(\exists y)Fxy \supset (\forall y)Fyx], (\exists x)(\exists y)Fxy\}/ \therefore (\forall x)(\forall y)Fxy$

7. $(\forall x)(Fx \equiv Gx)/ \therefore (\forall x)Fx \equiv (\forall x)Gx$

8. $(\forall x)(Fx \equiv Gx)/ \therefore (\exists x)Fx \equiv (\exists x)Gx$

9. $(\exists x)(Fx \supset Gx)/ \therefore (\forall x)Fx \supset (\exists x)Gx$

10. $\{(\exists x)(Fx \land (\forall y)(Gy \supset Hy)), (\forall x)(Fx \supset (\neg Lx \supset \neg(\exists z)(Kz \land Hz)))\}$
    $/ \therefore (\exists x)(Kx \land Gx) \supset (\exists x)Lx$

11. $\{(\exists x)(\forall y)[(\exists z)Fyz \supset Fyx], (\forall x)(\exists y)Fxy\}/ \therefore (\exists x)(\forall y)Fyx$

8.8 Identity

There are a lot of problems, philosophical and otherwise, about treating identity as what we have been calling a *logical word* (see page 13). Some people have even alleged that identity is not a logical word at all, but belongs to some less general science—mathematics perhaps. Even classical logicians are split on this point. What is the source of the controversy?

Notice that unlike the other logical words which are connectives,[5] identity is a *predicate*. Why should one predicate have the status of a logical word while another, set-membership for instance, be relegated

---

[5]Even the quantifiers, although the notion of connective must be attenuated to cover the case in which open sentences are connected.

to the status of a mathematical notion only? This is a tough question to answer, so tough that there have been logicians who thought that set-membership (in general, set-theory) is indeed a part of logic. They are in the minority.

Those who wish to argue on the side of identity being a logical word are quick to point out that nowhere is it made explicit that only connectives can be logical words. That is certainly no part of the classical approach, as it has come to be understood. They also point out that any of the other predicates which we wish to formalize, like set-membership, *require* that identity already be defined. If indeed the concept of identity has such *conceptual priority* then perhaps it does make sense to call it a logical notion.

On the other hand, what are the principles which govern reasoning about identity, and can they be replicated within elementary logic? This is a somewhat more difficult matter.

First we introduce some technical terminology. We shall assume that the symbol $=$ (read 'equals') has been added to the alphabet of our language, which expanded language will be called ELI and the definition of formula suitably amended.

Terminology. A formula of the kind $a = b$ is said to be an *equation*.

Terminology. A formula of the kind $(\forall x)(\forall y)x = y$ (in general any universally quantified '=' formula)is said to be an *identity assertion* or simply an *identity*.

We shall often indicate that the '=' relation doesn't hold by using the same symbol with a strike-through.

Definition 8.8.1. '$x \neq y$' for '$\neg(x = y)$'

Now we ask how an identity is to be introduced into a derivation. Most identities come from previously introduced identities. That is, most of what we count as reasoning using the symbol '=,' consists of reasoning from one identity (or batch of identities) to another. But there must be some way of getting the whole chain off the ground without appeal to the very thing we are trying to establish. There is indeed a *basic* identity which we might think of as the prototypical logical truth involving identity:

$(\forall x)x = x$

In effect the rule we adopt for introducing an identity says that this *is* a logical truth or theorem, and hence can be written anywhere in any derivation.

Identity Introduction [=I]

$$\vdots$$
$$(\forall x)x = x$$

When we eliminate an identity, we usually have an equation and from that we substitute equals for equals in some other expression which contains at least one of the terms mentioned in the equation. We shall stick close to this ordinary way of doing things but we must make precise what we mean by the substitution involved.

Terminology . If P is any formula then $P(a//b)$ is the formula which is like P except for having an occurrence of a in 0 or more places in which P has an occurrence of b.

Since equality is a symmetric relation, when we substitute equals for equals we have our choice of directions. In other words the rule of identity elimination has two possible forms.

Identity Elimination [=E]

$$
\begin{array}{|l}
\vdots \\
a = b* \\
\vdots \\
P* \\
P(a//b)
\end{array}
$$

$$
\begin{array}{|l}
\vdots \\
a = b* \\
\vdots \\
P* \\
P(b//a)
\end{array}
$$

Clearly these rules are not derivable in CEL so that by adding them we are producing a logic which extends the classical logic of elements. We shall refer to the new logic as CELI which suggests 'Classical Elementary Logic with Identity.' We assume the key definitions have been recast in terms of the extended logic.

8.9   Exercises

In each of the following construct a derivation of the conclusion from the premises using the derivation rules of CELI.

1. $a = b \land \neg Bab /\therefore \neg(\forall x)Bxx$

2. $\{Ge \supset d = e, Ge \supset He\}/\therefore Ge \supset Hd$

3. $\{(\forall z)[Gz \supset (\forall y)(Ky \supset Hzy)], (Ki \land Gj) \land i = j\}/\therefore Hii$

4. $\{(\exists x)(Hx \land Mx), Ms \land \neg Hs\}/\therefore (\exists x)[(Hx \land Mx) \land \neg(x = s)]$

5. $a = b/\therefore Ka \lor \neg Kb$

8.10 Some Puzzles

This is all very well, but is it *identity*? We could imagine objects satisfying some 'lesser' relation than identity, and still allowing these rules. What we mean by lesser here is that the relation in question identifies objects which aren't *really* identical.

Definition 8.10.1. Two objects a and b are said to be *indiscernible* if and only if, for every property **P**, a has **P** if and only if b does.

Indiscernible objects would satisfy the previously given rules for identity, but should we count these as identical?

Some might respond that this worry is a paranoid fantasy, that Leibnitz has shown us both that identicals are indiscernible and that indiscernibles are identical. But if these are both correct principles of reasoning about identity, then they must be the true rules of inference. [=E] might be thought of as a version of the rule of indiscernibility of identicals, but what of the other direction? The problem with that direction, with stating something like the rule of identity of indiscernibles, is that it can't really be *said* in the language of elementary logic.

The only way we have to translate 'property' is our notion of a predicate, and that notion seems to fit very well. What doesn't fit at all is *quantifying over* predicates. In elementary logic we are permitted to quantify over elements, and no other sort of quantification is permitted. Another, standard way of saying this is to classify quantification over individuals or elements as *first-order*. Quantification over predicates of individuals is said to be *second-order*, while quantification over predicates of predicates (of elements) is *third-order* and so on.

Somebody could argue that if we give up the identity of indiscernibles we might save ourselves a lot of worry about higher-order logic. This proposal would seem to suffer the defect of requiring us to give up something true. Certainly in its most intuitive form the principle must be true. One of the properties of a is *being identical to a*. So if b has every property of a it must follow that a and b are identical.

What we might say then is that the best we can do in CELI is to formalize a first-order *approximation* of the identity relation (on individuals). And that a full account of the identity relation on individuals actually requires a second-order formalization.

8.11   Relational Properties Revisited

The notion of identity is required when we want to present certain alternative ways of talking about the negative version of relations. Consider the property of symmetry for instance. If there are a pair of elements for which a relation, say R, holds between the two in one direction but not in the other, we say that the relation is *non-symmetric* (definition 7.6). If a relation is non-symmetric there may be objects which it relates in both directions, just so long as not all pairs satisfy that condition. We can make this negation stronger, if we were to say it never holds in both directions, to say that if it holds in one direction it doesn't hold in the other.

Recall definition 7.6 which says that a relation R is asymmetric if and only if

$$(\forall x)(\forall y)(Rxy \supset \neg Ryx)$$

That certainly won't permit the relation to hold in both directions, but at a certain cost which we might find burdensome. Suppose x and y are the same, then the condition forbids reflexivity. In other words, this version of 'strong' non-symmetry has the consequence that

$$(\forall x)(Rxx \supset \neg Rxx)$$

which is just another way of saying

$$(\forall x)(\neg Rxx)$$

See exercise 8.12.

To get round this unfortunate feature, we define the notion of anti-symmetry.

Definition 8.11.1. We say that a relation R is *antisymmetric* if no two distinct elements can each bear the relation to one another.

$$(\forall x)(\forall y)(Rxy \wedge Ryx \supset x = y)$$

So when we wish to prevent all symmetry except for the reflexive loops, the notion of antisymmetry is what we should use. This is all very theoretical.

For more concrete examples, the relations $\leq$ and $\geq$ (less than or equal, and greater than or equal, respectively) defined on the integers, and $\subseteq$ (subset) defined on sets, are all antisymmetric. The strict versions of these relations, $<$ (strictly less than), $>$ (strictly greater than) and $\subset$ (proper subset) are all asymmetric.

We defined the property of antisymmetry in order that we needn't ban reflexivity in our zeal to root out symmetry. Something similar is needed for transitive relations, although in the latter case we are more concerned about forcing reflexivity to hold *volens nolens*. If we ask that a relation be provided which is fitted out with symmetry and transitivity, we shall obtain reflexivity as a possibly unintended bonus (see number 4 of the next exercise). To prevent this, we define a variant of transitivity.

Definition 8.11.2. We say that a binary relation is *quasi-transitive* if and only if the relation is required to compose for distinct elements only. In other words:

$$(\forall x)(\forall y)(\forall z)((Rxy \wedge Ryz \wedge x \neq z) \supset Rxz)$$

For example, the relation of 'is different from' in any domain is quasi-transitive without also being transitive.

8.12 Exercises

In the following expressions we say 'relation' meaning 'binary relation,'

1. Show that an asymmetric relation cannot be reflexive.

2. Show that if a relation is symmetrical and intransitive, it is also irreflexive.

3. Show that if a relation is transitive and irreflexive, it is also asymmetric.

4. Show that for a transitive and symmetric relation, every pair of elements in the relation has both elements in the pair related to themselves.

8.13   Numerical Quantification

In ordinary life we often quantify using numbers in the manner of 'There are two lions in my backyard.' Now that we have admitted identity into the fold, we may translate such expressions. What we require that we didn't have before (see example 7.4.5 on page 226 for instance) is a way to express *distinctness*. Let Lx stand for x is a lion, and Bx for x is in my backyard. Then our translation would be:

[L2L] $(\exists x)(\exists y)(Lx \wedge Bx \wedge Ly \wedge By \wedge x \neq y))$

If we think about the matter a bit we shall see that we have taken a liberty or two in this translation. The formula we produced says 'There are *at least* two lions in my backyard.' Is that what 'There are two lions in my backyard.' really amounts to? It isn't clear. That certainly is a possibility but it may not be the intended reading—what we might think of as the *normal* reading. It depends, as do so many other translation questions, on the context.

> I could really use some lions—I don't suppose you might be able to help me out?
> Why yes, there are two lions in my backyard.

as opposed to

> I'd like to wrestle two lions, though I don't think I'd be able to manage more.
> Just drop by my place, there are two lions in my backyard.

In the second context, it seems to be implied that there are no more than two lions although this is not perhaps so clear in the first.

We clearly need to be able to use upper bounds as well as lower ones. To translate 'There are at most two lions in my backyard.' we should use the formula:

[M2L] $(\exists x)((\exists y)(Lx \wedge Bx \wedge Ly \wedge By) \wedge (\forall z)((Lz \wedge Bz) \supset (x = z \vee y = z)))$

We now define a useful predicate[6] which expresses that some items a_1 through a_n are all distinct from one another. The difference between this sort of predicate and the ones to which we have previously been exposed is that the earlier examples were of fixed degree, But the predicate DIS is defined for every finite degree greater than 1 (evidently no element can be distinct from itself). Such a predicate of no fixed degree, we shall call *schematic*.

Definition 8.13.1. We define the notion that two or more elements are distinct by means of a schematic predicate:

$\text{DIS}(a_1 \ldots a_n) \Longleftrightarrow$

$a_1 \neq a_2 \wedge \ldots a_1 \neq a_n \wedge$

$a_2 \neq a_3 \wedge \ldots \wedge a_2 \neq a_n \wedge$

$\vdots$

$a_{n-1} \neq a_n$

It should be obvious that if we put [L2L] and [M2L] together (which we can accomplish by simply adding the distinctness clause to the first list of conjuncts, i.e. adding $x \neq y$)), we can use the new formula to translate 'There are exactly two lions in my backyard.'

We shall generalize upon our examples to formalize 'There are at least n elements x, such that Fx.' 'There are at most n elements x, such that Fx.' and 'There are exactly n elements x such that Fx.' The formal definitions in order:

---

[6]This repairs an earlier unclear passage pointed out to me by Darren Abramson

---

Definition 8.13.2.

$$(\exists_n x)(Fx) \iff$$
$$(\exists x_1) \ldots (\exists x_n)(F x_1 \wedge \ldots \wedge F x_n \wedge \text{DIS}(x_1 \ldots x_n))$$

$$(\exists^n x)(Fx) \iff (\exists x_1) \ldots (\exists x_n)(F x_1 \wedge \ldots \wedge F x_n \wedge$$
$$(\forall y)(Fy \supset (y = x_1 \vee \ldots \vee y = x_n)))$$

$$(\exists! n x)(Fx) \iff (\exists x_1) \ldots (\exists x_n)(F x_1 \wedge \ldots \wedge F x_n \wedge$$
$$\text{DIS}(x_1 \ldots x_n) \wedge (\forall y)(Fy \supset (y = x_1 \vee \ldots \vee y = x_n)))$$

When n is 1, we usually omit the numerical sub or super-script.

8.14 Exercises

1. Translate 'All but two of the people in the room were happy.'

2. Translate 'No fewer than three people danced.'

8.15 Identity and Singular Terms

Introducing identity allows us to consider certain related issues involving *existence*. For example, look at the following inference:

John loves Mary.

Therefore, there is someone who is Mary.

We shall use the constants a, b to represent John and Mary respectively and the phrase 'someone who is Mary' we shall take to be translated by '$x = b$.' It follows that the inference should be translated as follows if 'L' represents 'loves:'

(Ex) $Lab \therefore (\exists x)(x = b)$

Is this a valid inference? We are pulled in two different directions.

On the one hand we want to say that the inference is as valid as 'John loves Mary, therefore someone loves Mary,' which is simply an application of [$\exists$I] in an intuitive setting. To say this is to say that singular terms have a property which is usually called *existential import*. This seems to be the classical view of things,[7] although in CELI the conclusion of the inference is a theorem, so the inference is indeed valid, but trivially.[8]

On the other hand, there seem to be plenty of sentences which we would count as true, in which there is no existential import. Consider the following examples:[9]

Zeus is not identical with Allah.

The ancient Greeks worshipped Zeus.

The accident was prevented.

The predicted storm did not occur.

True believers fear Beelzebub.

In so far as we wish to call any or all of these sentences true, to that extent do we incline toward a non-classical view of singular terms in which not all terms actually refer to something.

The term *free logic* has been used to refer to this kind of approach[10]— the idea being that such a logic has been freed of unwarranted existence assumptions.

---

[7]In *De Interpretatione* 21a, 26-28; Aristotle asks whether 'Homer is' follows from 'Homer is a poet.' Some commentators state that his answer is negative, which would mean that Aristotle's logic is non-classical.

[8]If one thought, which may or may not be compatible with the classical view, that 'John loves Mary' (or some similar premise) must play an essential role in the derivation of 'There is somebody who is Mary' then our account is stronger than the classical one.

[9]These examples are due to Bas van Fraassen and Karel Lambert, and may be found in their book van Fraassenn and Lambert (1972)

[10]Karel Lambert seems to have coined this term. The interested reader should consult the book: van Fraassenn and Lambert (1972). In the following passages, especially on the form of the quantifier rules in Free Logic and the question of whether or not definite descriptions are singular terms, we follow the book quite closely.

If we were to take the radical step of allowing that the individual constants may or may not refer to something, this must have consequences for our rules of inference. We wouldn't want to allow as valid:

Ponce de Leon was searching for the fountain of youth.

Therefore, there is something which is a fountain of youth.

This suggests what we take as a proviso to [∃I] that we can derive $(\exists x)Fx$ from Fa only provided $(\exists y)(a = y)$.

A side effect of this new rule is that in free logic we seem to be able to handle at least some of the translations involving intensional predicates without recourse to so-called big predicates. Contrast the treatment just given with the one on page 228.

Similarly we wouldn't want to allow:

Everything exists, therefore Pegasus exists.

So the same kind of proviso would be have to be imposed upon the rule [∀E].

In other words, in the free version of our logic we would have:

Universal Quantifier Elimination (free logic version) ([∀E(F)])

$$(\forall v)P*$$
$$\vdots$$
$$(\exists x)(x = a)*$$
$$\vdots$$
$$P(a/v)$$

Existential Quantifier Introduction (Free version) ([∃I(F)])

$$P(a/v)*$$
$$\vdots$$
$$(\exists x)(x = a)*$$
$$\vdots$$
$$(\exists v)P$$

These are subtle and difficult issues. If we are only allowed to instantiate a universally quantified formula using constants which refer, it would follow that only referring terms are self-identical—provided we keep the other rules the same. In other words $a = a$ if and only if $(\exists x)(x = a)$.[11] It has seemed to some people that such an equivalence is not part of the classical picture.

We shall refer to the 'free' version of CELI as FELI. In other words FELI is like CELI except that it uses the (F) version of the rules for universal quantifier elimination and existential quantifier introduction.

It was at the beginning of the 20th Century that these issues came to the fore in connection with formal logic. The philosopher and logician Bertrand Russell devised a theory which was designed to solve all (or at least most) of these problems about reference. That theory has come to be called *Russell's theory of definite descriptions*.[12]

Singular Terms and Definite Descriptions

Russell was concerned with what to him seemed the bizarre consequences of allowing singular terms which do not refer. These concerns arose in connection with a number of claims made by the Austrian philosopher Alexius Meinong[13] concerning truth and existence. Meinong's view is one which we have glanced at already, though not under that name. He remarks that even though a term may not refer, yet still it can participate in the construction of a true sentence. Meinong claims being thus-and-so (*Sosein* in German) is independent of being (*Sein*).[14] Even though the golden mountain does not exist, 'The golden mountain is golden' is true. Further, even though the round square *cannot* exist, it remains true that the round square is round. So the general principal to which Meinong subscribed could be put:

Meinong's Law [ML] The thing which is F, is F

---

[11] Since we would derive $a = a$ from $(\forall x)(x = x)$ introduced by [=I].

[12] This theory was first presented in Russell's 1905 paper 'On denoting' although many important features of the theory (all of them, according to R.J. Butler) were anticipated in Russell's famous *Principles of Mathematics*.

[13] The volume *Realism and the Background of Phenomenology*. R. Chisholm (ed.), The Free Press, 1960, contains a translation of some of the relevant work of Meinong.

[14] *Ibid.*, p.82.

And given the impossibility of 'the round square,' Meinong must side with Aristotle on the question of whether or not true predication implies existence; which is to say that both of them would reject 'If t is F, then t exists.'

What we notice first about definite descriptions is that it is very easy for them to fail. When we say 'The man on the corner is a fool', there are two situations in which we fail to refer to anybody in using those words. If there is nobody on the corner, then there is no man, and so the description does not refer. Similarly if there are two men on the corner then there is no *the* man, and once again our attempted description fails. So if we were to allow, as Meinong (and many others) suggest, that descriptions are terms, then we must allow that terms sometimes fail to refer to anything.

Russell objected[15] that [ML] has two unpleasant consequences that anybody would prefer to avoid. In the case of the round square, we have as a consequence of [ML] to the round square:

> M1: The thing which is round and not round is round, and it is also not round

while applying [ML] to the golden mountain gives us:

> M2: The existent golden mountain is an existent golden mountain.

Meinong's comeback was to say of M2 that the existent golden mountain is an existent, but that it doesn't exist. In response to M1, Meinong said that the law of non-contradiction does not apply to non-existents. It was generally thought in the Anglo-American philosophical world at least, that Meinong's response was inadequate.

Russell's diagnosis of the problem was that we have been misled by surface grammar. Once we realize that the *logical form* of a sentence can be very different from its surface or grammatical form, we can break free of the idea that definite descriptions are *any* kind of singular term. It *looks* as if an expression like 'The man on the corner' is a term; a

---

[15]Russell's side of this debate is reported in the articles he published in *Mind* during the years 1904-1905. This of course includes his famous *On Denoting* Russell (1905).

piece of language which is used to secure reference to some thing. But that is mere appearance. We can provide a logical form for sentences which embed that kind of expression and contain *nothing* referential at all. This frees us from the temptation to allow non-referring singular terms, and lets us settle the issue of [M] and related properties, in a more satisfactory way.

Russell proposes that the logical form of 'The such-and-such is so-and-so' is given by the conjunction of:

(1) There is at least one such-and-such

(2) there is at most one such-and -such

(3) Whatever is such-and-such is so-and-so

Let us introduce the notation ιx to stand for the definite descriptive 'the x.' We shall read '$(\iota x)Fx$' as 'The x such that F,' or more colloquially as 'The F.' The Russell proposal amounts to saying that any formula of the sort $G(\iota x)Fx$ will be true just in case

(Rus) $(\exists y)(Fy \wedge (\forall x)(Fx \supset x = y) \wedge Gy)$

is true.

We can see that on this translation of sentences containing definite descriptions, if the description fails to refer then the sentence is false. If there is no golden mountain, then the first conjunct is false and so is the whole conjunction.

There remains a problem for Russell which we might put this way: Whether or not the golden mountain is made of gold, the golden mountain is the golden mountain. Everything is identical to itself, after all— we have made that one of our rules of inference for $=$. Suppose Gx stands for 'x is a golden mountain', then 'The golden mountain is identical to the golden mountain' would be translated by:

$$(\exists y)(Gy \wedge (\forall x)(Gx \supset x = y) \wedge Hy)$$

where Hy stands for the expression 'y is identical to the golden mountain.' We don't need to worry about how to unpack H because we already know that the whole sentence is false since the first conjunct is. Russell would agree that this looks bad but, he would go on to say, it *only looks* bad. It looks as if we are attempting to deny that $t = t$ for some term t, and thus flying in the face of our own introduction rule for identity, but we have to remember that *there isn't any term* in the sentence. 'The golden mountain' is the grammatical subject to be sure but that doesn't mean that it's a term; what Russell would call a *logical subject*. The whole point of Russell's theory is to deny that definite descriptions are terms at all, and thus to avoid falling into Meinong's swamp of being.

Russell's position on the issue of whether or not definite descriptions are singular terms has so far been all *negative*. He has listed the bad consequences of saying that they are and tried to deal with what might be thought a bad consequence of *his* view. But we should consider also two *positive* arguments in favor of the view.

In the first argument he considers the statement that 'George IV wished to know whether Scott was the author of *Waverly*, but he did not wish to know whether Scott was Scott.' He says:

> As we have just seen, you may turn a true proposition into a false one by substituting "Scott" for "the author of *Waverly*." This shows that it is necessary to distinguish between a name and a description: "Scott" is a name, but "the author of *Waverly*" is a description.[16]

For Russell, names (it would be better to say *purely referential names* here[17]) are the only real singular terms, so this argument establishes that descriptions cannot be terms.

His second argument:

> The central point of the theory of descriptions was that a phrase may contribute to the meaning of a sentence without having any meaning at all in isolation. Of this, in the

---

[16]*My Philosophical Development* (London: George Allen & Unwin, 1959) p. 84.

[17]In the end Russell coins the term 'logically proper names' to describe what he means. These are in such short supply that Russell was reduced to the demonstratives 'this' and 'that' as his entire stock

case of descriptions, there is a precise proof: If the "author of *Waverly*" meant anything other than "Scott," "Scott is the author of *Waverly*" would be false, which it is not. If "the author of *Waverly*" meant "Scott," "Scott is the author of *Waverly*" would be a tautology [i.e., a logically true sentence], which it is not. Therefore, "the author of *Waverly*" means neither "Scott" nor anything else—i.e. "the author of *Waverly*" means nothing.[18]

As van Fraassen and Lambert argue, the first of Russell's arguments fails to show any great gap between names and descriptions. Precisely the same sort of argument can be generated over 'Jim wants to know whether Tony Curtis is Bernie Swartz, but he does not wish to know whether Tony Curtis is Tony Curtis.'

We can turn a truth into a falsehood by substituting one name for another (with the same reference.) Does this show that we must distinguish between one name and another? Does it show anything at all about what we are substituting for what, or does it show something about the context in which the substitutions are being made?

The second argument rests on an ambiguity in the term 'meaning.' For

(1) 'If the "author of *Waverly*" meant anything other than "Scott," "Scott is the author of *Waverly*" would be false, which it is not.'

to be true, then 't_1 means t_2' must be short for '$t_1 = t_2$', i.e., the two *refer* to the same thing. But then

(2) 'If "the author of *Waverly*" meant "Scott," "Scott is the author of *Waverly*" would be a tautology [i.e. a logically true sentence], which it is not.'

would be false since for it to be true, 't_1 means t_2' must amount to the *logical truth* of $t_1 = t_2$ as opposed to the two terms merely having the same reference. But this version of 't_1 means t_2' would make (1) false. To see this, perform the substitution. (1) becomes:

---

[18]*Ibid.*, p.85.

(1*) 'If the "author of *Waverly* = Scott" is a not a logical truth, "Scott is the author of *Waverly* would be false, which it is not.'

But even if $t_1 = t_2$ is not a logical truth, the possibility yet remains that it is true nevertheless. And if so, then (1*) is clearly false.

So it seems that Russell has not shown after all that definite descriptions cannot be terms, but only that the principle [ML] cannot be correct. From that it doesn't follow that being thus-and-so is entirely dependent upon being.[19]

There remains one more comment on Russell's account of the correct form of sentences like 'The F is G.' We must be extremely careful when stating the conditions which give the supposed logical form of this. A common way of doing it was: 'There is exactly one F, and it is G.' Russell himself seems to have favored such a gloss on more than one occasion.[20] The problem is, such a way of speaking does not eliminate the description in the sense of eliminating "everything referential"[21]—something referential remains in the "it." The same goes for such forms of words as 'There is only one thing which is F and *that thing* is G,' which were also used by Russell(emphasis added). It seems that our account has avoided this trap since all we say is 'whatever is F, is G.' There remains at least a trace of unease at 'whatever.' But if we look again at the formula (Rus), it might be a stretch to recover the third conjunct which is translated as 'Gy.' Now the first two conjuncts of (Rus) clearly say that 'there is exactly one thing which is F' but if we weren't thinking about avoiding traps, wouldn't we translate the remaining '$\wedge\ Gy$' as simply 'and it is G?' After all, the standard way of translating 'Whatever is F, is G' would be '$(\forall x)(Fx \supset Gx)$.'

All this is meant to make us wonder if there could be any account of (singular) definite descriptions which, like Russell's was supposed to do, *eliminates* anything referential. This is emphatically not to say that

---

[19]It might well be one of the requirements of the classical approach, as we have noted above in connection with (Ex), although it seems safer to regard this whole matter as a gray area in which (otherwise) classical logicians may disagree.

[20]For example in Russell (1905) he says "Scott was the author of *Waverly* [] becomes One and only one entity wrote *Waverly* and Scott was identical with *that one*. (emphasis added)

[21]This criticism was first raised by L. Susan Stebbing.

(Rus) doesn't translate 'The F is G.' But a translation can work without eliminating terms.

We remind ourselves that one of the consequences of accepting descriptions as terms, is the recognition that some terms don't actually refer. We can think of descriptions as providing lots of examples of cases in which reference goes awry.

Essay or Discussion Questions and Topics

1. Russell's supporters often say that his theory provides an *analysis* of definite descriptions. To use this expression, which suggests 'taking apart'[22] is to imply that some deep structure or meaning has been provided for the thing analyzed. But isn't the only thing the Russell can claim, is that he has provided a formula which is logically equivalent to the one containing the description? Is this enough to satisfy the demands of analysis?

2. Linguists count sentences like

   > The boy who deserves it will get the prize he wants.

   as defective enough to be only marginally grammatical because when trying to resolve the reference of the pronouns 'it' and 'he', we find ourselves in an infinite loop. The reference of each pronoun contains the other. Thus when we put in 'the boy who deserves it' for 'he', we now have 'it' to resolve, but the resolution of the latter re-introduces 'he' and so on. Sentences of this kind are usually called 'Bach-Peters' sentences. [23] Now consider

   > The natural number which is greater than the natural number less than it, is even. (Example due to Richmond Thomason)

   If this is also a Bach-Peters sentence and if Russell's theory makes this sentence true, then it would seem to provide an example of a sentence which the theory regards as true but that we shouldn't.

---

[22] Analysis is the converse of synthesis.
[23] See especially Bach and Partee (1980),

3. Suppose that Russell's account really shows that definite descriptions do not contain what Russell called 'denoting complexes'—what we have been calling singular referring expressions. It has also been proposed by Russell, Quine and others, that *names* can be eliminated by definite descriptions, with 'John' being replaced by 'the man on the corner', and 'Mary' by 'the thinnest person in the room' for example. It would seem to follow that a great deal of our language, perhaps even all of it, need not refer to anything at all.[24] In his *Lectures on Logical Atomism* Russell suggests that only demonstratives like 'this' and 'that' can function as what he calls 'logically proper names,'

Rules for Free Descriptions

Since we have discovered the whole area of description theory to be something of a gray area, we shall have to be quite careful in stating introduction and elimination rules. The first thing to say, is that for followers of Russell, we don't need any rules. Descriptions aren't terms and every sentence which contains a description can (and should be) translated into a form which doesn't.

On the other hand, we might want to allow that (singular) descriptions are indeed (singular) terms, but they may fail to refer to anything in some cases. We can then see how much of what Russell wants to say is true of the case in which the descriptions actually manage to refer. We shall refer to the logic we construct as *Free Description Theory*. We present it as an extension of the logic FELI:

Description Elimination ($[IE]$)

$$
\begin{array}{|l}
a = (\imath v)P \\
\vdots \\
P(a/v) \wedge (\forall x)(Px \supset x = a)
\end{array}
$$

---

[24]Something like this might be thought to be a theme of certain existentialist authors.

Description Introduction ([II])

$$
\begin{array}{|l}
P(a/v)* \\
\vdots \\
(\forall x)(Px \supset x = a)* \\
\vdots \\
a = (\iota v)P
\end{array}
$$

In these statements, v is supposed to be a variable different from x.

8.16 Exercises

In the following derive the conclusion from the premises, if any.

1. $(\exists x)Fx \supset F((\iota x)F)$

2. $(\exists y)(y = (\iota x)Fx)/ \therefore G(\iota x)Fx \equiv [(\exists y)(Fy \wedge (\forall x)(Fx \supset x = y) \wedge Gy)]$

   (Notice that this shows that Russell's theory of descriptions is correct for those descriptions which actually refer)

3. $\{a = (\iota x)Fx, b = a \wedge (\exists y)(y = b)\}/ \therefore Fb$

4. $(\exists y)(Fy \wedge (\forall x)(Fy \supset x = y) \wedge Gy/ \therefore G(\iota x)Fx$

8.17   Rules Quick Reference

Universal Quantifier Elimination ([∀E])

$$
\begin{array}{c|l}
n & (\forall v)P \\
0 & \vdots \\
Ae1m & P(a/v)
\end{array}
$$

Existential Quantifier Introduction ([∃I])

$$
\begin{array}{c|l}
n & P(a/v) \\
0 & \vdots \\
Ei1m & (\exists v)P
\end{array}
$$

Universal Quantifier Introduction ([∀I])

$$
\begin{array}{c|l}
n & P(a/v) \\
0 & \vdots \\
Ai1m & (\forall v)P
\end{array}
$$

Provided

(i) a does not occur in any assumption of the line on which $P(a/v)$ is derived, and

(ii) a does not occur in $(\forall v)P$

Existential Quantifier Elimination ([∃E])

$$
\begin{array}{lll}
n & (\exists v)\,P & \\
n+1 & \quad P(a/x) & \\
& \quad \vdots & \\
m & \quad Q & \\
m+1 & Q & [\exists E],\, n,\, n+1\text{--}m
\end{array}
$$

Provided

(i) *a* does not occur in any assumption of the line on which $P(a/x)$ is derived, and

(ii) *a* does not occur in $(\exists v)\,P$ and

(iii) *a* does not occur in Q

Quantifier Negation [QN]

$$\neg(\forall v)\,P \longleftrightarrow (\exists v)\neg P$$

$$\neg(\exists v)\,P \longleftrightarrow (\forall v)\neg P$$

Identity Introduction [=I]

$$
\begin{array}{ll}
\vdots & \\
(\forall x)x = x & [=I] \\
\vdots &
\end{array}
$$

Identity Elimination [=E]

$$
\begin{array}{ll}
 & \vdots \\
m & a = b \\
 & \vdots \\
m & P \\
m + 1 & P(a//b) \qquad \text{[=I]}, m, m
\end{array}
$$

$$
\begin{array}{ll}
 & \vdots \\
m & a = b \\
 & \vdots \\
m & P \\
m + 1 & P(b//a) \qquad \text{[=I]}, m, m
\end{array}
$$

Universal Quantifier Elimination (Free version) ([∀E(F)])

$$
\begin{array}{l}
(\forall v) P * \\
\vdots \\
(\exists x)(x = a) * \\
\vdots \\
P(a/v)
\end{array}
$$

Existential Quantifier Introduction (Free Version) ([∃I(F)])

$$
\begin{array}{l}
P(a/v) * \\
\vdots \\
(\exists x)(x = a) * \\
\vdots \\
(\exists v) P
\end{array}
$$

Description Elimination ([IE])

$$
\begin{array}{|l}
a = (Iv)P \\
\vdots \\
P(a/v) \wedge (\forall x)(Px \supset x = a)
\end{array}
$$

Description Introduction ([II])

$$
\begin{array}{|l}
P(a/v)* \\
\vdots \\
(\forall x)(Px \supset x = a)* \\
\vdots \\
a = (Iv)P
\end{array}
$$

In these statements, v is supposed to be a variable different from x.

8.18   Solutions to Selected Exercises

The following selected assignment questions are presented without line justifications (such 'solutions' would be marked as wrong on an examination). Keep in mind that even short derivations can usually be done in *many* different ways so that if yours fails to match the one given here, it doesn't follow that yours is wrong.

Exercise 8.4

4.1

1	$Ga \supset (\forall x)Fx$	
2	$(\exists x)Fx \supset Ga$	
3	Ga	
4	$(\forall x)Fx$	[$\supset$E], 1, 3
5	Fb	[$\forall$E], 4
6	Fb	
7	$(\exists x)Fx$	[$\exists$I], 6
8	Ga	[$\supset$E], 2, 7
9	$Ga \equiv Fb$	[$\equiv$I], 3–5, 6–8
10	$(\forall x)(Ga \equiv Fx)$	[$\forall$I], 9

4.3

1	$(\forall x)(\neg Fx \supset Gx)$	
2	$(\forall x)[(\neg Gx \vee Fx) \equiv \neg Gx]$	
3	$(\exists x)(Hx \equiv Fx)$	
4	$(\forall x)(Hx \equiv Gx)$	
5	$Ha \equiv Fa$	
6	$\neg Fa \supset Ga$	$[\forall E], 1$
7	$Ha \equiv Ga$	$[\forall E], 4$
8	$\neg Fa$	
9	Ga	$[\supset E], 6, 8$
10	Ha	$[\equiv E], 7, 9$
11	Fa	$[\equiv E], 5, 10$
12	Fa	$[\neg E], 8–11$
13	Ha	$[\equiv E], 5, 12$
14	Ga	$[\equiv E], 7, 13$
15	$(\neg Ga \vee Fa) \equiv \neg Ga$	$[\forall E], 2$
16	$\neg Ga \vee Fa$	$[\vee I], 12$
17	$\neg Ga$	$[\equiv E], 15, 16$
18	$\bot$	$[\bot E], 14, 17$
19	$\bot$	$[\exists E], 3, 5–18$
20	$\neg(\forall x)(Hx \equiv Gx)$	$[\neg I], 4–19$

4.8

1	$(\forall x)(Fx \supset \neg Gx)$	
2	$(\forall x)(Fx \wedge Hx)$	
3	$\neg(\exists x)\neg Gx$	
4	$Fa \wedge Ha$	[∀E], 2
5	Fa	[∧E], 4
6	$Fa \supset \neg Ga$	[∀E], 1
7	$\neg Ga$	[⊃E], 6, 5
8	$(\exists x)\neg Gx$	[∃I], 7
9	$\neg(\exists x)\neg Gx$	[R], 3
10	$(\exists x)\neg Gx$	[¬E], 3–9

4.10

1	$(\exists x)Fx \supset (\forall x)Gx$	
2	$\neg Ga$	
3	Fa	
4	$(\exists x)Fx$	[∃I], 3
5	$(\forall x)Gx$	[⊃E], 1, 4
6	Ga	[∀E], 5
7	$\neg Fa$	[¬E], 3–6
8	$\neg Ga \supset \neg Fa$	[⊃I], 2–7
9	$(\forall x)(\neg Gx \supset \neg Fx)$	[∀I], 8

4.16

1	$(\exists x)[Fx \supset (\exists y)Gy]$	
2	$(\forall x)Fx$	
3	$Fa \supset (\exists y)Gy$	
4	Fa	[∀E], 2
5	$(\exists y)Gy$	[⊃E], 3, 4
6	Gb	
7	$(\exists x)Gx$	[∃I], 6
8	$(\exists x)Gx$	[∃E], 5, 6–7
9	$(\exists x)Gx$	[∃E], 1, 3–8
10	$(\forall x)Fx \supset (\exists x)Gx$	[⊃I], 2–9

Exercise 8.7

7.1

1	$(\forall x)(Fx \supset (\forall y)(Gy \supset Hxy))$	
2	$(\forall x)(Dx \supset (\forall y)(Hxy \supset Cy))$	
3	$(\exists x)(Fx \wedge Dx)$	
4	$Fa \wedge Da$	
5	Gb	
6	$Fa \supset (\forall y)(Gy \supset Hay)$	[∀E], 1
7	Fa	[∧E], 4
8	$(\forall y)(Gy \supset Hay)$	[⊃E], 6, 7
9	$Gb \supset Hab$	[∀E], 8
10	Hab	[⊃E], 9, 5
11	$Da \supset (\forall y)(Hay \supset Cy)$	[∀E], 2
12	Da	[∧E], 4
13	$(\forall y)(Hay \supset Cb)$	[⊃E], 11, 12
14	$Hab \supset Cb$	[∀E], 13
15	Cb	[⊃E], 14, 10
16	$Gb \supset Cb$	[⊃I], 5–15
17	$(\forall y)(Gy \supset Cy)$	[∀I], 16
18	$(\forall y)(Gy \supset Cy)$	[∃E], 3, 4–17
19	$(\exists x)(Fx \wedge Dx) \supset (\forall y)(Gy \supset Cy)$	[⊃I], 3–18

7.2

1	$(\forall x)((Fx \lor Hx) \supset (Gx \land Kx))$	
2	$\neg(\forall x)(Kx \land Gx)$	
3	$(\exists x)\neg(Kx \land Gx)$	[rep], 2
4	$\neg(Ka \land Ga)$	
5	$(Fa \lor Ha) \supset (Ga \land Ka)$	[∀E], 1
6	$\neg(Fa \lor Ha)$	[MT], 5, 4
7	$\neg Fa \land \neg Ha$	[rep], 6
8	$\neg Ha$	[∧E], 7
9	$(\exists x)\neg Hx$	[∃I], 8
10	$(\exists x)\neg Hx$	[∃E], 3, 4–9

7.4

1	$(\forall x)(\forall y)(Gxy \equiv (Fy \supset Hx))$
2	$(\forall z)Gaz$
3	$(\exists x)Fx$
4	Fb
5	$(\forall y)(Gay \equiv (Fy \supset Ha))$ [$\forall$E], 1
6	$Gab \equiv (Fb \supset Ha)$ [$\forall$E], 5
7	Gab [$\forall$E], 2
8	$Fb \supset Ha$ [$\equiv$E], 6, 7
9	Ha [$\supset$E], 8. 4
10	$(\exists x)Hx$ [$\exists$I], 9
11	$(\exists x)Hx$ [$\exists$E], 3, 4–10
12	$(\exists x)Fx \supset (\exists x)Hx$ [$\supset$I], 3–11

7.7

1	$(\forall x)[(\exists y)Fxy \supset (\forall y)Fyx]$	
2	$(\exists x)(\exists y)Fxy$	
3	$(\exists y)Fay$	
4	$(\exists y)Fay \supset (\forall y)Fya$	[$\forall$E], 1
5	$(\forall y)Fya$	[$\supset$E], 4, 3
6	Fba	[$\forall$E], 5
7	$(\exists y)Fby \supset (\forall y)Fyb$	[$\forall$E], 1
8	$(\exists y)Fby$	[$\exists$I], 6
9	$(\forall y)Fyb$	[$\supset$E], 7, 8
10	$(\forall x)(\forall y)Fyx$	[$\forall$I], 9
11	$(\forall y)Fyd$	[$\forall$E], 10
12	Fcd	[$\forall$E], 11
13	$(\forall y)Fcy$	[$\forall$I], 12
14	$(\forall x)(\forall y)Fxy$	[$\forall$I], 13
15	$(\forall x)(\forall y)Fxy$	[$\exists$E], 2, 3–14

7.12

1	$(\exists x)(\forall y)[(\exists z)Fyz \supset Fyx]$	
2	$(\forall x)(\exists y)Fxy$	
3	$(\forall y)[(\exists z)Fyz \supset Fya]$	
4	$(\exists z)Fbz \supset Fba$	[∀E], 3
5	$(\exists y)Fby$	[∀E], 2
6	Fbc	
7	$(\exists z)Fbz$	[∃I], 6
8	$(\exists z)Fbz$	[∃E], 5, 6–8
9	Fba	[⊃E], 4, 8
10	$(\forall y)Fya$	[∀I], 9
11	$(\exists x)(\forall y)Fyx$	[∃I], 10
12	$(\exists x)(\forall y)Fyx$	[∃E], 1, 3–11

Exercise 8.9

9.1

1	$a = b \wedge \neg Bab$	
2	$(\forall x)Bxx$	
3	Baa	[∀E], 2
4	$a = b$	[∧E], 1
5	Bab	[=E], 3, 4
6	$\neg Bab$	[∧E], 1
7	$\neg(\forall x)Bxx$	[¬I], 2–6

Chapter 9

Model Theory: Semantics of Elementary Logic

9.1 Introduction

In this chapter we take up the semantics of elementary logic, usually known as *model theory*. The central concern here, as with the semantics of sentence logic, is the definition of *truth* (relative to some or other structure). Once possessed of this, we can go on to define the others: e.g. *entailment*, *logical truth*, etc. Of course this is not a difficult matter, these latter definitions—in fact they go the way anybody would expect who had seen our previous semantic studies. The hard part is that first step, providing an adequate definition of truth. So hard in fact, that it wasn't adequately framed until the 1930's. [1]

Why is this task so much more difficult than the corresponding task for the logic of sentences? The answer to this is easy to see. Let our semantic structure be represented by $\mathbb{S}$, for the time being. The difficulty is not that we cannot see straight away how the truth-condition for universal quantification should go, but rather that we *can*. It's obvious to most people that the condition should be:

---

[1] Most authorities agree that the first adequate definition of truth was carried out in Alfred Tarski's paper Tarski (1936) the title of which is usually translated as 'The Concept of Truth in Formalized Languages.'

$$\mathbb{S} \models (\forall v)P \iff \mathbb{S} \models Px \text{ for every value of } x$$

since '∀' is supposed to mean 'all,' The problem is that it is equally obvious that the condition cannot be this one. The reason is, that the expression Px cannot be true at all, let alone for every value of x, since Px is not a sentence. Tarski's answer is to suggest that we first define a more primitive predicate called *satisfaction*. We can then say things like Px is satisfied by certain values of x. After that we can define truth in terms of satisfaction and all will be well—provided of course, that the details can be worked out.

Before we get to the actual semantics, it is necessary to be a little less inclusive in the matter of the language (of elementary logic) which we use. In fact, we now officially abandon the idea that there is one unique object, *the* language. Instead we shall introduce the notion of *a* language for elementary logic.

Definition 9.1.1. We define the concept of a language $\mathcal{L}$, for elementary logic (alternatively, the concept of an elementary language) as a family of disjoint sets of *symbols* as follows.

$$\mathcal{L} = \mathbf{Pred}(\mathcal{L}) \cup \mathbf{Con}(\mathcal{L})$$

where the first set is called the set of *predicate* (alternatively *predicate* and *relation*) symbols of $\mathcal{L}$ and the second set is called the set of *individual constant* symbols of $\mathcal{L}$.

If the sets of symbols just mentioned are finite sets, we might choose to display them more explicitly, along the lines of:

$$\mathcal{L} = \{F_0, \ldots, F_n\} \cup \{c_0, \ldots, c_q\}$$

Given two Languages, $\mathcal{L}_1$ and $\mathcal{L}_2$

> **Definition 9.1.2.** We define the notion that $\mathcal{L}_2$ is an *expansion* of $\mathcal{L}_1$ (alternatively, that $\mathcal{L}_1$ is a *reduction* of $\mathcal{L}_2$) by
>
> $$\mathcal{L}_1 \sqsubset \mathcal{L}_2 \iff \mathcal{L}_1 \subset \mathcal{L}_2$$
>
> When $\mathcal{L}_2$ is exactly like $\mathcal{L}_1$ except for having more individual constant symbols, then it is said to be a *simple* expansion.

We carry over the notion of 'formula of elementary logic' from the previous account, except that now the definition is $\mathcal{L}$relativized to a particular language $\mathcal{L}$.

Next we specify the semantic structures we shall be using. Following a certain tradition, we use capital Gothic letters $\mathfrak{A}$, $\mathfrak{B}$, $\mathfrak{C}$, with and without subscripts, to denote these structures, which are called *models*.

Elementary logic requires for its semantics not just truth-values, but also *elements*. We thus require, for each model $\mathfrak{A}$, a set of elements which we shall call the *domain* of $\mathfrak{A}$, indicated by the same capital Roman letter, in this case A. Individual constants of an elementary language $\mathcal{L}$ correspond to elements of the domain and predicates (including relations) correspond to predicates and relations defined over A.

We need something now to specify this mysterious correspondence just mentioned. That something is a function $\mathbf{I}$, called the *interpretation* of the model. Since each model for an elementary language consists of just these two ingredients, we often write things like
$\mathfrak{A} = (A, \mathbf{I})$, $\mathfrak{B} = (B, \mathbf{J})$, $\mathfrak{C} = (C, \mathbf{K})$ etc.

It should be obvious that we want the value of $\mathbf{I}(a)$ to be the element of A which a 'names'(according to $\mathbf{I}$). It may not be so obvious how to display the value of $\mathbf{I}$ for predicates.

We want 'John is happy' to come out true (on an interpretation) when the individual named by 'John' has the property indicated by 'happy' (presumably that property is 'happiness'). Given that the interpretation of 'John' is an element of the domain, it seems most natural to interpret the predicate 'is happy' by means of a *subset* of A. In other words, we interpret the predicate PRED as 'the set of all elements of the domain

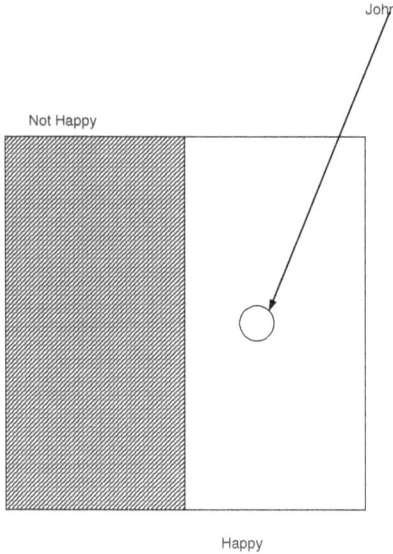

Figure 9.1: Graphic Depiction of the truth of 'John is Happy'

which have the property indicated by PRED.'[2] Then the truth condition for 'John is happy' will be simply $\mathbf{I}(john) \in \mathbf{I}(is\ happy)$. We may represent this graphically in the manner of figure 9.1

The advantage of this approach is that it extends to cover the case of relational predicates quite easily. Consider a relation like 'loves': We want 'Jack loves Marnie' to come out true on an interpretation when the individual named by 'Jack' loves the individual named by 'Marnie.' This suggest that we interpret the predicate 'loves' as a set, not of individuals but of *pairs* of individuals—lover-lovee pairs, so to speak. This can be represented by a *directed graph* as in figure 9.2.

Then 'Jack loves Marnie' will be true if and only if

$$<\mathbf{I}(jack), \mathbf{I}(marnie)> \in \mathbf{I}(loves)$$

---

[2]This set is often referred to as the *extension* of the predicate. When predicates are interpreted as sets in this way, the approach is said to be *extensional*.

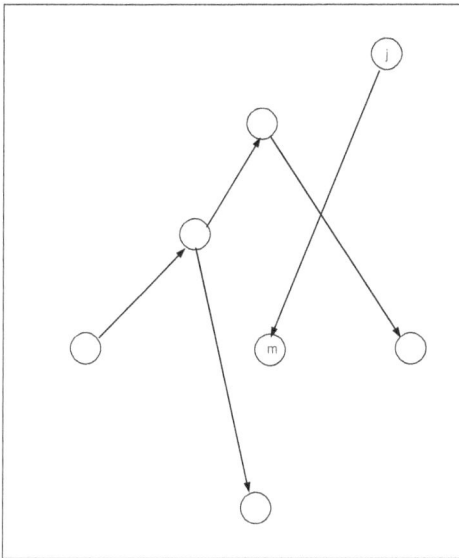

Figure 9.2: Graphic Depiction of the 'loves' relation

Here we use $< x, y >$ to denote the *ordered pair* which contains as *first* element x, and as *second* element y.[3] The order is represented graphically by arrows, with the first element of the pair at the tail of the arrow and the second element at the head. Figure 9.2 is a picture of an interpretation of the relation 'loves', i.e. of what we just called '$\mathbf{I}(loves)$', 'John loves Mary' is true on this interpretation since there is an arrow from the element named by 'John' to the element named by 'Mary.'

For ternary relations, the interpretation will be sets of ordered triples, and in general the interpretation of an n-ary relation will be a set of n-termed ordered sets (usually called ordered n-tuples).

We have been talking as if we already had a definition of truth relative to a model, but of course we began this section by pointing out a

---

[3]To say that the pair is ordered is to say that the order is constitutive. In other words, while $\{x, y\}$ is the identical to $\{y, x\}$, $<x, y>$ is a different object from $<y, x>$. For 'raw' sets, order makes no difference, but for ordered sets, it does.

problem with that project, one involving framing a truth-condition for quantified sentences. But we can quite easily define truth for the other types of sentences, as follows:

9.2   A Partial Truth Definition and Satisfaction

First, we produce the clause for atomic sentences along the lines that we have already telegraphed. Using '$\mathfrak{A} \models P$' to represent 'The sentence P is true in the model $\mathfrak{A}$', we write:

$$\mathfrak{A} \models F^n a_1 \ldots a_n \iff \langle \mathbf{I}(a_1), \ldots, \mathbf{I}(a_n) \rangle \in \mathbf{I}(F^n)$$

We also want to form compound sentences using the truth-functional connectives, but we need not strain ourselves. We can simply recycle the truth-conditions from our previous truth definition (substituting $\mathfrak{M} \models$ for $\models_v$).

$$(\mathfrak{A} \models P \wedge Q) \iff (\mathfrak{A} \models P \ \& \ \mathfrak{A} \models Q)$$

$$(\mathfrak{A} \models P \vee Q) \iff (\mathfrak{A} \models P \ \text{or} \ \mathfrak{A} \models Q)$$

$$(\mathfrak{A} \models P \supset Q) \iff (\mathfrak{A} \models P \implies \mathfrak{A} \models Q)$$

$$(\mathfrak{A} \models P \equiv Q) \iff (\mathfrak{A} \models P \iff \mathfrak{A} \models Q)$$

$$\mathfrak{A} \models \neg P \iff \mathfrak{A} \not\models P$$

But now we encounter the problem of finding the truth-condition for quantified formulas. Our method of writing down such conditions has always been to say that a compound formula is true if and only if the parts out of which the compound is formed, themselves satisfy some truth condition. But the parts of a quantified sentence consist of the quantifier ($\forall x$ and $\exists x$ e.g.) along with the unquantified open sentence e.g. Fx. Neither of these *could* be true or false. They aren't sentences.

The answer, at which we hinted earlier, is to define some other predicate, a predicate which we call *satisfaction*. Under what conditions will an open sentence be satisfied? The most obvious approach would be to say that a formula Fx is satisfied *by an element of a domain* if and only if that element belongs to the interpretation of F. At least this is obvious if we happen to have a model handy. But even having a model on hand, doesn't solve the problem of how to assign an element of the domain to an individual variable like x. To do that, another *function* will have to be deployed,[4] this one assigning elements of the domain of some model to the individual variables. We shall call this a *variable assignment function* and represent them by means of the notation d, with and without subscripts.

Before we go on to satisfaction, we require a definition:

Definition 9.2.1. Relative to the model $\mathfrak{A}$, for every variable assignment function d and element e of A and individual variable v, $d(e/v)$ is the variable assignment function such that for every variable v', If $v' \neq v$ then $d(e/v)(v') = d(v')$. And $d(e/v)(v) = e$.

In other words: $d(e/v)$ agrees with d on every variable different from v, and to v, assigns the element e. It is important to notice that there is no assumption here that d assigns v some element distinct from e (and neither is there any presumption that it doesn't). We also need some notion of the semantic evaluation of individual terms.

Definition 9.2.2. Relative to a model $\mathfrak{A}$, variable assignment d, and individual term t, the expression $|t|^{\mathfrak{A}_d}$ is defined to be $\mathbf{I}(t)$ if t is an individual constant, and $d(t)$ if t is an individual variable.

When the superscript '$\mathfrak{A}_d$' is clear from the context, it will often be omitted. With these preliminaries out of the way, it is now possible to define satisfaction.

---

[4]In his original paper, cited earlier, Tarski uses *sequences* instead of functions. However one may think of an infinite sequence of domain elements as another way of writing out a function specification: the first element is the value of the function for x_0, the next for x_1, and so on.

Definition 9.2.3. [Satisfaction]
The predicate '$\mathfrak{A} \models_d P$,' read 'd satisfies the formula P in the
model $\mathfrak{A}$,' is defined recursively as follows:

$\mathfrak{A} \models_d Pt \iff |t| \in \mathbf{I}(P)$ if Pt is an atomic formula.

If P is a truth-functional compound, $\mathfrak{A} \models_d P$ is defined by
the usual clauses.

$\mathfrak{A} \models_d (\forall v)P \iff$ for every element e, of A, $\mathfrak{A} \models_{d(e/v)} P$

$\mathfrak{A} \models_d (\exists v)P \iff$ there exists an element e of A such that
$\mathfrak{A} \models_{d(e/v)} P$.

This definition often looks strange to beginners because it looks as
if satisfaction is being defined for one-place predicates only, and not for
relations. To see that this isn't true, let's consider a concrete example—a
language with a single binary relation F.

Let $\mathfrak{A}$ be a model for this language, so that $\mathbf{I}(F)$ will be a set of
ordered pairs of elements of A (in graphical terms, a set of arrows between nodes which represent domain elements). Using the definition of
satisfaction,

we see that the sentence '$(\forall x)(\forall y)Fxy$' is satisfied by the variable assignment function d in the model $\mathfrak{A}$ if and only if

for every element e of A $\mathfrak{A} \models_{d(e/x)} (\forall y)Fxy$ which means, iter-
ating the satisfaction condition again, if and only if

for every element e of A (for every element e' of A)
$\mathfrak{A} \models_{d(e/x)(e'/y)} Fxy$) which is clearly the same as

for every pair of elements $<e, e'>(\mathfrak{A} \models_{d(e/x)(e'/y)} Fxy)$

We shall soon finish the definition of truth, but before we do, we
shall require this result:

Theorem 9.2.4. *If* $\mathfrak{A} \models_d P$ *for some variable assignment d, then* $\mathfrak{A} \models_{d'} P$ *for every variable assignment d', for any sentence P, of the language of EL.*

Proof. It is crucial to notice that P must be a sentence in the statement of the theorem, rather than a formula. In other words, all occurrences of variables in P must be bound occurrences.

  1 If P is an atomic sentence or any truth-functional compound of sentences, then $\mathfrak{A} \models_d P$ if and only if $\mathfrak{A} \models P$ by the definition of satisfaction and hence P must be satisfied by every variable assignment d or by none, according as P is true in $\mathfrak{A}$ or not.

  2 Consider now the case in which P has the form $(\forall v)Q$. In this case P is satisfied by a variable assignment d if and only if Q is satisfied by $d(e/v)$ for every element e of A. Here $d(e/v)$ is the variable assignment which matches d on all the variables other than v and gives v the value e. But v is the only freely occurring variable in Q since $(\forall v)Q$ was required to be a sentence. So the only thing which counts toward the satisfaction or otherwise of Q, is what value is given to v. So any variable assignment will satisfy $(\forall v)Q$ if and only if every element of A satisfies Q, and if not every element of A has this property, then no variable assignment satisfies $(\forall v)Q$.

  3 The case in which P has the form $(\exists v)Q$ is left as an exercise.

Remark 9.2.5. Even though we restrict ourselves to sentences in the above theorem, the result can be strengthened to cover formulas as well, but in that case the statement would have to change from 'every variable assignment d',' to 'every assignment d' which agrees with the assignment d on every variable which occurs freely in P.' In such a case the proof we have offered would have to be replaced by a proof by induction on the length $\ell(P)$ of the formula P.

The construction of such a proof is left as an exercise.

$\square$

We shall also require the following obvious result when it comes time to deploy some models.

Proposition 9.2.6. *For every formula P, model $\mathfrak{A}$ and variable assignment d:*
$$\mathfrak{A} \models_d P(a/x) \iff \mathfrak{A} \models_{d(\mathbf{I}(a)/x)} P.$$

9.3   The Key Definitions

We can now utter the central definitions beginning with truth.

Definition 9.3.1. [Truth]

For every model $\mathfrak{A}$ and sentence P

$\mathfrak{A} \models P \iff \mathfrak{A} \models_d P$ for every variable assignment d.

So we get truth by 'quantifying away' satisfaction. Of course this is not such a stringent definition as might at first appear, in view of Theorem 9.2.4.

The remaining concepts don't change at all.

Definition 9.3.2. [Entailment] Entailment is defined as truth-preservation:

$\Gamma \models P \iff [\mathfrak{A} \models \Gamma \implies \mathfrak{A} \models P]$ for every model $\mathfrak{A}$.

Definition 9.3.3. [Logical Truth] The logical truths are defined to be the consequences of the empty set:

$$\models P \iff \varnothing \models P$$

Chapter 10

Metalogic of Elementary Logic

10.1 Special Sets

We shall use the same strategy as in the earlier study of metalogic, which we somewhat fancifully described as 'reconstructing the semantics inside the proof theory.' We employ this strategy to the same end, namely deriving a certain equivalence result.

At the very heart of this endeavor then, is the project of finding, for every model $\mathfrak{A}$ for an elementary language $\mathcal{L}$, a set $\Delta_{\mathfrak{A}}$ of sentences of $\mathcal{L}$, such that $\mathfrak{A} \models P$ if and only if $\Delta_{\mathfrak{A}} \vdash P$, for every sentence P.

For the metalogic of classical sentence logic, it turned out that the Δ in question was a member of $\mathbf{T}_I$, and since the notion of truth in a model matches the notion of truth relative to a truth-value assignment, we shall need the Δ mentioned above to be maximally consistent (in terms of the CEL account of deduction). But for elementary logic, maximal consistency won't be enough. The reason is that the set $\{(\exists x)F\} \cup \{\neg Fa_1, \ldots, \neg Fa_i, \ldots\}$ for every individual constant a_i, is consistent. How can it be consistent to assert that something is F but it isn't the first thing we can name, nor is it the second, ... nor the nth, ... ? A moment's thought will show that even if we throw all the names we have into the breach, that will avail us nothing unless we also say that we have named all that can be named. Thus 'I'm wearing a glove but it isn't on my left hand and it isn't on my right hand.' is consistent even if we stipulate that gloves can only be worn on hands, until we say explicitly that I have no other hands except my left and my right. But while we can say that I have only two hands, we have no way of saying that $a_1, \ldots, a_n, \ldots$ names everything that there is.

It will turn out that in order that $\Delta \vdash$ match $\mathfrak{A} \models$, Δ cannot be like the set mentioned above, even though it is consistent. This leads to the definition of a new property of sets of sentences.

Definition 10.1.1. A set Σ of sentences of $\mathfrak{L}$, is said to be *omega-complete* if and only if $\Sigma \vdash (\exists v) P \implies \Sigma \vdash P(a/v)$ for some individual constant a of $\mathfrak{L}$.

As mentioned in chapter 8 a constant like a which is used to produce an instance of an existentially quantified sentence is often referred to as a witness. We use that terminology in the following:

Definition 10.1.2. If Σ is a set of sentences of an elementary language $\mathfrak{L}$, and $\mathbf{C}$ a set of individual constants then Σ is said to *have witnesses in* $\mathbf{C}$ if and only if $\Sigma \vdash (\exists v) P \implies \Sigma \vdash P(c/v)$ for some constant c in $\mathbf{C}$.

Evidently every set which has this property is omega-complete. Now we fold this into our existing account of special sets.

Definition 10.1.3. The class $\Omega_{\mathfrak{L}}$ is defined to be the class of all sets of sentences of $\mathfrak{L}$ which are (CEL) maximally consistent and omega-complete.

When no confusion will result, we usually drop the subscript $\mathfrak{L}$ and the qualification CEL.

Terminology. We say $\Omega(\Delta)$ or that Δ has the *omega property* when Δ is both maximally consistent and omega-complete.

Defining is all very well, but we must now assure ourselves that the class Ω is non-empty. We shall undertake to show this by means of the same kind of construction that we used in lemma 5.8.1. As before, we begin with a set Σ of sentences of $\mathcal{L}$ which is stipulated to be consistent. There is a large difference between the new construction and the old. In the old one, we had a fixed language. But we need to construct omega sets now, and $\mathcal{L}$ might be a language without the resources to provide witnessing constants. In that case we must provide ourselves with a stock of individual constants sufficient to our needs. This means expanding the language $\mathcal{L}$.

Lemma 10.1.4. *Suppose that $\mathcal{L}$ is an elementary language, Σ a consistent set of $\mathcal{L}$ sentences, $\mathbf{C}$ a countable set of new constants, and $\mathcal{L}^*$ the simple expansion of $\mathcal{L}$ formed by adding $\mathbf{C}$, then Σ can be extended to a maximally consistent set Σ^* of sentences of $\mathcal{L}^*$ with witnesses in $\mathbf{C}$.*

Proof. We order all the sentences of $\mathcal{L}^*$ in some fixed but arbitrary way, which we shall refer to by means of $1st, 2nd, 3rd, \ldots$. This much is familiar but now we move into uncharted waters. It will turn out that in order to construct a set with the omega property, we must add witnessing constants whenever we add an existentially quantified sentence.

This is accomplished in the following sequence:

$$\Sigma_0 = \Sigma$$

$$\vdots$$

$$\Sigma_k = \begin{cases} \Sigma_{k-1} \cup \{kth\} & \text{if consistent and } kth \neq (\exists v)F, \\ \Sigma_{k-1} \cup \{kth, F(a/v)\} & \text{if consistent and } kth \text{ has the form } (\exists v)F, \\ \Sigma_{k-1} & \text{otherwise.} \end{cases}$$

$$\vdots$$

Define Σ^+ to be $\bigcup_i \Sigma_i$.

In this construction the witness added at the kth stage is stipulated to be the (alphabetically) first member of $\mathbf{C}$ which does not occur in any formula of the set constructed so far. The terminology *foreign* is often used to describe such non-occurring constants. Since Σ is stipulated not to contain any members of $\mathbf{C}$, it should be obvious that we won't run out of constants since there can be at most countably many witnesses to find.

Terminology. If Γ is any set of sentences of $\mathcal{L}$, Γ^+ refers to any result of putting Γ through the kind of construction just detailed.[1] Of course, given the construction, the set Γ^+ will contain sentences of the $\mathcal{L} \cup \mathbf{C}$ simple expansion of $\mathcal{L}$, as well as the set Γ of sentences of $\mathcal{L}$.

Putting a plus on a set does not denote some unique omega set containing the set in question, since the construction will give a distinct set, in general, for each distinct ordering 1st, 2nd, ... of sentences.

It is clear that for every Γ, Γ^+ is omega complete and will thus be an omega-set provided only that it is consistent.

The earlier arguments showing that the construction of $\mathbb{M}$ sets preserves consistency can be recycled here which leaves only one new case—the case in which we add not only kth but also $F(a/v)$. We argue indirectly that consistency must be preserved in this case also.

(1) $\Gamma_{k-1}, (\exists x)P \nvdash \bot$ since otherwise we didn't add $(\exists x)P$ and

(2) $\Gamma_{k-1}, (\exists x)P, P(a/x) \vdash \bot$ from which

(3) $\Gamma_{k-1}, (\exists x)P \vdash \neg P(a/x)$ by [¬I] and since a is foreign

(4) $\Gamma_{k-1}, (\exists x)P \vdash (\forall x)\neg P$ and by [QN]

(5) $\Gamma_{k-1}, (\exists x)P \vdash \neg(\exists x)P$ So

(6) $\Gamma_{k-1}, (\exists x)P \vdash \bot$ contrary to (1).

(7) So Γ^+ must be consistent after all and hence $\Omega(\Gamma^+)$.

$\square$

10.2   Overview of Metalogical Results

To organize our thinking about matters metalogical, we bring back the diagram used previously, mutated in the obvious way by replacing truth-value assignments with models. First some definitions.

---

[1]This terminology was earlier used to denote the (or more properly 'a') result of converting the base set into a maximally consistent set. We can reassign the notation now, since it will always be clear from the context which flavor of 'plus' is intended.

Definition 10.2.1. We say that of a set Δ of sentences of $\mathcal{L}^+$ is an *omega extension* of a set Γ of sentences of $\mathcal{L}$, indicated by $\Gamma \subseteq^\Omega \Delta$, if and only if $\Gamma \subseteq \Delta$ & $\Omega(\Delta)$

Definition 10.2.2. We say that a set Γ of sentences of an elementary language $\mathcal{L}$ *omega proves* a sentence P, indicated by $\Gamma \vdash^\Omega P$, if and only if for every Δ, if $\Gamma \subseteq^\Omega \Delta$ then $\Delta \vdash P$

We shall also use the abbreviation

Notation. '$\Gamma \models^\mathfrak{A} P$' for 'For every $\mathfrak{A}$, if $\mathfrak{A} \models \Gamma$ then $\mathfrak{A} \models P$'

The later is a bit confusing since we already have an abbreviation for 'For every $\mathfrak{A}$, if $\mathfrak{A} \models \Gamma$ then $\mathfrak{A} \models P$', namely $\Gamma \models P$. This secondary abbreviation makes the figure 10.1 nicer.

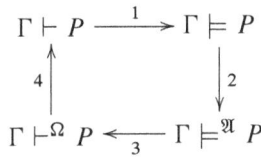

$$\begin{array}{ccc} \Gamma \vdash P & \xrightarrow{\quad 1 \quad} & \Gamma \models P \\ {\scriptstyle 4}\big\uparrow & & \big\downarrow{\scriptstyle 2} \\ \Gamma \vdash^\Omega P & \xleftarrow{\quad 3 \quad} & \Gamma \models^\mathfrak{A} P \end{array}$$

Figure 10.1: The Equivalence Diagram for CEL

We shall once again consider two ways of showing that this diagram 'commutes.' The first way, the normal way we might say, is to show that each of the arrows labelled 1 through 4 represents an implication.

Theorem 10.2.3 (Consistency of CEL). *For every set Γ of sentences and every sentence P of an elementary language $\mathcal{L}$:*
$\Gamma \vdash P \implies \Gamma \models P$.

Notice that this asserts that the arrow labelled 1 stands for an implication.

Proof. We see that the only thing that we need to do is to show that the quantifier introduction and elimination rules preserve entailment.

[∀E] preserves entailment. i.e.
  $\Gamma \models (\forall x)P \implies \Gamma \models P(a/x)$ for any individual constant a.

> *Proof.* Let $\mathfrak{A}$ be some arbitrarily selected model. Clearly, the truth of $(\forall x)P$ in $\mathfrak{A}$ implies that for every element e of the domain A, $e \in \mathbf{I}(P)$. But since, in $\mathfrak{A}$ every constant must be interpreted as some or other element of A, it follows that every constant a must be interpreted as a member of $\mathbf{I}(P)$. But then $P(a/x)$ must be true in $\mathfrak{A}$ for every a.
>
> $\square$

[∀I] preserves entailment, i.e.
  $\Gamma \models P(a/x) \implies \Gamma \models (\forall x)P$
  provided that a does not occur in

  (i) any sentence of Γ

  (ii) $(\forall x)P$

> *Proof.* Suppose, for reductio, that $\Gamma \not\models (\forall x)P$. Then there must be some model, $\mathfrak{A}$ such that $\mathfrak{A} \models \Gamma$ and $\mathfrak{A} \not\models (\forall x)P$. From the latter it follows that there must be some variable assignment d and element e of the domain such that $d(e/x)(x) \notin I(P)$ (since otherwise $(\forall x)P$ would be satisfied in $\mathfrak{A}$ by every variable assignment, and hence would be true in $\mathfrak{A}$, contrary to hypothesis). It is easily seen that this amounts to saying that $e \notin I(P)$. Construct a new model $\mathfrak{A}'$, which has the same domain as $\mathfrak{A}$ and for which $\mathbf{I}' = \mathbf{I}$ except only that $I'(a) = e$. It can now be seen that:
> $\mathfrak{A}' \models \Gamma$, since $\mathfrak{A} \models \Gamma$, $\mathfrak{A}$ and $\mathfrak{A}'$ differ only on a and a does not occur in Γ.
> $\mathfrak{A}' \not\models P(a/x)$ since $e \notin I(P)$ and a does not occur in P, so $e \notin I'(P)$.

Thus $\Gamma \nvDash P(a/x)$ contrary to hypothesis, so it must be the case that $\Gamma \vDash (\forall x)P$.

□

[∃I] preserves entailment, i.e.
$$\Gamma \vDash P(a/x) \implies \Gamma \vDash (\exists x)P$$

The proof is left as an exercise.

[∃E] preserves entailment, i.e.
$$[\Gamma \vDash (\exists x)P \ \& \ \Gamma, P(a/x) \vDash Q] \implies \Gamma \vDash Q \text{ provided } a \text{ does}$$
not occur in

(i) any sentence of Γ

(ii) $(\exists x)P$

(iii) Q

The proof is left as an exercise

□

Once again the arrow labeled 2 is simply the model-theoretic definition of entailment so that arrow must represent an implication (in fact we get the stronger assertion that it represents an equivalence) trivially.

The arrow marked 3 is 'hard.' In order that we can prove the implication, it will be necessary to update the first correspondence theorem for CSL. First a definition:

Definition 10.2.4. For any $\Delta \in \Omega$, the (*canonical*) model (*for* Δ) $\mathfrak{A}_\Delta$ is defined

A_Δ = the set of individual constants occurring in some sentence of Δ

$\mathbf{I}_\Delta(a) = a$ for every individual constant a

$\mathbf{I}_\Delta(F^n) = \{<a_1, \ldots, a_n> \mid \Delta \vdash F^n a_1 \ldots a_n\}$

Now we can show that for every omega-set Δ, there is a corresponding model, where the sense of correspondence here is the same as it was for the earlier sentential result. In other words:

Theorem 10.2.5 (First Correspondence Theorem for CEL). *For every sentence P of* EL *and every* $\Delta \in \Omega$: $\Delta \vdash P \iff \mathfrak{A}_\Delta \models P$

Proof. We prove the first correspondence theorem by induction on $\ell(P)$ the length of the sentence P.

(α) When $\ell(P) = 0$, and P is therefore an atomic sentence, say $F^n a_1 \ldots a_n$. Then the result holds trivially by definition of $\mathfrak{A}_\Delta$, since:

    1. $\Delta \vdash F^n a_1 \ldots a_n$ if and only if

    2. $<a_1, \ldots, a_n> \in I_\Delta(F^n)$ by definition of I_Δ which holds if and only if

    3. $\mathfrak{A}_\Delta \models F^n a_1 \ldots a_n$ by the truth definition. QED

(β) Assume the result for $\ell(P) < k$. When $\ell(P) = k$ we have the usual cases. The cases in which P is truth-functional compound are dealt with in the same manner as those cases in the first correspondence theorem for CSL.

We must prove the result for the cases [∃] $P = (\exists x)F$ and [∀] $P = (\forall x)F$.

    [∃] It must be shown that $\Delta \vdash (\exists x)F \iff \mathfrak{A}_\Delta \models (\exists x)F$
    Proof:

        1. $\Delta \vdash (\exists x)F$ if and only if
        2. $\Delta \vdash F(a/x)$ for some constant a by the omega property ($\Rightarrow$) and by [∃I] ($\Leftarrow$). And this is if and only if
        3. $\mathfrak{A}_\Delta \models F(a/x)$ for some constant a, by the hypothesis of induction. Which implies and is implied by
        4. $a \in I_\Delta(F)$ for some constant a, by the definition of truth in a model. But this means that

5. There is some assignment d such that $d(a/x)$ satisfies F in $\mathfrak{A}_\Delta$ for some element a of A_Δ, and by the definition of truth in a model, this is equivalent to

6. $\mathfrak{A}_\Delta \models (\exists x) F$. QED

[∀] It must be shown that $\Delta \vdash (\forall x) F \iff \mathfrak{A}_\Delta \models (\forall x) F$
Proof:
The proof is left as an exercise

□

Corollary 10.2.6. *The arrow marked 3 in the equivalence diagram represents an implication.*

Proof. Assume that there is some omega set Δ which contains the set Γ and which does not prove the sentence P. It follows from the theorem that there is a model $\mathfrak{A}_\Delta$ in which every member of Γ is true, but P is false. So if every model in which Γ is true makes P true, it must be the case that every omega set which contains Γ proves P.

□

Theorem 10.2.7 (Omega Provability Theorem). *If $\Gamma \vdash^\Omega P$ then $\Gamma \vdash P$.*

Proof. The proof is indirect.

1. Suppose that $\Gamma \nvdash P$. Then

2. $\Gamma \cup \{\neg P\} \nvdash \bot$ or else $\Gamma \vdash P$ by [¬E] contra 1. So

3. There must be at least one omega set, Δ containing $\Gamma \cup \{\neg P\}$, by the construction of page 307.

4. $\Delta \nvdash P$ since Δ is consistent.

5. So, by contraposition, If every omega set containing Γ proves P, so does Γ. QED

□

Corollary 10.2.8. *The arrow marked 4 in the equivalence diagram of page 309 represents an implication.*

Proof. The proof is immediate.   □

Theorem 10.2.9 (Equivalence Theorem for CEL**).** *The following are equivalent*

1. $\Gamma \vdash P$

2. $\Gamma \models P$

3. $\Gamma \models^{\mathfrak{A}} P$

4. $\Gamma \vdash^{\Omega} P$

Proof. Since it has been shown that each of the arrows in the equivalence diagram represents an implication, the result is immediate.   □

Here again, we see at once that the arrows marked 2 and 4 in the equivalence diagram, represent equivalences. In the former case we get the converse of the implication because of the definition of entailment and in the latter case because of the rule [M] of monotonicity. In parallel with the metalogic of CSL, we notice the possibility of deriving the converse of the implication represented by arrow 3, without using the consistency theorem. As before, this would give us the equivalence theorem by the transitivity of the biconditional. The converse of arrow 3 requires that we prove a new version of the correspondence theorem (which is a kind of converse of the first correspondence theorem). For elementary logic this is rather more of a chore than it was for sentence logic.

A little thought will suggest that one requirement will be the semantic equivalent of the omega property. In order for a model $\mathfrak{A}$ to correspond to an omega set it must have the property that whenever $\mathfrak{A} \models (\exists v)P$ there is some witnessing constant c such that $\mathfrak{A} \models P(c/v)$. It is easy to see that an arbitrary model need not enjoy this property since in order that $(\exists v)P$ be true in a model it is only necessary that there be some or other element of the domain which belongs to the interpretation of P. There is exactly one circumstance in which the latter condition implies the existence of a witness, and that is the circumstance in which every element of the domain is named by some constant symbol c. In other words, for every domain element e, there is some constant c, such the $\mathbf{I}(c) = e$. We now cast this idea in ink.

Definition 10.2.10. A model $\mathfrak{A}$ is said to be *nominatious* if and only if For every $e \in A$ there is some constant c such that $\mathbf{I}(c) = e$.

But how to come by such a virtuous model? We can't say 'by adding new constants' since that only makes sense for languages, not for models. We begin with a model, say $\mathfrak{A}$, which is a model for an elementary language say $\mathfrak{L}$. It is the language $\mathfrak{L}$ which expands to suit our needs by the addition of the set $\{c_e | e \in A\}$ of new constants indexed by the domain of the model $\mathfrak{A}$. We shall call the expanded language $\mathfrak{L}^{\mathfrak{A}}$. We must also expand the original model to interpret the new constants. We shall refer to the original model expanded in this way, by $\mathfrak{A}^+$. The obvious way to effect the expansion is to add the following to the interpretation which $\mathfrak{A}^+$ inherits from $\mathfrak{A}$.

For every $e \in A, \mathbf{I}^+(c_e) = e$.

Evidently $\mathfrak{A}^+$ is nominatious. On the way to defining 'the corresponding set' we require another definition:

Definition 10.2.11. The notion of the *diagram* of a model $\mathfrak{A}$ is defined
$$\{P | \mathfrak{A}^+ \models P\} \cup \{\neg Q | \mathfrak{A}^+ \not\models Q\}$$
where P and Q are atomic sentences of $\mathfrak{L}^{\mathfrak{A}}$

We shall use the expression $\mathbb{D}(\mathfrak{A})$ to refer to the diagram of $\mathfrak{A}$.

Definition 10.2.12. For every model $\mathfrak{A}$, the set $\Delta_\mathfrak{A}$, the *theory* of $\mathfrak{A}$, is defined in two stages. First:
$$\Delta_\mathfrak{A}^- = \mathbb{C}_\vdash(\mathbb{D}(\mathfrak{A}))$$

The equivalent construction for CSL results in a complete theory, but alas, the quantifiers aren't truth-functional operators. For example, suppose that we have constructed a given model $\mathfrak{A}^+$ and that there is a unary predicate F in the language $\mathcal{L}$ such that for every constant c, $\mathfrak{A}^+ \models Fc$. In this case, by the construction of $\mathfrak{A}^+$, it must be the case that $\mathfrak{A}^+ \models (\forall x)F$. But although $\Delta_\mathfrak{A}^- \vdash Fc$ for every c, it does *not* prove[2] $(\forall x)F$ and neither does it prove $\neg(\forall x)F$.[3] So $\Delta_\mathfrak{A}^-$ is not complete (and fails at the same time to have the omega property).

Finally, we 'throw in' the missing generalizations.

$$\Delta_\mathfrak{A} = \Delta_\mathfrak{A}^- \cup \left\{ (\forall v)P \,|\, \Delta_\mathfrak{A}^- \vdash P(c/v) \text{for every constant } c \right\}$$

Proposition 10.2.13. $\Delta_\mathfrak{A} \nvdash \bot$

Proof. $\Delta_\mathfrak{A}^-$ is evidently consistent either by appeal to soundness or to some version of [W] for atomic sentences. There is no similar principle to which we can appeal in order to establish the consistency of the entire $\Delta_\mathfrak{A}$, at least not unless we wish to go beyond CEL.[4] For that project we must argue that $\mathfrak{A}^+$ is a model of this set but not a model of $\bot$. Consistency then follows from soundness.   □

---

[2]Perhaps the easiest way to convince oneself of this is use the soundness result heuristically (since we are trying at this point to do without it) and see that it would be easy to construct a model for $\mathcal{L}^\mathfrak{A}$ which made all the instances true without making the universal true.

[3]Since, we remark heuristically, the model $\mathfrak{A}^+$ makes everything in $\Delta_\mathfrak{A}^-$ true, and makes $\neg(\forall x)F$ false.

[4]An alternative diagnosis would be that the problem is with CEL not offering enough proof resources. We might wish that the deductive closure of $\mathbb{D}(\mathfrak{A})$ *should* have the omega property. To ensure this we could add the rule:

   $[\omega]\,[\Gamma \vdash P(c/v) \text{ for every constant } c] \implies \Gamma \vdash (\forall v)P$

However in order for this rule to do the work we require of it, we must allow that proofs may be infinitely long. CEL strengthened in this way is usually called ω-logic.

Proposition 10.2.14. $\Delta_{\mathfrak{A}}$ *is maximal.*

Proof. This is easy to show by induction on the length of P such that $P \notin \Delta_{\mathfrak{A}}$.

$\square$

Proposition 10.2.15. $\Omega(\Delta_{\mathfrak{A}})$

Proof. Suppose that $\Delta_{\mathfrak{A}} \vdash (\exists x)P$. If there is no witness then, in view of the maximality just shown, it must be the case that $\Delta_{\mathfrak{A}} \vdash \neg P(c/v)$ for every constant c. But in that case, by the construction of $\Delta_{\mathfrak{A}}$, we have that $\Delta_{\mathfrak{A}} \vdash (\forall x)\neg P$. But this is just to say that $\Delta_{\mathfrak{A}} \vdash \neg(\exists x)P$, which is impossible unless $\Delta \vdash\perp$. So there must be a witness after all. $\square$

Now we can show that this object really is the theory of $\mathfrak{A}$.

Theorem 10.2.16 (Second Correspondence Theorem for CEL). *For every model $\mathfrak{A}$ and sentence P:* $\mathfrak{A}^+ \models P \iff \Delta_{\mathfrak{A}} \vdash P$.

Proof. We prove the second correspondence theorem in the same way as we proved the first: by induction on $\ell(P)$.

(α) When $\ell(P) = 0$, i.e. P is an atomic sentence, the result holds trivially since by the definition of $\Delta_{\mathfrak{A}}$, that set contains $\mathbb{D}(\mathfrak{A})$.

(β) Assume that the result holds for $\ell(P) < k$. When $\ell(P) = k$ there are the usual cases. The truth-functional connective ones handled in the usual way by appeal to primeness etc. This leaves the quantification cases.

($P = (\exists x)F$) 1. Suppose $\mathfrak{A}_+ \models (\exists x)F$. This is equivalent to:

2. $\mathfrak{A}_+ \models F(a/x)$ for some constant a, since $\mathfrak{A}_+$ is nominatious (necessity) and by the truth-condition for $\exists$ (sufficiency). But this in turn is equivalent to

3. $\Delta_{\mathfrak{A}} \vdash Fa$, for some constant a, by the hypothesis of induction (since $\ell(F(a/x)) < k$). And this in turn implies

4. $\Delta_{\mathfrak{A}} \vdash (\exists x) F$ (by [$\exists$I]) and must also be implied by the same. Otherwise, $\Delta_{\mathfrak{A}} \vdash \neg F a$ for every constant a, since $\Delta_{\mathfrak{A}}$ is maximal. But then $\Delta_{\mathfrak{A}} \vdash (\forall x) \neg F$ by construction of $\Delta_{\mathfrak{A}}$, from which it would follow that $\Delta_{\mathfrak{A}} \vdash \perp$ which is impossible.

$(P = (\forall x) F)$ This case is left as an exercise.

$\square$

Corollary 10.2.17. *The arrow marked 3 in the equivalence diagram, represents an equivalence.*

Proof. Since we already have the implication from right to left, we only require the one from left to right. From, that is

$$\Gamma \vdash^{\Omega} P \text{ (for every } \Delta : \Gamma \subseteq \Delta \ \& \ \Omega(\Delta) \implies \Delta \vdash P)$$

to

$$\Gamma \models^{\mathfrak{A}} P \text{ (for every } \mathfrak{A} : \mathfrak{A} \models \Gamma \implies \mathfrak{A} \models P)$$

We argue indirectly once more.

1. Assume that for some model $\mathfrak{A}$, $\mathfrak{A} \models \Gamma$ but $\mathfrak{A} \not\models P$. Then

2. Form $\mathfrak{A}^{+}$ as described on page 315. Clearly $\mathfrak{A}^{+} \models \Gamma$ and $\mathfrak{A}^{+} \not\models P$. Then, by the second correspondence theorem and proposition 10.2.15 :

3. $\Gamma \subseteq \Delta_{\mathfrak{A}} \ \& \ \Omega(\Delta_{\mathfrak{A}}) \ \& \ \Delta_{\mathfrak{A}} \not\vdash P$, which is to say that $\Gamma \not\vdash^{\Omega} P$.

4. So $\Gamma \vdash^{\Omega} P \implies \Gamma \models^{\mathfrak{A}} P$. QED

$\square$

10.3   Dealing with Identity

When identity is added to the language, the interpretation function must give the right meaning to '=.' This comes down to adding the following clause to the definition of satisfaction.

Let $t_1 = t_2$ be an atomic formula in which t_1 and t_2 are terms. Then

$\mathfrak{A} \models_d t_1 = t_2$ (d satisfies $t_1 = t_2$ in $\mathfrak{A}$) $\Longleftrightarrow$ $e_1 = e_2$

where e_i is that element of the domain such that $e_i = I(a_i)$ if t_i is the constant a_i, and $e_i = d(x_i)$ if t_i is the variable x_i.

Alternatively, we could simply give the extension of the identity predicate under every interpretation:

for every model $\mathfrak{A}$ for an elementary language $\mathcal{L}$ with identity, $I_{\mathfrak{A}}(=) = \{<e, e> | e \in A\}$.

A set of ordered pairs like this, with the two entries identical, is often called a *diagonal* set.

How will this change affect the results we have already proved? In each of the induction proofs, there will be another case to deal with in the basis case, i.e. when P is atomic, it might be of the form $a = b$. Similarly, when an induction proof, like the consistency proof, appeals to how some sentence was derived, the rules for identity introduction and elimination must also be included. In the latter proof the basis step considers the shortest, i.e. 1 step, derivations. Those must now include the 1 step derivation of sentences like $(\forall x)x = x$, together with all those derivations in which the sentence derived on line 1, is an assumption. The proof that the former derivation has a corresponding entailment is only a bit less trivial than showing that the latter derivation does, it requires showing that every model makes $(\forall x)x = x$ true.

It is an easy matter to show that the results in metalogic that we have already obtained, survive the enrichment of the language of elementary logic to contain the identity symbol, with one exception. The correspondence results need some work. In particular, the construction of $\mathfrak{A}_\Delta$ needs to be changed.

Extensionalizing Omega Sets

In view of what was just pointed out concerning the interpretation of the the $=$ symbol, there cannot be any members of any omega set of the form $a_i = a_j$ if $i \neq j$, since that would result in $I_\Delta(=)$ containing pairs $<a_i, a_j>$ which are 'off the diagonal.' We shall deal with this problem by changing the nature of the elements of A_Δ. This in turn will require a change to the construction detailed on page 307. First a definition.

Definition 10.3.1. Whenever a set Σ of sentences of an elementary language $\mathfrak{L}$ (with identity) contains $a_i = a_j$ the set $\Sigma_=$, called the *extensionalization* of Σ, contains the result of replacing every occurrence of a_i by an occurrence of a_j, as well as the result of replacing every occurrence of a_j by an occurrence of a_i. Evidently we must be careful in specifying how these substitutions are to be made otherwise we shall lose half the sentences. Let b be any constant which doesn't occur in Σ and replace all occurrences of both a_i and a_j by occurrences of b. Then $\Sigma(a_i/b) \cup \Sigma(a_j/b)$ is the set we want.

So if Δ contains $a_i = a_j$ then $\Delta_=$ contains $a_j = a_j$ and $a_i = a_i$ but no longer contains $a_i = a_j$.

To make the construction of $\mathfrak{A}_\Delta$ work in the enriched environment then, only extensionalized omega sets can be used.

An Alternative Method for Dealing with Identity

There is an alternative approach to constructing canonical models, one which might well be called the standard method. To carry this out, one changes the nature of the elements in the canonical domain.

First we define a certain equivalence relation.

Definition 10.3.2. The constants c_1 and c_2 are said to be *equivalent in the set* Δ, indicated by $c_1 \sim_\Delta c_2$, if and only if $\Delta \vdash c_1 = c_2$

Next we introduce a certain useful kind of equivalence class.

> **Definition 10.3.3.** The constant c_1 is said to belong to the class $[c_2]_\Delta$ if and only if $\Delta \vdash c_1 = c_2$

The idea is that A_Δ is to consist not of all the constants c mentioned in Δ, but rather of all the distinct classes $[c]_\Delta$. We often omit the subscript when confusion is unlikely to follow. That this solves our problem is shown by the following.

Proposition 10.3.4. *If* $\Delta \vdash c_1 = c_2$ *then* $[c_1]_\Delta = [c_2]_\Delta$

Of course we still need to (re)define truth for atomic sentences in a Δ canonical model under this change. This is hardly a difficult matter. We call the version of the canonical model which uses equivalence classes as elements, $\mathfrak{A}_\Delta^=$.

> **Definition 10.3.5.** We shall say that $\mathfrak{A}_\Delta^=$ makes a predicate true of a sequence of equivalence classes if and only if Δ proves that the predicate holds of a sequence of representative elements, which is to say specimens drawn from the classes. Formally:
> $$\mathfrak{A}_\Delta^= \models F[a_1]\ldots[a_n] \iff \Delta \vdash Fa_1\ldots a_n$$

There may be a small doubt that this definition is coherent. Might it be possible, for example, that $\mathfrak{A}_\Delta^=$ makes $F[a]$ true because $\Delta \vdash Fa$ but also make $F[a]$ not true because for some *other* specimen $a*$ also drawn from the class $[a]$, $\Delta \not\vdash Fa*$? A little thought will remove any such doubt. Since $a*$ is a member of $[a]$, and since the only members of that class are elements for which Δ proves their identity to a, it follows that $\Delta \vdash Fa*$ by simple application of the rule [=E].

That the two approaches give the same result is the burden of:

Theorem 10.3.6. *If* $\Delta \in \Omega$ *then for every sentence* P,
$$\mathfrak{A}_{\Delta_=} \models P \iff \mathfrak{A}_\Delta^= \models P$$

In the construction of $\Delta_\mathfrak{A}$, there is a different problem. In order to show that the base set is consistent, we appealed to [W]. But if we admit any predicates into the stock of logical words, that principle no longer holds. So for an elementary language $\mathcal{L}$ with identity, there *can* be logical relations between atomic sentences. E.g. $a = a \vdash b = b$. The fast way out of this problem, and perhaps the only way, is to establish that the rules for identity cannot reverse the consistency result that has already been established. The easiest way to do this is to show that the identity rules are also rules for entailment. In other words:

> $\models (\forall x)x = x$ [the rule [=I] preserves entailment].
> By (the semantic version of) monotonicity,
> if $\models (\forall x)x = x$ then $\Gamma \models (\forall x)x = x$, for every Γ.
> But this is just to say that $(\forall x)x = x$ can be introduced on any line of a derivation and the result has a corresponding entailment i.e. that the rule [=I] preserves entailment. So let $\mathfrak{A}$ be an arbitrarily selected model. Then by the definition of satisfaction relative to a model for CELI, it must be the case that $x = x$ is satisfied by every variable assignment d and hence that $\mathfrak{A} \models (\forall x)x = x$. Since $\mathfrak{A}$ was arbitrary, this must hold for every model and hence $\models (\forall x)x = x$. QED

> $[\Gamma \models a = b \ \& \ \Gamma \models P] \implies [\Gamma \models P(a//b) \ \& \ \Gamma \models P(b//a)]$ [The rule [=E] preserves entailment].
> The proof is left as an exercise.

This is not, of course, a proof of the second correspondence theorem, it is instead a proof the consistency theorem which relies upon the previously established consistency result for elementary logic without identity. We could now prove the second correspondence theorem since it can be seen to follow from the consistency theorem.

10.4   Model Theory for Free Logic

There are a number of ways in which we might attempt semantics for the variation on the logic of elements (with identity) earlier called 'free.' Most of these involve using two distinct kinds of domains, sometimes called 'inner and outer' domains. This sounds better than calling them e.g. 'existent and non-existent elements.' But perhaps the most intuitive sounding terminology uses the name 'Story,'[5] which we emulate in the following definition. First for languages without the identity symbol:

Definition 10.4.1. A *model for a free logic FEL* is a triple $\mathfrak{A}^{\mathfrak{F}} = (A_{\mathfrak{A}^{\mathfrak{F}}}, \mathbf{I}_{\mathfrak{A}^{\mathfrak{F}}}, \mathbb{S}_{\mathfrak{A}^{\mathfrak{F}}})$ in which

$A_{\mathfrak{A}^{\mathfrak{F}}}$, the domain of $\mathfrak{A}^{\mathfrak{F}}$, is a non-empty set.

$\mathbf{I}_{\mathfrak{A}^{\mathfrak{F}}}$, the interpretation function of $\mathfrak{A}^{\mathfrak{F}}$, is

> a *partial* function from the set of individual constants to $A_{\mathfrak{A}^{\mathfrak{F}}}$ and
>
> A function from the predicate symbols carrying each n-ary predicate F^n to some set of ordered n-tuples of elements of $\mathfrak{D}_{\mathfrak{A}^{\mathfrak{F}}}$.

$\mathbb{S}_{\mathfrak{A}^{\mathfrak{F}}}$, the *story* of $\mathfrak{A}^{\mathfrak{F}}$, is a set (empty or non-empty) of atomic sentences such that each contains some occurrence of at least one constant which is not in the domain of $\mathbf{I}_{\mathfrak{A}^{\mathfrak{F}}}$.

To say that the function $\mathbf{I}_{\mathfrak{A}^{\mathfrak{F}}}$ is partial (on the constants), is just to say that not every constant need receive a value. The ones that do, are said to lie in the domain of the partial function. This is confusing as well as awkward since we already use the term 'domain' to stand for the set of elements used to interpret the constants. In view of this we shall say from now on that any constant which does receive an element of the domain under $\mathbf{I}_{\mathfrak{A}^{\mathfrak{F}}}$, *refers* (relative to the model $\mathfrak{A}^{\mathfrak{F}}$).

This model theory isn't actually very helpful since the rules for quantifiers in the proof theory of free logic require '$=$' for their statement. We can't simply say that $\mathbf{I}_{\mathfrak{A}^{\mathfrak{F}}}$ assigns $=$ the diagonal in $A_{\mathfrak{A}^{\mathfrak{F}}}$ and leave it at that, since the story now has a part to play, (which part we shall soon see). The thing that must be avoided, is that the story contain any atomic sentences of the form $b = b$ in which the constant b refers. The

---

[5] see van Fraassenn and Lambert (1972) Chapter 9.

thing to be ensured is that whenever the story has it that $a = b$, then all the required substitutions of one for the other are also in the story. Here is the final form of the definition of model for FELI

Definition 10.4.2. A *model for a free logic with identity* FELI, is a model $\mathfrak{A}^{\mathfrak{F}}$ for a free logic in which

$$\mathbf{I}_{\mathfrak{A}^{\mathfrak{F}}}(=) = \{<e, e> \,|\, e \in \mathfrak{D}_{\mathfrak{A}^{\mathfrak{F}}}\}$$

$$(b = c \in S_{\mathfrak{A}^{\mathfrak{F}}} \,\&\, P \in S_{\mathfrak{A}^{\mathfrak{F}}}) \implies (P(b//c) \in S_{\mathfrak{A}^{\mathfrak{F}}} \,\&\, P(c//b) \in S_{\mathfrak{A}^{\mathfrak{F}}}).$$

$b = b \in S_{\mathfrak{A}^{\mathfrak{F}}}$ if and only if b doesn't refer

We now pursue the same strategy as we did earlier. Since truth is not defined for open sentences, we shall begin by defining something truth-like which does apply in that case, namely the notion of satisfaction. After that, truth may be defined in terms of satisfaction in a manner parallel to the original presentation. In the following definition we re-use the notation $|t|$ which was introduced earlier.

Definition 10.4.3. The expression '$\mathfrak{A}^{\mathfrak{F}} \models_d P$,' read 'The variable assignment d satisfies the formula P relative to the model $\mathfrak{A}^{\mathfrak{F}}$' (for $\mathfrak{A}^{\mathfrak{F}}$ a model for a free logic with identity), is defined inductively.

When P is an atomic formula, (including an equation) it is of the form
$Ft_1 \ldots t_n$ for F an n-ary predicate, and the t_i all individual terms.
$\mathfrak{A}^{\mathfrak{F}} \models_d Ft_1 \ldots t_n$ if and only if either

$<|t_1|,\ldots,|t_n|> \in \mathbf{I}_{\mathfrak{A}^{\mathfrak{F}}}$ or (if all the terms are individual constants)

$F t_1 \ldots t_n \in \mathbb{S}_{\mathfrak{A}^{\mathfrak{F}}}$.

When P is not an atomic formula it is either a truth-functional compound, or a quantified sentence. These cases are handled in the same way as in 'regular' model theory.

Now we can define truth relative to a model $\mathfrak{A}^{\mathfrak{F}}$ in the usual way by quantifying away variable assignments in satisfaction. In other words:

Definition 10.4.4. The sentence P is true relative to the model $\mathfrak{A}^{\mathfrak{F}}$ (for a free logic with identity), written $\mathfrak{A}^{\mathfrak{F}} \models P$, if and only if for every variable assignment d,
$\mathfrak{A}^{\mathfrak{F}} \models_d P$.

Like truth, the concepts: entailment, logical truth, and semantic consistency are unaffected by the somewhat changed semantic structures.

But in order to re-prove some of the earlier results, the equivalence theorem for example, we shall have to change the omega-set construction adding the stipulation that the witnessing constants added during the formation of an omega set, all refer. The new class of omega sets will be denoted by $\Omega^{\mathfrak{F}}$. What was called the Δ-canonical model, $\mathfrak{M}_\Delta$ must also be re-defined.

Definition 10.4.5. By the canonical model for an omega set (relative to a free logic with identity) Δ, we understand the model:

$\mathfrak{A}^{\mathfrak{F}}{}_\Delta = (\mathfrak{D}_\Delta, \mathbf{I}_\Delta, \mathbb{S}_\Delta)$ where

$\mathfrak{D}_\Delta$ and $\mathbf{I}_\Delta$ are defined as before and

> $\mathbb{S}_\Delta$ is the set of atomic sentences $Fa_1 \ldots a_n$ such that for at least one constant a_i ($1 \leq i \leq n$), there is no variable v such that $\Delta \vdash (\exists v)(v = a_i)$.

The next step is to re-prove the first correspondence theorem.

Theorem 10.4.6 (First Correspondence Theorem for FELI). *For every sentence P of FELI and every* $\Delta \in \Omega^{\mathfrak{F}}$: $\Delta \vdash P \iff \mathfrak{A}^{\mathfrak{F}}{}_\Delta \models P$

This proof and the rest of the metalogical results up to the equivalence theorem for FELI are left as an exercise for the reader. Given the definitions and the example of the results for ELI there are no surprises.

References

Bach, E. and B. Partee (1980). Anaphora and semantic structure. In *CLS Parasession on Pronouns and Anaphora*, pp. 1–28.

Fitch, F. B. (1952). *Symbolic Logic*. New York: Ronald Press.

Gentzen, G. (1969). *Collected Works of Gerhard Gentzen*. North Holland.

Henkin, L. (1949, Sep). The completeness of first-order functional calculus. *Journal of Symbolic Logic 14*(3), 159–166.

Henkin, L. (1996, June). The discovery of my completeness proofs. *The Bulletin of Symbolic Logic 2*(2), 127–158.

Howe, M. L. and F. M. Rabinowitz (1996). Reasoning from memory: A lifespan inquiry into the necessity of remembering when reasoning about class inclusion. *Journal of Experimental Child Psychology*, 1–42.

Howe, M. L., F. M. Rabinowitz, and T. L. Powell (1998). Individual differences in working memory and reasoning-remembering relationships in solving class-inclusion problems. *Memory and Cognition*, 1089–1101.

Poincaré, H. (1960). *Science and Hypothesis* (2nd ed.). New York: Dover.

Post, E. L. (1994). *Collected Works of Emil L. Post*. Boston: Birkhäuser.

Quine, W. V. O. (1970). *Philosophy of Logic*. Foundations of Philosophy. Englewood Cliffs, New Jersey: Prentice-Hall.

Quine, W. V. O. and J. S. Ullian (1970). *The Web of Belief* (2nd (1978) ed.). McGraw Hill.

Rosser, J. B. and A. R. Turquette (1952). *Many-valued Logics*. Amsterdam: North Holland Publishing Co.

Russell, B. (1903). *The Principles of Mathematics* (2nd ed.). Cambridge.

Russell, B. (1905). On denoting. *Mind 14*.

Schotch, P. (2004). *A Course in Philosophical Logic*. http://www.schotch.ca/pdf/Course.pdf: Schotch.

Tarski, A. (1936). Der Wahrheitsbegriff in den formalisierten Sprachen. *Studia Philosophica 1*, 261–405.

van Fraassenn, B. and K. Lambert (1972). *Derivation and Counterexample*. Encino, California: Dickenson.

Worrall, J. and G. Come (Eds.) (1978). *The Philosophical Papers of Imre Lakatos*. Cambridge: Cambridge University Press.

Index

Index of Symbols

$'$ successor function, page 16

$(\exists^n x)(Fx)$ there are at most n F's, page 268

$(\exists_n x)(Fx)$ there are at least n F's, page 268

$+$ recursive definition of addition, page 17

$=$ The identity symbol, page 260

$\mathfrak{A}^+$ Expanded model, page 315

$\mathfrak{A}_\Delta^=$ canonical model for identity, page 321

$\mathfrak{A}_\Delta$ Δ canonical model, page 311

α step   basis step of an induction, page 162

β step   inductive step of an induction, page 162

$\cap$ set intersection, page 160

CELI   Classical Elementary Logic with Identity, page 262

COMP   completeness property for theories, page 169

CSL   classical sentence logic—semantic mode, page 126

CSL   classical sentence logic—syntactical mode, page 21

$\cup$ set union, page 160

$\Delta_\mathfrak{A}$ Theory of the model $\mathfrak{A}$, page 316

$\mathbb{D}(\mathfrak{A})$ the diagram of the model $\mathfrak{A}$, page 315

337

$\mathbb{D}_I$ the class of diagrams spanning the index I, page 170

$\mathbb{D}_i$ Diagram of a subset i of an index I, page 170

EL   Language of Elementary Logic, page 213

ELI   Language of Elementary Logic with Identity, page 260

$\ell(P)$ Length of the formula P, page 16

$\models P$ P is a logical truth, page 131

$\models_v \Gamma$ the set Γ is true at v, page 130

$\models_v \Gamma$ for some v Γ is semantically consistent, page 132

$\models_v$ true relative to the truth-value assignment v, page 128

$\equiv$ truth-table for biconditional, page 125

&   metalinguistic conjunction, page 18

$\exists$ existential quantifier, page 215

$\perp$ falsum symbol, page 125

FELI   Classical Elementary Logic (Proof theory mode) with Identity (Free version), page 271

$\forall$ universal quantifier, page 215

$\Gamma \models P$ the set of premises Γ semantically entails the conclusion P, page 130

$\Gamma \models^i P$ truth-preservation, entailment (alternative notation), page 179

$\Gamma \models^{\mathfrak{A}} P$ $\mathfrak{A}$-entailment, page 309

$\Gamma \models_{\otimes} P$ entailment for classical product logic, page 207

$\Gamma \nvdash P$ Post's definition of consistency, page 40

$\Gamma \vdash P$ Gamma proves P, page 39

$\Gamma \vdash^{\Omega} P$ omega-provability, page 309

$\Gamma \vdash^i P$ proof-preservation, page 179

$\Gamma \subseteq^{\Omega} \Delta$ Δ is an omega extension of Γ, page 309

Γ^+ Turning Γ into an omega set, page 308

I   interpretation function, page 297

$\Longleftrightarrow$ metalinguistic biconditional, page 18

IMPLIC   implication property for theories, page 169

$\Longrightarrow$ metalinguistic conditional, page 18

$\in$ set membership symbol, page 18

$\mathcal{L}$ language for elementary logic, page 296

$\mathcal{L}^{\mathfrak{A}}$ Elementary language with added constants, page 315

$\mathcal{L}_1 \sqsubset \mathcal{L}_2$ $\mathcal{L}_2$ is an expansion of $\mathcal{L}_1$, page 297

$\mathfrak{A}^{\mathfrak{F}}$ model for a free logic, page 323

$\neg$ truth-table for negation, page 124

$\neg_{\otimes}$ product truth-table for negation, page 205

$\neq$ negated =, page 260

$\Omega(\Delta)$ Δ has the omega property, page 306

$\Omega_{\mathcal{L}}$ the class of maximally consistent omega-complete sets, page 306

$<x, y>$ the ordered pair of x and y in that order, page 298

PRIME   disjunctive property for theories, page 169

$\vdash P$ P is a theorem, page 39

$\Sigma_=$ extensionalization of Σ, page 320

SL   Language of Sentence Logic, page 14

$\subset$ proper set inclusion, page 161

$\subseteq$ set inclusion, page 161

$\supset$ truth-table for the conditional, page 123

$\mathfrak{T}_i$ deductive closure of $\mathbb{D}_i$, page 170

ιx Definite description, page 273

THEORY(Δ) Δ is a theory, page 167

$\mathbf{T}_I$ indexed class of theories spanning SL_I, page 171

$\mathbb{V}_I$ indexed class of truth-value assignments for SL_I, page 170

$\varnothing$ empty set symbol, page 18

$\vee$ truth-table for disjunction, page 115

$\wedge$ truth-table for conjunction, page 113

$\wedge_{\otimes}$ product truth-table for negation, page 205

$\underline{\vee}$ truth-table for exclusive disjunction, page 117

A domain of individuals for model $\mathfrak{A}$, page 297

a individual constant, page 213

At set of atomic formulas, page 160

$c_1 \in [c_2]_\Delta$ c_1 belongs to the c_2 Δ equivalence class, page 321

$c_1 \sim_\Delta c_2$ c_1 and c_2 are equivalent in Δ,, page 320

d variable assignment function, page 301

$d(e/x)$ matching assignment except for x, page 301

F predicate symbols, page 215

I index for an indexed language for sentence logic, page 170

i_Γ subset of index determined by Γ, page 177

$P \in \mathcal{A}(D,i)$ P is an assumption active at line i in derivation D, page 39

$P \dashv\vdash Q$ P and Q are syntactically equivalent, page 40

$P(a/x)$ a is substituted for x everywhere in P, page 242

$P(a//b)$ a is substituted for b in P at 0 or more places , page 261

$P :: Q$ P and Q are semantically equivalent, page 133

SL_I language for sentence logic indexed by I, page 170

T,F the truth-values truth and falsehood, page 113

T_Γ Closure of diagram of i_Γ, page 178

v truth-value assignment function, page 128

$X \rightleftharpoons Y$ X and Y are isomorphic, page 176

$\mathfrak{A} \models_d P$ d satisfies P in $\mathfrak{A}$, page 302

$\mathbb{C}_\vdash$ deductive closure operator, page 168

*   mark for required premise in a rule, page 24

[=E]   Rule of Identity Elimination, page 262

[=I]   Rule of Identity Introduction, page 261

[≡E]   rule of Biconditional Elimination, page 30

[∃E]   Rule of Existential Quantifier Elimination, page 245

[∃I(F)]   Rule of Existential Quantifier Introduction for Free Logic, page 270

[∃I]   Rule of Existential Quantifier Introduction, page 242

[⊥E]   rule of Falsum elimination, page 33

[⊥I]   rule of Falsum Introduction, page 33

[∀E(F)]   Rule of Universal Quantifier Elimination for Free Logic, page 270

[∀E]   Rule of Universal Quantifier Elimination, page 242

[∀I]   Rule of Universal Quantifier Introduction, page 244

[¬E]   rule of Negation Elimination, page 34

[¬I]   rule of Negation Introduction, page 34

[⊃E]   rule Conditional Elimination, page 29

[⊃I]   rule of Conditional Introduction, page 30

[∨E]   rule of Disjunction Elimination, page 28

[∨I]   rule of Disjunction Introduction, page 26

[∧E]   rule of Conjunction Elimination, page 25

[∧I]   rule of Conjunction Introduction, page 24

[IE]   Rule of Description Elimination, page 278

[II]   Rule of Description Elimination, page 278

[Assoc] (replacement) rule of Associativity, page 61

[Com]   (replacement) rule of Commutativity, page 61

[Contra] (replacement) rule of Contraposition, page 61

[DeM]   replacement) DeMorgan's rule, page 61

[Dist]   (replacement) rule of Distribution, page 61

[DN]   (replacement) rule of Double Negation, page 61

[DS]   rule of Disjunctive Syllogism, page 59

[Equiv] (replacement) rule of Equivalence, page 61

[Exp]   (replacement) rule of Exportation, page 61

[HS]   rule of Hypothetical Syllogism, page 59

[Id]   (replacement) rule of Idempotence, page 61

[Impl]   (replacement) rule of Implication, page 61

[M]   Structural Rule Monotonicity, page 166

[ML]   Meinong's Law, page 271

[MT]   rule of Modus Tollens, page 60

[R]   rule of reiteration, page 37

[T]   Structural Rule: Cut, page 166

[TRAN]   Structural Rule of Transitivity, page 166

[W]   Wittgenstein's Law, page 171

the logic CEL the set of pairs Γ, P, such that $\Gamma \vdash P$ in CEL, page 257

The logic CSL, syntactical mode the set of pairs Γ, P such that $\Gamma \vdash P$, page 39

the semantic version of the logic CSL The set of pairs Γ, P such that $\Gamma \models P$, page 133

www.ingramcontent.com/pod-product-compliance
Lightning Source LLC
Chambersburg PA
CBHW020846090426
42736CB00008B/257